John's Gospel

Recovering Authorial Intent

Fr. Peter Grover, OMV

En Route Books and Media, LLC
Saint Louis, MO

✺ENROUTE
Make the time

En Route Books and Media, LLC

5705 Rhodes Avenue

St. Louis, MO 63109

Contact us at contactus@enroutebooksandmedia.com

Cover art by John Michael Grover.

Copyright 2024 Fr. Peter Grover, OMV

ISBN: 979-8-88870-320-5

Library of Congress Control Number: 2024952095

All rights reserved. No part of this book may be reproduced, stored in a retrieval system, or transmitted in any form, or by any means, electronic, mechanical, photocopying, or otherwise, without the prior written permission of the author.

Table of Contents

Abbreviations v
Introduction 1
   Defining Intratextuality or Composition Theory 2
   The Problem of Isolating Texts and Importing Meaning from Outside Sources 4
   Advantages of Intratextual Analysis 10
   Guidelines Governing the Use of Intratextuality 11
Part 1: The Prologue (1:1-18) 21
   The Purpose of the Prologue.. 23
   The Divine Plan 33
Part 2: The Books of Signs (Revelation Accessible to Particular Groups) 49
   Section 1: Believers 51
      Seven Days (1:19–2:11) 51
      The First Day: Introducing the rejecters of the Word (1:19-28) 58
      The Second Day: Introducing Christ (1:29-31) 64
      The Third Day: Introducing the believers (1:35-42) 71
      The Fourth Day: Confirming Jesus' Origin (1:43-51) 73
      The Seventh Day, Creating Believers (2:1-12)................... 81
      Signs.. 92
      The Temple (2:13-23)... 98
      The "Jews" 98

Nicodemus (3:1-21) 103
John and Jesus (3:22-30) 117
Jesus and the Samaritan Woman (4:1-42) 120
The Royal Official (4:46-54) 130
Section II: Non-Believers.. 135
The Sign at Sheep Pool (5:1-47) 135
The Bread of Life (6:1-71) 141
Festival of Booths (7:1–8:59) 158
Before the Feast (7:1-9) 161
Middle of the Feast (7:14-36) 163
The Last Day of the Feast (part 1): Living Water (7:37ff) 165
The Last Day of the Feast (part 2): Light of the World 180
The Man Born Blind: First Words (Water, Light), Now
    Deeds... 185
The Good Shepherd... 200
The Feast of Dedication 206
The Sleep of Lazarus 208
Mary and Judas 216
The Welcome in Jerusalem... 221
Part 3: Book of Glory (World Access to Revelation)...................... 223
The Greeks Want to "See" 225
Washing Feet (13:1-38) 231
- Obedience 242
- Humility... 245
- Knowing Jesus Origin 246

Table of Contents

- The Details 249
- Judas, the Beloved Disciple, and Peter 256

The Final Discourse (13:31–17:26) 258
The True Vine (John 15) 272
Joy (acceptance) versus Sin (rejection) 274
Death Wish: Jesus' Prayer before the Arrest 279
The Arrest: Jesus, Judas, and Peter 282
The Trials: The Crowd, Pilate, and Jesus 289
The Crucifixion 304
- The Inscription 305
- The Outside Garment and the Inside Garment 308
- "I Thirst" 311
- "It Is Finished" 313

The Burial of Jesus 316
The Empty Tomb 319
Appearance to Mary Magdalene 321
Jesus Appears to His Disciples 323
Peter and Jesus: Fear to Love 325
Closing Thought 329
Appendix: Woman Caught in Adultery 333
Bibliography of Texts Used 335

Abbreviations

ABR	*Australian Biblical Review*
AnBib	*Analecta biblica*
ATK	
AusBR	
AUSS	*Andrews University Seminary Studies*
BBR	*Bulletin for Biblical Research*
BDAG	Bauer, W., G. W. Danker, W. F. Arndt, and F. W. Gingrich. *Greek-English Lexicon of the New Testament and Other Early Christian Literature.* 3rd ed. Chicago, 2000.
Bib	*Biblica*
BibInt	*Biblical Interpretation*
BJRL	*Bulletin of the John Rylands Library*
BNTC	*Black's New Testament Commentaries*
BSac	*Bibliotheca sacra*
BVC	*Bible et vie chrétienne*
BZ	*Biblische Zeitschrift*
CTQ	*Concordia Theological Quarterly*
CUP	
EDNT	*Exegetical Dictionary of the New Testament*
EvQ	*Evangelical Quarterly*
ExpTim	*Expository Times*
JBL	*Journal of Biblical Literature*
JETS	*Journal of the Evangelical Theological Society*
JSNT	*Journal for the Studies of the New Testament*

JSNTSup	*Journal for the Study of the New Testament Supplement Series*
JSS	*Journal of Semitic Studies*
JTS	*Journal of Theological Studies*
Neot	*Neotestamentica*
NovT	*Novum Testamentum*
NTS	*New Testament Studies*
RB	*Revue biblique*
RevExp	*Review and Expositor*
RivB	*Rivista biblica italiana*
SBLSP	*Society of Biblical Literature Seminar Paper*
SJT	*Scottish Journal of Theology*
SupNT	Supplements to the New Testament
TynBul	*Tyndale Bulletin*
TDNT	*Theological Dictionary of the New Testament*
TZ	*Theologische Zeitschrift*
WTJ	*Westminster Theological Journal*
WUNT	*Wissenschaftliche Untersuchungen zum Neuen Testament*
ZNW	*Zeitschrift für die neutestamentliche Wissenschaft und die Kunde der älteren Kirche*

All translations of biblical texts are taken from the New Revised Standard Version. Translations of classical authors are taken from the editions in the Loeb Classical Library unless otherwise noted. Abbreviations for ancient texts generally follow the guidelines in P. H. Alexander et al., eds., *The SBL Handbook of Style*. Peabody, MA: Hendrickson, 1999.

Introduction

Many who read the Gospel of John seek to find a connection with the divine by way of the God's conversation partner: the human author of John's Gospel. Is there a study that really concentrates solely on finding authorial intent? And what is the best methodology for such a task? The methodologies used today in the study and interpretation of biblical texts are predominantly forms of historical criticism. They contribute to understanding the historical situation of the author, the significance of cultural influences, and the *Sitz im Leben* of the authors and their communities. These studies rely heavily on what is outside the text itself and tend to focus on isolated pericopes. In this study, I propose a reading of John's Gospel with a methodology known as intratextuality, or composition theory, with the purpose of interpreting the Gospel as intended by the author/redactor of the final canonical text.[1] Rather than focusing primarily on the historical factors and influences, it looks at the text itself as the product of human agency and therefore the most complete evidence of authorial intent. This method treats the text as an integral literary composition that itself provides the most complete and reliable evidence of authorial intent, particularly by coherence in the narrative. Finding the consistent message in the Gospel of John allows the reader to understand the author's theology.

---

[1] The definition of authorial intent is classically understood as the examination of a text within its own historical circumstances. One reconstructs as accurately as possible the meaning that was intended for the original audience by the human author/redactor of the final canonical text.

Defining Intratextuality or Composition Theory

Using the intratextual method to read the Gospel of John depends on approaching it as a complete and integral work of literature in which the author presents a narrative that actively engages the reader. As the narrative advances, the reader picks up interpretive data: information presented by the author as clues to interpret subsequent texts. The engaged reader will be attentive to details which are important for the flow of the argument and the narrative's teaching. For example, a murder mystery typically begins by offering clues, character development, and situational drama to engage the reader. Not everything is explained, loose ends are not always connected, and questions are not immediately answered. The author uses the narrative to tease the reader to figure out the sequence of events, motive, and other such matters that are not explicitly clarified until the end of the book. But unlike a mystery novel, the Gospel of John begins with a thesis and then expands on the themes presented. With such *leitmotif* in place, the author can embellish his narrative with a variety of images, symbols, puzzling dialogues, and clever irony without leaving the reader in confusion.[2] Of course, the reader must understand that his or her role is to recall details and

---

[2] On the use of irony in the gospel of John, see W. Gingrich, "Ambiguity of Word Meaning in John's Gospel," *Classical Weekly* 37 (1943): 77; Oscar Cullmann, "Der johannische Gebrauch doppeldeutiger Ausdriicke als Schliissel zum Verstandnis des vierten Evangeliums," *TZ* 4 (1948): 360-72; David Wead, "The Johannine Double Meaning," *Restoration Quarterly* 13 (1970): 106-20; Earl Richard, "Expressions of Double Meaning and Their Function in the Gospel of John," *NTS* 31 (1985): 96-112.

make connections. The intended audience must perceive that the coherence found in the text is for a hermeneutical purpose.

This presupposes that the prologue, the opening eighteen verses, introduces the audience to the theological themes of the Gospel. It provides a thematic blueprint giving an interpretation to the narrative that follows and clarifies texts that seem incongruous. With such a roadmap, the reader can interpret the collection of stories, narratives, and exhortations in light of one unifying theme. The prologue presents a rather ambitious divine project to produce children of God (1:12). In order to execute this plan, God will send his Word into the world. Those who accept and believe the sent Word will become God's children and receive all the benefits that come with the relationship. Once the reader knows this plan, the stories, dialogue, and imagery will be understandable with reference to the blueprint.

For example, if the divine plan is to create children of God, as stated in the prologue, then it is not surprising that the Gospel begins with a wedding, the traditional path for having children. During the feast of Cana, Jesus takes on the role of the bridegroom as observed by the head waiter: "You have saved the better wine until now." The next concern after the wedding is typically housing and children. In the same chapter, Jesus enters the temple and must reclaim a marketplace as the Father's house (2:16). When this home is eventually destroyed, a new one will be rebuilt (2:19). In the next chapter, Jesus meets a Pharisee to discuss birth: "You must be born from above" (3:7). Then, in the same chapter, Jesus is called the "bridegroom" by John the Baptist (3:29). Next, Jesus, the bridegroom meets a Samaritan woman with "marital issues" at one of the ancient wells, a common place for patriarchs to meet future wives

(Gen 24:10-66: 29:9-12). The woman engages in a theologically weighty discussion about worship, a topic that addresses fidelity and appropriate covenant relations with God. Often the prophets spoke of such fidelity in terms of marriage. She goes back to her village where the inhabitants become believers. According to the prologue, believers and those who receive the Word, as the villagers do, will have access to eternal life, recalling the prologue and the children of God. Later Jesus will describe the pain of the disciples with the analogy of a woman in labor, who suffers only a little while before she feels great joy at the birth of a child (16:21). The attentive reader thus perceives coherence in the narrative which all goes back to the themes of the prologue. All this of course is not a new hermeneutical insight. Scholarship has long worked with the premise that good storytelling maintains strong thematic relationships between the whole and the parts so that the audience's understanding of a part is informed by the whole and the understanding of the parts is strengthened by a growing understanding of the whole. No one to my knowledge has done this systematically for the Gospel of John as this study.

The Problem of Isolating Texts and Importing Meaning from Outside Sources

Most scholarly interpretations analyze passages by isolating them and seeking interpretive keys from outside sources, but this approach often interrupts the theological as well as the narrative flow of the author's composition and obscures the overall themes and patterns worked into the structure of the text. Separating passages from the rest of the text and interpreting one author through other authors of different sources can be hermeneutically risky for those who seek authorial intent. For example, the author/redactor may use a word differently than other authors. This is especially true when generic words have been recast in a theological or philosophical context (i.e. "Word," "light," "water"). One must avoid taking a general term that has been given theological significance from one source and import that theological meaning into another text such as the Gospel of John.[3] In contrast, the intratextual approach uses the context of a word or phrase in the text to determine its meaning. It seeks meaning by studying the relationship between words, symbols, phrases and how they are used in the composition. For example, there are numerous studies that try to determine the meaning of water in the Gospel of John by using the Old Testament, composi-

---

[3] James Barr, *The Semantics of Biblical Language* (Philadelphia: Trinity Press International, 1991), 107.

tions from the Covenanters (Dead Sea Scrolls), and classical literature.[4] But not all literature uses the term "water" as a symbol of divine revelation or truth like the author of John.[5] Some scholars assert that the text uses water as a symbol of purification rather than revelation, and back this assertion with evidence from outside sources only. One purpose of this study is to show that interpreting the text through its original context gives a consistent and coherent exegesis, whereas using outside sources can yield a wide variety of conflicting

---

[4] Dale C. Allison, Jr. "The Living Water (John 4:10-14, 6:35c, 7:37-39)," *St Vladimir's Theological Quarterly* 30 (1986), 143-157; Steven Bouma-Prediger, "Water in Biblical Reflection," *Word & World* 32 (2012): 42-50; Larry P. Jones, "The Symbol of Water in the Gospel of John," *JSNT* Sup 145 (Sheffield: Sheffield Academic Press, 1997); Gerald Klingbeil, "Water," in *The New Interpreters Dictionary of the Bible*, ed. Katharine Sakenfeld; Vol 5 (Nashville: Abingdon, 2009), 818-21; J. A. Kowalski, "On Water and Spirit: Narrative Structure and Theological Development in the Gospel of John," (Ph.D. diss., Marquette University, 1987); and Wai-yee Ng, *Water Symbolism in John: An Eschatological Interpretation* (New York: Peter Lang, 2001); Marianne Mey Thompson, "Baptism with Water and with Holy Spirit: Purification in the Gospel of John" in *Historical, Literary, and Theological Readings from the Colloquium Ioanneum 2015 in Ephesus* (Wissenschaftliche Untersuchungen zum Neuen Testament 385) ed. R. Alan Culpepper and Jörg Frey (Tübingen: Mohr Siebeck, 2017), 59-78. For purification and ablutions in Greco-Roman society and cultic practice, see L. Moulinier, *Le pur et L'impur dans la pensée des Grecs d'Homère à Aristote* (Paris: Klincksieck, 1952).

[5] "Any study of Johannine revelation that ignores the form, style, and mode of Johannine revelatory language will always miss the mark." J. Bryan Born, "Literary Features in The Gospel of John (An Analysis of John 3:1-21)," *Direction* 17 (1988): 4.

interpretations. For example, H. J. Harrington understands the baptism of John as a washing with water that, like the ritual ablutions in the Dead Sea scrolls, "preceded and anticipated the world of the Spirit to generate life, provide atonement, bring divine revelation and usher in the eschaton."[6]

Conversely, the special meaning of certain words can be identified when they are seen in context, as an author can use individual words with a special meaning unique to his text. For example, Jesus addresses his mother at the wedding of Cana with the term "woman." Scholars debate why Jesus would call his mother "woman." Many suppose that it is an appropriate expression although unusual in either Hellenistic or Jewish tradition.[7] Raymond E. Brown asserts that Jesus uses it as a polite expression.[8] However, if one looks elsewhere in the Gospel, one notes that Jesus also calls the Samaritan woman (4:21) and Mary Magdalene (20:15) "woman." All three share a common feature: they give testimony. The Mother of Jesus tells the servants to do whatever he tells them, the Samaritan woman gives witness to the people in her village, and Mary is sent to testify to the disciples about Jesus' resurrection from the dead. The expression "woman" appears to be used as a title for

---

[6] H. K. Harrington, "Purification in the Fourth Gospel in light of Qumran," In *John, Qumran, and the Dead Sea Scrolls: Sixty Years of Discovery and Debate* (ed. M. L. Cole et al.; SBLEJL 32; Atlanta: Society of Biblical Literature, 2011), 117-38.

[7] Raymond Edward Brown, *A Commentary on the Gospel of John* (2 vols. Garden City, NY: Doubleday, 1966), 99.

[8] Ibid. Craig Keener maintains that addressing one's mother with the expression "women" would be considered rude. See his *The Gospel of John: A Commentary* (Peabody, Mass: Hendrickson, 2003), 503.

one who testifies to the truth. Addressing his mother as "woman" means Jesus is confirming that she is not acting as a mother requesting a favor from a son, but as a witness who gives testimony about the Divine Word: "Do whatever he tells you" (2:5). The importance of witnessing is attested in the prologue by reference to John the Baptist, who is sent to witness to the light. This theme continues to be significant throughout the Gospel. If the term "woman" is a clue to the role played by characters in the Gospel, then it would be very likely that the author intended the expression to stand out as a title rather than use it as a polite expression. Such interpretive meaning can be discovered when the reader uses information from the prologue and narrative that were placed there by the author.

There are numerous symbols in the Gospel used to represent divine revelation/truth, such as living water, bread that comes down from heaven, and light. The reader is informed, before chapter 6, that the welcomed reception of living water and light (i.e., revelation) generates eternal life; one must accept revelation to receive eternal life, just as one drinks living water to live or uses light to perform the works of God. Analogies, metaphors, and symbols exhibit a pattern with a consistent theological message; that is why a reader can understand that eating the body and drinking the blood of Christ are analogous to accepting and receiving revelation that can bring one to eternal life because it has appeared before with other metaphors (e.g., light and living water).[9] This interpretation is consistent with the theological argument of the Gospel and coheres with

---

[9] Brandon Scott described the metaphor in its simplest terms as "understanding and experiencing one reality in terms of another." See his *The Word of God in Words* (Philadelphia: Fortress, 1985), 76.

Introduction

the mission of the prologue, where acceptance of the Word enables one to become a child of God (1:12). With this approach, one does not run the risk of importing information from outside sources that can alter or add to the meaning that was originally intended. Scholars who read the text (6:51-58) with a Eucharistic optic need information about the Lord's Supper from Synoptic and Pauline writings to reach this conclusion, using information that is not given in the Gospel of John.[10] The author, I argue, communicates his intention by way of coherence, whereby all the information necessary for the reader's interpretation is provided in the Gospel. Taking all of these

---

[10] This is not to say that the flesh and blood narrative (51-58) does not have legitimate sacramental meaning beyond authorial intent especially when the text is read in the context of liturgical gatherings and/or in respect to its place in the New Testament canon. The canon allows Christians to read the passage in context to other books of the New Testament which clearly articulate a Eucharistic theology. This, of course, entails an interpretation that goes beyond the human author. After a strong endorsement of literary and historical methods for understanding Scripture, *Dei verbum* 12 insists on a theological reading: "No less serious attention must be devoted to the content and unity of the whole of Scripture, taking into account the entire living tradition of the Church and the analogy of faith." The Pontifical Commission in 1994 further states that "(T)he fuller sense is defined as a deeper meaning of the text, intended by God but not clearly expressed by the human author. Its existence in the biblical text comes to be known when one studies the text in the light of other biblical texts which utilize it or in its relationship with the internal development of revelation." See the Pontifical Biblical Commission, "The Interpretation of the Bible in the Church" (1994), 34. That said, my analysis is less expansive. I want to restrict my findings to what the author/redactor intended by using intratextuality to isolate the Gospel from other sacred or profane works and canons in order to find the author's intention by way of coherence found within the narrative progression.

examples into consideration shows how following the narrative structure from beginning to end can bring out details otherwise overlooked.[11] No commentary to my knowledge discusses these matters and presents them as a consistent theme in the Gospel.

Advantages of Intratextual Analysis

The author of the Gospel seems to have intentionally placed literary and thematic ties in the text so that the reader will find coherence in the narrative. With intratextuality, distinctive literary features such as words, phrases, and motifs that are repeated are seen to contribute to a particular theological viewpoint "rather than mere evidence of numerous redactors."[12] Literary analysis offers discriminating attention to the artful use of language and to the shifting play

---

[11] Authors can use common words and phrases for different meanings. For example, the phrase "the New England Patriots had a perfect regular season with sixteen wins" can have different meanings depending on the author who uses it. If a New England fan said it, then the phrase is understood as a positive evaluation of the organization. If, on the other hand, a New York Giants fan said it, the phrase is most likely intended as an insult, since what good is a perfect season if the team loses the Super Bowl to the New York Giants? In the same way, the author of John may use a word that is shared in other literature but with a different meaning. In contrast to these approaches, the intratextual approach employs semantics which means understanding the context of a word, symbol, or phrase in the text to determine its meaning.

[12] JoAnn Davidson, "John 4: Another Look at the Samaritan Woman," *AUSS* 43 (2005): 159. See similar opinions that call attention to the sophisticated nature of narrative writing: Phyllis Trible, *Rhetorical Criticism: Context, Method, and the Book of Jonah* (Minneapolis: Fortress, 1994); idem, *Texts of Terror: Literary-Feminist Readings of Biblical Narratives*

of ideas, conventions, tone, sound, imagery, syntax, narrative viewpoint, compositional units, and much else.[13] Such connections indicate a conscious effort on the part of the author or redactor to weave a theme, assuming that the reader is attuned to clues that establish the narrative's meaning. This methodology treats the text as a window to see the author's thoughts.[14]

Guidelines Governing the Use of Intratextuality

But how can one be sure that efforts to find *leitmotifs* in the text do not impose more than what the author intended, making these findings inconsequential to the original intent?[15] There are numerous terms and phrases that are repeated in the Gospel; should one assume they are all probative? Even if the author uses rare terms, should one assume there is a connection between texts so that one passage should be read in the light of another? For example, twice in the Gospel, the author uses the phrase "the hour was around noon"

(Philadelphia: Fortress, 1984); J. P. Fokkelman, *Reading Biblical Narrative: An Introductory Guide*, trans. Ineke Smit (Louisville, KY: Westminster John Knox, 1999); idem, *Narrative Art in Genesis: Specimens of Stylistic and Structural Analysis* (Sheffield: JSOT Press, 1991); Meir Steinberg, *The Poetics of Biblical Narrative: Ideological Literature and the Drama of Reading* (Bloomington: Indiana University Press, 1987); Roberts Alter, *The Art of Biblical Narrative* (New York: Basic, 1981), 312.

[13] Ibid., 312.
[14] Trible, *Rhetorical Criticism*, 96.
[15] "The intentionalist understanding of meaning extends from the original arbitration of the notion of texts, implicit in an author's act of writing or speaking." John C. Poirier, "Some Detracting Considerations for Reader-Response Theory," *CBQ* 62 (2000): 253.

(ὥρα ἦν ὡς ἕκτη): at Jacob's Well (4:6) and the trial of Pilate (19:14). Should one make a connection between the two passages, or is noontime during the passion narrative a reference for when the lambs begin to be slaughtered in preparation for the Passover? How does one avoid making arbitrary links when reading passages in the light of others to formulate an interpretation? The methodology needs to have certain controls in place to prevent conclusions that are arbitrary or fanciful. What methods and rules can be used to demonstrate solid textual support?

I propose three methods: multiple connections, prologue themes, and textual recurrence. First, there must be numerous literary and thematic links between passages before one can say with any certainty that one passage should be interpreted in light of an earlier one. Take, for example, the expression "it was about noon" (ὥρα ἦν ὡς ἕκτη, 4:6; 19:14). One can note numerous other ties between the passages that cite this phrase: both mention the action of sitting ("and Jesus, tired out by his journey, was sitting by the well" 4:6, and "When Pilate heard these words, he brought Jesus outside and sat on the judge's bench" 19:13); both scenes we read of Jesus' physical thirst (4:7; 19:28); in both scenes, we can assume that Jesus is the giver and source of the living water (4:10; 7:37-38);[16] both discuss moments of physical weakness (Jesus' fatique "from long journey" (4:6), and flogged, crowned with thorns, struck on his face (19:1-3);[17] both share the same verb to express Jesus' intention to finish his

---

[16] Robert H. Lightfoot, *St. John's Gospel: A Commentary*, (Oxford: Clarendon, 1983), 122.

[17] Bernadeta Jojko, "Eternity and Time in the Gospel of John," *Verbum Vitae* 35 (2019): 264.

work ("My food is to do the will of him who sent me and to complete [τελειόω] his work" (4:34), and "After this, when Jesus knew that all was now finished" [τελειόω] 19:28);[18] both narratives have characters who call Jesus a "man" (4:29; 19:5); both narratives have characters calling Jesus the messiah/king (4:29; 19:14); and both have a water container (Jacob's Well and the Messianic pierced side). Finally, both texts discuss living water. The Samaritan asks Jesus where to find living water: "Where do you get that living water?" (4;11). The passion narrative seems to answer this question when the side of Jesus is pierced: the source of living water is Jesus' testimony. Both texts exhibit testimony which produces believers. The woman testified to the people of her village, and they became believers. At the cross, the disciple whom Jesus loved testifies "So that you also may believe" (19:35). There appear to be numerous literary and thematic ties between the two passages. I will argue later that the Samaritan woman scene provides vital interpretive information for understanding Jesus' trial and death.

Second, the texts must comply with themes of the prologue. This methodology assumes that the Gospel is intended to be a complete and an integral literary unit. The prologue is a theological and literary guide given by the author/redactor, and each passage is a road that is first mapped in 1:1-18. For example, the Samaritan woman is offered a gift of living water that will bring her eternal life. Water, again, is a symbol of revelation/truth; when one receives the gift of truth and believes, then they will have access to eternal life. This complies with the prologue. The Word (revelation/truth) comes

---

[18] Ibid.; Thompson, The Humanity of Jesus, 3-4.

into the world, and those who receive him and believe will become children of God. In 1:18 Jesus who is at the bosom of the Father, makes him known (1:18). In 1:5, 9 the Word is described as light, a metaphor for revelation.[19] The Word, pre-existent with God, comes into the world (σκηνόω) to make him known (ἐξηγέομαι). No one else can reveal the truth because no one else "has ever seen God" (1:18). Likewise, in the passion narrative, Jesus explains to Pilate that he came into the world, to testify to the truth (18:37). Jesus tells him, "Everyone who belongs to the truth listens to my voice" (19:37). Again the theme is revelation. From the cross, blood and water flow from the pierced side, which causes the disciple to testify to the truth so that the reader will believe (19:35). Once again, water represents revelation and when it is believed it will provide eternal life. Both texts are connected to the theological program of the prologue.

Lastly, the theological meaning must be repeated at other places in the text besides the two passages in question. For example, the symbol of water that is used in both the Samaritan and the passion narrative is found in other places in the Gospel. The symbolism of water is used during the festival of booths: "Let anyone who is thirsty come to me and let the one who believes in me drink" (7:27-28). Water represents revelation because it is the believer that possesses living water: "Out of the believer's heart shall flow rivers of living water" (7:38). Water is also referenced in the story of Nicodemus as a requirement for one to be born from above: "No one can enter the kingdom of God without being born of water and Spirit" (3:5). Jesus explains the symbolic language of water and Spirit as revelation: "I

---

[19] See Ps 36:9; Bar 4:2-4; Wis 7:21-26; 1QS 11:5-8.

tell you, we speak of what we know and testify to what we have seen; yet you do not receive our testimony...How can you believe if I tell you about heavenly things?" (3:11-12). Water consistently represents revelation throughout the Gospel.

These three principles will allow one to identify coherence in the text which reveals the author's rhetorical strategy. I maintain that a text ought to be interpreted by placing it in the complex network of its context, and the purpose of the study is to make a connection with the author's intentions by way of coherence. This study does not derogate varied and legitimate methods of criticism (textual, literary, redaction, rhetorical, form, source, semiotics).[20] Biblical study encompasses a wide range of topics on matters such as the historical Jesus, literary and oral stages of development, history of the primitive church, socio-political conditions, history of interpretation and reception, comparison of texts and translations, other various analysis (cultural, anthropological, psychological, feminist, liberationist), and so forth. However, it is infrequent that a study focuses exclusively on the intention of the author/redactor. When it does, I maintain that intratextuality or composition theory is the method of

---

[20] For milestone source-critical studies of John's Gospel, see Rudolf Bultmann, *The Gospel of John: A Commentary* (trans. G. R. Beasley-Murray, R. W. N. Hoare, and J. K. Riches; Philadelphia: Fortress, 1971); Robert T. Forma, *The Gospel of Signs: A Reconstruction of the Narrative Source Underlying the Fourth Gospel* (SNTSMS 11; Cambridge: Cambridge University Press, 1970); D. Moody Smith, "The Setting and Shape of a Johannine Narrative Source" pages 80-93 in *Johannine Christianity: Essays on Its Setting, Sources, and Theology* (Columbia: University of South Carolina Press, 1984).

choice, without the exclusion of others. Why value the human author? In my faith-based opinion, he or she acts as a direct line to the divine author. God inspired the human author of each book of Scripture as well as the faith traditions that forged together the canon. It is not my intention to enter the "inspiration of Scripture" debate, but the human author remains a legitimate subject for the school of interpretation.

That is, the author has to be understood as a historical figure who addresses an audience in a socio-historical setting. This study proposes a solution to a specific problem – namely, how intratextuality can shed light on authorial intent. None of the historical-critical methods is specifically interested in or addresses this subject. Rhetorical analysis focuses on the "art of composing discourse aimed at persuasion."[21] It determines the mode of speech from influential classical Greco-Roman rhetorical modes of speaking (judicial, deliberative, and demonstrative), but it can never be fully determined if the author was exposed to higher education and how much attention was given to procedural guidelines that were outlined in ancient grammar manuals. Narrative analysis focuses on the perception of the reader; source criticism seeks to understand the stages of composition of a text; historical criticism in general considers the text as a window giving access to the situation which the story relates and to the community for whom the story is told.[22] None of these

---

[21] Pontifical Biblical commission, "The Interpretation of the Bible in the Church," (1994), 4B1.

[22] "Narrative criticism explores the ways in which an implied author determines an implied reader's response (through the medium of the text) rather than on ways in which the [actual] reader determines meaning."

Introduction

disciplines seeks directly to understand the author's intentions. Our method is generally ahistorical, yet it is not motivated by an expressly antihistorical bias and agenda.

To be clear, this study is not an exercise in audience-response whereby the reader separates the text from the author.[23] Nor is it an effort to discern the contemporary meaning of the text. Some may argue that it is more legitimate to ask, "What does the text say?"[24] For example, Sandra M. Schneiders states: "In biblical interpretation (or interpretation of texts) we are concerned primarily with the meaning of the text itself, not with the author's meaning."[25] However, separating the author from the text opens the door to reader-reconstructions, a multiplicity of potentially contradictory interpretations, eisegesis—in short, chaos. The interpretive approaches today have limitations if they are applied for the purpose of gleaning

---

M.C. de Boer, "Narrative Criticism, Historical Criticism, and the Gospel of John," *JSNT* 47 (1992): 39.

[23] Paul Ricoeur claims that the semantic autonomy does not imply the "absolute text," which means that the "author's intention and the meaning of the text cease to coincide." He continues, "What the text means now matters more than what the author means when he wrote it." See his, *Interpretation Theory: Discourse and the Surplus of Meaning* (Fort Worth: Texas Christian University Press, 1976), 32-32. For a sampling of post-structural and reader-oriented approaches, see Fernando F. Segovia, ed., What Is John? Readers and Readings of the Fourth Gospel (SBLSymS 3; Atlanta: Scholars Press, 1996).

[24] Northrop Frye, "Literary Criticism," in *The Aims and Methods of Scholarship in Modern Languages and Literatures* (ed. James Thorpe; New York: Modern Language Association of America, 1963), 59.

[25] Sandra M. Schneiders, *Written That You May Believe: Encountering Jesus in the Fourth Gospel* (New York: Crossroad, 2003), 186.

the meaning intended by the author/final redactor. Intratextuality affords the interpreter the opportunity to read the text as one coherent unit rather than divide the text into fragments while importing data from outside.

In this study, I seek to validate the method of intratextuality as a tool for interpreting authorial intent from the *textus receptus*, the text as received by us today. To my knowledge, no commentary or analysis has ever attempted such a reading of the Gospel of John. To accomplish this, I base arguments on multiple connections between texts that also comply with the author's consistent theme and conform with the divine plan described in the prologue. Numerous authors maintain that the prologue provides a thematic map or blueprint of the Gospel, yet rarely refer back to it in their analysis of the narrative. In this study, the prologue will be referred to when treating each passage. I will use existing scholarship as a measure of comparison as well as support to my claims. There will be times when my findings differ from others, primarily because other studies introduced data from outside sources. Information that does not comply with the structure, themes, and style of the author.

Finally, this study is written to address a wide audience, with particular attention to seminarians, students, and those who have a specific interest in John's Gospel. It is difficult to offer an analysis without some recourse to the original Greek. I do not want the use of Greek to intimidate potential readers or restrict the readership to only those who have a working knowledge of the New Testament language. I am painfully aware of the reader who has to struggle through language barriers and technical terminology. So that the study can be offered to a wider audience, I will always provide an

English translation. I will also offer definitions and explanations when I use technical terminology thereby presenting a reader friendly study that can reach both a general audience and experts in the field.

Part 1

The Prologue (1:1-18)

Part I

The Prologue (1:1-13)

The Purpose of the Prologue

I intend to show in this section that the purpose of the prologue is to provide a theological guide for the rest of the Gospel. I will then offer a verse-by-verse analysis to underscore this theological theme.

The function of the opening 18 verses has been long debated. For a number of reasons, not all scholars see the prologue as the thesis statement of the Gospel. This is because there are dissimilarities between the prologue and the Gospel. In fact, some go so far as to question its integrity.[26] Scholars such as R. Bultmann and E. Käsemann discuss the original form and provenance of the prologue, treating it as an independent unit.[27] Once the authenticity of the prologue is in

---

[26] The coexistence of both similarities and dissimilarities between the prologue and Gospel has produced a number of theories. Those who favor the dissimilarities such as Schnackenburg are in favor of the prologue as an independent source. They provide reconstructions and often identify later additions or interpolations that have Johannine characteristics. Harnack claims that the prologue was later added to accommodate Hellenistic readers. See A. von Harnack, "Über das Verhältnis des prologs des vierten Evangeliums zum ganzen Werk," *ATK* 2 (1892): 189-231. J.A.T. Robinson argues that the prologue was a polemical response to Docetism and added to the Gospel in a later addition. See his "The Relation of the Prologue to the Gospel of St. John," *NTS* 9 (1962-63): 120-29.

[27] R. Bultmann, "Der religionsgeschichtliche Hintergrund des Prologs zum Johannes-Evangelium," in *Eucharisterion: für H. Gunkel II* (Göttingen: Vandenhoeck &Ruprecht, 1923), 1-26; E. Käsemann, "The Structure and Purpose of the Prologue to John's Gospel," *New Testament Questions of Today* (Philadelphia: Fortress, 1969), 138-67. Lindars suggest that that the portions that treat John the Baptist were original to the Gospel as was the practice in other Gospels, and only later in a second edition the poetic

doubt, one needs to raise questions about its relationship with the rest of the Gospel. Are the prologue and the Gospel two independent parts superficially juxtaposed, or do they form a coherent unity? The interest in this study is to argue whether the author/redactor of the canonical text intended the hymn-like prologue to introduce the theological themes of the Gospel. The question of whether it was original or added later may never be resolved with certitude. This problem I leave for other experts. To see if the prologue has anything to do with the Gospel, one has to decide whether or not the similarities compensate for the differences. There are legitimate reasons why scholars cast doubt on the prologue's relation with the narrative proper. First, we will look at the style and textual differences, then examine the prologue's likeness and parallels to the rest of the Gospel.

The style of the prologue is radically different from the Gospel narrative. Raymond Brown points out the unusual nature for an ancient work to begin with a poetic introduction with respect to either classical Hellenistic or biblical traditions.[28] Such hymn-like features that are found in the prologue are not replicated in the Gospel proper. John 1:1-5 adopts a parallelism, which some label as the "staircase," whereby the author takes the last word of the previous sentence and repeats it in the next. (I.e., note the repeated words "life," "light," "darkness" in 1:4-5: "in him was **life**, and the **life** was the **light** of all people. The **light** shines in the **darkness**, and the **darkness** did not overcome it"). Although there are examples of this

---

sections of the hymn were added. Lindars, *John* (New Century Bible; London: Marshall, Morgan &Scott, 1972), 76-77.

[28] Brown, *John*, 18.

parallelism in the Gospel (6:37; 8:32; 13:20; 14:21), none are as prominent as in the prologue. Even so, it is still possible the author wanted to stylistically distinguish the prologue from the Gospel narrative. The introduction to Luke's Gospel, for example, begins with an elegant classical Greek style before shifting to a narrative that matches the Old Testament style of storytelling. Few of the words in Luke's first four verses are found in the body of his work. In both Gospels, the introduction is nicely identified and distinct from the main body of their respective Gospels.

Second, there are theologically significant terms in the prologue not found in the Gospel proper, something that is also true for the opening verses in Luke. They include the Christological title "the Word" (ὁ λόγος), "grace" (χάρις occurs 4 times in 1:14-17), "full" (πλήρης, 14) "fullness" (πλήρωμα, 16), and the verb "to tabernacle" (σκηνόω, 14). The term οἱ ἴδιοι is employed again in 13:1 but not with the same meaning. Why would the author allow such differences to infiltrate a text if the intention was to project coherence? To begin to answer this, I need to show that (1) the concepts of these above terms are well represented and (2) that the similarities substantially outnumber the dissimilarities.

First, it is true that there are terms in the prologue which are not repeated in the Gospel, yet the meaning they symbolize is well represented. For example, although ὁ λόγος (the Word) is not used as a Christological title in the Gospel, the significance of the title λόγος ("Word") as the pre-existent divine being is well attested there. In the prologue, the λόγος ("Word") enjoys a personal union and relationship with God (ὁ λόγος ἦν πρὸς τὸν θεόν, 1:1, 2), which is further clarified by the phrase "the word was God" (1:1). Verses 3-4 further characterize the Word as non-created, as well as the creator of all the living. In the Gospel, Jesus is confessed as the Son of God (20:31) who has the words of everlasting life (6:68). In addition to pre-existence, the prologue firmly establishes the origin of the Word "with God" (1:1, 2) and "in the bosom of the Father" (1:18). The Gospel confirms this as well: Jesus was sent "from above" (8:23), "from heaven" (3:13; 6:31-58), is "not of this world" (8:23; 17:14, 16), is "from God" (7:17), is not his own (7:16, 18), and is the one who has been sent by the Father.[29]

In the prologue, the function of the word is to testify to the truth. The "Word" is also the revealer of God. By its very essence, "Word" is the authentic revelation of God.[30] Just the nature of the term "Word" indicates disclosure or communication, as opposed to sealed lips, inaccessibility, or being hidden. Christ is the only one who can make God known (ἐξηγέομαι, 1:18)—a true contribution to the world because no one has ever seen God. In the Gospel, the ones who believe that Jesus is the revealer from above understand his claims of origin (16:30), know the Father (8:19; 14:6-7), or see the Father (12:45; 14:9). Jesus is the only begotten Son of God (3:16-18). His testimony is described as light coming into the world (1:9, 15, 30; 3:8; 19:31; 4:25; 5:43; 8:14; 14:3).[31] **The Word is God's agent**

---

[29] See John 4:34; 5:23, 24, 30, 37; 6:29, 38-40, 44, 57; 7:16, 18, 28, 29, 33; 8:16, 18, 26, 29, 42; 9:4; 10:36; 11:42; 12:44, 45, 49; 13:20; 14:24; 15:21; 16:5; 17:3, 8, 18, 21, 23, 25; 20:21.

[30] Warren Carter, "The Prologue and John's Gospel: Function, Symbol and the Definitive Word," *JSNT* 39 (1990): 35-58.

[31] There are 38 uses of the term "world" (κόσμος) having negative force found in the main body of the Gospel.

Part 1: The Prologue (1:1-18)

in the creation. The Word is also the light. Later Jesus will describe himself as "the light of the world" (8:12,9:5; similarly 12:46) and by so doing will associate himself with the light of day, as in 11:9: "There are twelve hours of day, aren't there? If anyone walks about during the day, he/she doesn't stumble, because he/she sees the light of this world."

Jesus is the truth (3:21; 4:23-24; 5:33; 8;32; 14:6, 17; 15:26; 16:7, 13; 17:17, 19; 18:37), and is a gift of God (3:33; 4:18; 5:31-32; 6:55; 7:18; 8:13-14, 7, 26; 10:41; 19:35; 21:24). I agree with John E. O'Grady who concludes that "The theology of the logos dominates the entire Gospel and should not be limited to the prologue."

The term "one's own" (οἱ ἴδιοι) is only used once to refer to the opposition in the prologue: "He came to what was his own, but his people did not accept him" (1:11). There are numerous times in chapter 5–12 that describe the rejection of Jesus when he comes in contact with his own people. The only other use of the term is found in 13:1. Here, it refers, not to rejecters, but believers, "having loved his own who were in the world, he loved them to the end," so it is used twice in the Gospel, but in different ways. Stephen Voorwinde points out that the adjective "his own" (τὰ ἴδια) is mentioned two times to refer to Christ's sheep (10:3, 4),[32] indicating that the meaning of the term has flipped since the prologue.[33] Therefore, when the

---

[32] Stephen Voorwinde, "John's Prologue: Beyond Some Impasses of Twentieth-Century Scholarship," *WTJ* (2002): 20.

[33] John F. O'Grady, "The Prologue and Chapter 17 of the Gospel of John," in *What We Have Heard from the Beginning: The Past, Present, and Future of Johannine Studies* (ed. Tom Thatcher; Waco: Baylor University Press, 2007), 227.

term is used in 13:1, it has already undergone a total transformation, no longer referring to opponents but receivers of the word. The shift of meaning seems intentional according to Voorwinde.[34]

The words "full" (πλήρης, 14) and "fullness" (πλήρωμα, 16) are likewise not repeated in the Gospel. However, the Gospel does describe Jesus' works and gifts as complete, without reserve, with a sense of totality. He gives his life for the benefit of others as a shepherd lays down his life for the sheep (10:11). And, "He loved his own until to the end" (13:1). He completes his work on the cross: "it is finished" (19:30). He gives the fullness of joy to his disciples (15:11; 16:24; 17:13). His revelation of God is described as a stream of living water (4:10, 14; 7:37-38). He also gives life (10:10), gives food to the crowds (6:1-15) and drink at the wedding (2:1-11) in great abundance.

Also the term "grace" (χάρις occurs 4 times in 1:14-17), is never seen again in the Gospel. In the prologue, the expression "grace and truth" is often understood epexegetically, or as a *hendiadys*, meaning that they are conjoined as one entity because the first term is used to describe the second.[35] An epexegetical sense in this case would mean that "truth" is understood as a divine "gift."[36] This is certainly true in the Gospel. Jesus offers light, living water, his body and blood for

---

[34] Ibid.

[35] Moloney, *John*, 45. Grace and truth are often found together in the Old Testament particularly in the psalter.

[36] See de la Potterie, "*Charis* paulinienne et *charis* johannique," in *Jesus und Paulus: Festschrift für Werner Georg Kümmel zum 70. Geburtstag* (eds. E. Earle Ellis and Erich Grässer; Göttingen: Vandenhoeck & Ruprecht, 1975), 265-82; R. B. Edwards, "Charin anti charitos (John 1:16): Grace and Law in the Johannine Prologue," *JSNT* 32 (1988): 3-15.

eternal life, which are all symbols of revelation or truth. For example, Jesus offers the Samaritan woman the gift of living water as a gift from God: "If you knew the gift of God, and who it is that is saying to you, 'give me a drink,' you would have asked him, and he would have given you living water" (4:10). He also promises to send the Spirit of truth as a free gift who comes from the Father (15:26).

Finally, the last word of the prologue, "to make known" (ἐξηγήσατο, 1:18), is never employed in the Gospel, but Jesus' entire ministry can be summed up as the one who reveals the Father (cf. 10:37, 38; 12:45; 14:8-10). There are terms in the prologue that are not repeated verbally, but it has been argued extensively by scholars that these terms are represented symbolically or transformed in the Gospel.

While there are numerous differences between the text of the prologue and that of the rest of the Gospel, the similarities seem to outnumber the dissimilarities. One can note the number of terms that are prominently found in both the prologue and the Gospel.[37]

---

[37] Note such terms and expressions such as "life" (ζωή, 3:15-16, 36; 4:14, 36; 5:24, 26, 29, 39, 40; 6:27; 8:12; 10:10;, 28; 11:25; 12:25, 50; 14:6; 17:2-3; 20:31), "light" (φῶς, 3:19-21; 8:12; 9:5 11:9-10; 12:35, 36, 46), "one who is sent with continuing effects" (ἀπεσταλμένος 9:7), "darkness" (σκοτία, 3:21), "witness" (μαρτυρία, 1:19; 3:11, 32, 33; 5:31, 32, 34, 36; 8:13, 14 17; 19:35; 21:24), "world" (κόσμος, 3:16, 17, 19; 4:42, 6:14, 33, 51; 7:4, 7; 8:12, 23, 26; 9:5, 39; 1036; 11:9, 27; 12:19, 25, 31, 46, 47; 13:1, 14:17, 19, 22, 27, 30, 31; 15:18, 19; 16:8, 11, 20, 21, 28, 33; 17:5, 6, 9, 11, 13, 1415, 16, 18, 21, 23, 24, 25; 18:20, 36, 37; 21:25), "to know" (γινώσκω, 1:48; 2:24, 25; 3:10; 4:1, 53; 5:6, 42; 6:15, 69; 7:17, 36, 2749, 51; 8:27, 28, 32, 43, 52, 55; 10:6, 14, 15, 27, 38; 11:57; 12:9, 16; 13:7, 12, 28, 35; 14:7, 9, 17, 20, 31; 15:18; 16:3, 19; 17:3, 7, 8, 23, 25; 19:4; 21:17), and "glory" (δόξα, 2:11; 5:41, 44; 7:18; 8:50, 54; 9:24; 11:4, 40; 12:41, 43; 17:5, 22, 24).

Besides terms, there are also themes from the prologue that echo through the Gospel. As mentioned above, according to the prologue, there are two responses to revelation: opposition and acceptance. Both are well represented in the Gospel, by those who reject Jesus (1:50; 2:24-25; 5:42; 6:15, 70; 8:28, 32, 55; 10:14; 16:3; 17:3) and those who accept him (2:23; 4:19; 6:2, 40, 62; 7:3; 12:45; 14:17, 19; 16:10; 17:24). In the prologue, rejection is treated first: "His own people did not receive him" (1:11).[38] Those who reject are condemned to death (3:18), and divine wrath (3:36). They do not know God (7:28; 8:55; 16:3), live a life in darkness (3:21), are not from God (8:47; 10:26), and are identified as the devil (8:44). Terms such as "darkness" (σκοτία), the "world" (κόσμος), "own people" (οἱ ἴδιοι) underscore both the proximity and imminence of the opposition. Those, however, who receive the Word are even closer to God because they become His children. (1:18), and have life in them (6:35-51; 3:15-18; 5:24; 6:40; 11:26; 20:31).

In both the prologue and the Gospel, John the Baptist and Moses have a relationship with the Word and are discussed in relation to Jesus.[39] John is the second of two who is sent to witness. (1:19-23, 27; 3:30). Twice, John the Baptist claims that there is one mightier than he who comes after him, once in the prologue and once in the Gospel proper. Moses is subordinated to Jesus by witnessing to Him

---

[38] See E. Haenchen, *John I* (Hermeneia; Philadelphia: Fortress, 1984), 118.

[39] The proper name of Moses (Μωϋσῆς) occurs thirteen times in the Gospel of John in eight separate sections all within the first nine chapters of the Gospel.

(1:45; 5:45-47).⁴⁰ God sends bread to feed the Israelites; Jesus is sent as food for everlasting life. Moses lifted up the serpent while Jesus himself is lifted up (see 3:14).⁴¹ Both Jesus and Moses are rejected. The Pharisees use Moses to validate their rejection of Jesus (9:29) but it is based on the fact that they do not know Jesus' origin (9:33), while the blind man recognizes and accepts Jesus because he knows he is "from God" (παρὰ θεοῦ, 9:33), a similar expression to verse 1 in the prologue: with God (πρὸς τὸν θεόν).

Whether or not the prologue was original to the Gospel, there are enough similarities to safely assume that the prologue was at least added or edited to introduce the theological objectives of the Gospel, thus supporting the theory of a unity between the Gospel and the prologue. Numerous scholars have concluded as such.⁴² As

---

⁴⁰ Further treatments of Moses's role in the Gospel see Marie-Emile Boismard, *Moses or Jesus: An Essay in Johannine Christology* (trans. B.T. Viviano; Leuven, Belgium: Leuven University Press, 1993), 93-98; Stefan Schapdick, "Religious Authority Re-Evaluated: The Character of Moses in the Fourth Gospel," in *Moses in Biblical and Extra-Biblical Traditions* (ed. Axel Graupner and Michael Wolter; Berlin: Walter de Gruyter, 2007), 188-189; Wayne A. Meeks, *The Prophet-King: Moses Traditions and the Johannine Christology* (Leiden: E.J. Brill, 1967), 287.

⁴¹ There are three texts in John that speak of Jesus' death as "being lifted up": 3:14; 8:28; 12:32-34.

⁴² Charles K. Barrett contends that coherence is perceived through unity of theme and subject matter. See his *The Prologue of John* (London, Athlone, 1971), 29. See also Luke T. Johnson, "The Writings of the New Testament: An Interpretation" (London: SCM, 1986), 474-75; Stephen Voorwinde, "John's Prologue: Beyond Some Impasses of Twentieth-Century Scholarship," *WTJ* (2002): 15-44. Theobald argued that the Prologue was produced after, not before, the Gospel to serve as an abstract. See Michael Theobald, Die Fleischwerdung des Logos: Studien zum Verhältnis

Voorwinde maintains, "The prologue, therefore, cannot be divorced from the remainder of the Gospel, but the two are linked in the most intimate and intricate ways. Even terms which are unique to the prologue can, upon closer examination, be shown to anticipate major emphases that emerge as the Gospel unfolds."[43] Voorwinde also cites James Dennison:

John has woven his Prologue and his gospel into a seamless garment. What is highlighted in the Prologue is exegeted in the gospel. What is displayed by the gospel is epexegetical of the Prologue. The Prologue is more than an introduction to the gospel. It is a thematic summary of the eschatological character embodied in the life and ministry of the incarnate Logos. New life, new light, new order of the cosmos—all this has appeared with the advent of the Logos-

---

des Johannesprologs zum Corpus des Evangeliums und zu I Joh (Münster: Aschendorff, 1988), 373. Benedict T. Viviano states "(t)he prologue and the rest of the gospel mutually explain one another; they are unintelligible without one another....The prologue and the rest of the Gospel need each other." See his "The Structure of the Prologue of John (1:1-18): A Note," *RB* (1998): 184. See also John F. O'Grady, "The Prologue and Chapter 17 of the Gospel of John," in *What We Have Heard from the Beginning: The Past, Present, and Future of Johannine Studies*, ed. Tom Thatcher (Waco: Baylor University Press, 2007), 219. See other works that regard the prologue as the interpretive key to the Gospel: R. Alan Culpepper, *Anatomy of the Fourth Gospel: A Study in Literary Design* (Philadelphia: Fortress, 1983), 116-20; Martin Hengel, "The Prologue of the Gospel as the Key to Christological Truth," in *The Gospel of John and Christian Theology* (eds. R. Bauckham & C. Mosser; Grand Rapids: Eerdmans, 2008), 265-94; D T. Barrosse, "The Seven Days of the New Creation in St. Johns Gospel," *CBQ* 21 (1959): 507-16.

[43] Voorwinde, "John's Prologue," 22.

Theos. The Prologue is proleptic of the gospel. One must read the *gospel* retrospectively (to the Prologue). Yet one must also read the *Prologue* prospectively (anticipatory of the gospel as a whole).[44]

Simon R. Valentine likewise agrees that the prologue provides "the exegetical key to the right understanding of the entire book."[45] Although many studies claim the relevance of the prologue, none of them have systematically read through the Gospel with a prologue lens. It does not make sense to turn to outside sources for interpretive background if the narrative already has coherence built into its structure.[46] I now propose to highlight the prologue as a divine plan in order to follow the interpretive path of the Gospel, which executes this project.

The Divine Plan

According to Brown, the prologue shares many of the same characteristics as other New Testament hymns.[47] Philippians 2:6-11 appears as a hymn describing similar thematic features as the pro-

---

[44] James Dennison, "The Prologue of John's Gospel," *Kerux: A Journal of Biblical-Theological Preaching* 8 (1993): 6.

[45] Simon R. Valentine, "The Johannine Prologue—a Micorocosm of the Gospel," *EvQ* 68 (1996): 293.

[46] According to Michael J. Gorman the first eighteen verses "reveal the narrative and theological starting point of the entire Gospel and the fundamental reality that makes the *missio Dei* what it is." Michael J. Gorman, "John: The Nonsectarian, Missional Gospel," *Canadian-American Theological Review* 7 (2018): 147.

[47] Brown, *John*, 20.

logue of John, including Jesus' status as a man, his rejection, acceptance, and glorification. Col 1:15-20, another hymn, depicts an only Son of the invisible God like the prologue's only begotten son who alone can see God. Both also claim that all things were created through the Son/Word. The Philippians' and Colossian hymns offer a brief summary of the Christ story. The prologue similarly condenses a story of the Word by describing its origin, function, and effect on others. I will now read the prologue as a story, with the purpose of exhibiting a divine plan that will be carried out by Christ in the Gospel.

The Gospel begins with the first words of the [LXX] Bible. The expression "In the beginning" immediately calls to mind the God who created the world by the power of his spoken Word in Genesis 1:1. God's word is existential. That is, when God speaks, divine power brings into existence whatever it wills. To appreciate such power, one can compare God's word to the human voice, which is merely epistemological. For example, I can say the word "water" and never cause the basement to flood. In the creation story in Genesis, the Word of God represents existential power that affects the universe. In the prologue, the Word once again is acknowledged as the source of creation. As the prologue states, without the Word nothing came into being (1:3). In addition to the first words of the prologue and the role of the Word in creation, the prologue also recalls the story of Genesis with the Greek term γίνομαι ("genesis"), employed seven times: 1:3 [twice], 6, 10, 12, 14, 15. Finally, both the Genesis creation story and the prologue make numerous references to light

(1:5, 7, 8) and life (1:4).[48] So there is enough evidence to tie the two texts together legitimately. With the creation story in the background, the reader has a biblical reference to the extensive and limitless creative power of the Word. After introducing John the Baptist, God's creative word now reenters the world, and the reader anticipates that something will come forth, but what? Did not God already create the world? Why recall Genesis and introduce the world to more productivity? What is missing from the first six days?[49] John 1:12 provides the purpose for the Word entering the world: children of God. The reentry of the Word provides divine truth to all. If believed, he or she will receive power to become children of God. Why is this creative act new? Did not God already produce children from

---

[48] R. Alan Culpepper, *The Gospel and Letters of John* (Nashville, Tn: Abingdon), 111.

[49] "The prologue demonstrates that the story about to be told is, from one angle, the ongoing narrative of God's dynamic relationship to the world—this time to transfigure creation. It is a narrative, moreover, in which light and darkness, life and death, contend with the ultimate, eschatological victory of life and light assured (1:5). The creation story is thus established as the backdrop to the Gospel, without which its understanding of salvation cannot adequately be grasped." Dorothy A. Lee, "Creation, Matter, and the Image of God in the Gospel of John," *St Vladimir's Theological Quarterly* 62 (2018): 103. On creation themes in John, see especially Carlos Raúl Sosa Siliezar, *Creation Imagery in the Gospel of John* (LNTS; London: Bloomsbury T&T Clark, 2015), 1-22; and Dorothy A. Lee, "Creation, Ethics, and the Gospel of John," in *John and Ethics* (eds. S. Brown & C. Skinner; Philadelphia: Fortress, 2017); John Painter, "Earth Made Whole: John's Reading of Genesis," in *Word, Theology, and Community in John* (eds. R. A. Culpepper, F. F. Segovia & J. Painter; St Louis, MO: Chalice, 2002), 65-84.

the tribes of Israel. Where not the patriarch considered God's children? I will argue that to be children of God, one must have access to eternal life, something that the patriarchs or the Israelites did not have. The reader anticipates a creative act but before the prologue reveals what it will produce in verse 12, the reader needs more background data. I ventured ahead to find the purpose of the creation theme, yet we need to return to the first verses to examine more closely the role of the Word.

Most commentaries focus on the linguistic problems of the first four verses because questions of translation need to be resolved. For example, In 1:1 the relation between the Word and God is expressed by the preposition "to" or "toward," (πρὸς) but most translations reflect this relationship as a static presence ("with") rather than a movement or orientation "toward." However, the accusative case of πρὸς ("to" or "toward") generally refers to a spatial (motion) relationship: one thing is moving toward another.[50] The preposition best expresses the mission of the Word, which is sent forth from God to create.[51] In the Gospel, Christ was sent on a mission by the Father and anticipates his return to the Father. The Word, while on mission, thus requires movement from the Father only to return "to" the Father, the place of origin. A grammatical preposition of motion

---

[50] See Moloney, *John*, 35, 42.

[51] The perception of the "Word" being "toward God" expresses an intimate relationship. See Francis J. Moloney, "'In the Bosom of' or 'Turned towards' the Father," *AusBR* 31 (1983): 63-71; Ignace de la Potterie, "L'emploi de eis dans Saint Jean et ses incidences theologiques," Biblica 43 (1962): 366-87; and Andrew T. Lincoln, *The Gospel According to Saint John* (BNTC. Peabody, MA: Hendrickson, 2005), 97.

such as πρὸς ("to" or "toward") best reflects the Word while on a mission to create. While the Word is on mission, it is distinct from God, though still acting as divine. The relationship between the Word and God is best described in the phrase "the Word was God."

To the untrained eye, this phrase appears simple and unassuming. To appreciate its complexity, one needs to understand how the Greek definite article is used. The predicate, "Word," has the definite article while the subject of "God" is anarthrous. This means that God and the Word are distinct; they are not the same reality.[52] This phrase is one of the most impressive and provocative Greek constructions in the New Testament. If the wording is not perfect, two egregious theological errors can result. On the one hand, the present construction does not say that the "Word" is just another way of saying "God," making them synonymous. They are, in fact, two different beings even though they share equal divine value. This is reflected by giving one a define article and the other remains without one. Moreover, the phrase does not say that the Word is a god among many gods. This would result if the order of the nouns were switched. This phrase is one of the most evasive yet meaningful theological statements in the Bible, condensed and packaged in the most unassuming structure. Before the first verse is even put in the rearview mirror, the reader has a grasp of the author's skills. Why highlight the distinction between "Word" and "God?" The Word is sent forth from God on a mission to create.

---

[52] See Warren Carter, "The Prologue and John's Gospel: Function, Symbol and the Definitive Word," *JSNT* 39 (1990): 37.

Another debated issue comes at the break between verses 3 and 4.[53] There are two possible readings. One is to include all three mentions of the verb "to be' in one sentence: "All things came to be (aorist) through him, and without him came to be (aorist) nothing that has come to be (perfect). In him was life..." The other option is to separate the final two verbs "to be" because of the tense shift: "All things came into being (aorist) through him, and without him not one thing came into being (aorist). What has come into being (perfect) in him was life...." The perfect tense indicates that whatever happened in the past has consequences in the present. That is, the word not only created the world but continues to offer life in the present. Some argue that the shift from the aorist tense to the perfect tense refers to the incarnation rather than primordial creation.[54] There is no way of knowing the intention of the author with certainty in this case, which is why the issue is so disputed. The prologue seems to have clear breaks between celestial and earthly spheres that nicely compartmentalize each section. It is easier to understand the text before the discussion of John the Baptist in verse 5 as an explanation of the effects of the Word in creation both past and present. The verb "came into being" in verse 3 reflects creation. Brown writes: "The fact that the "Word" creates means that creation

---

[53] The punctuation of the third line of the second strophe has been long debated. For overviews, see Ignace de la Potterie, "De punctuatie en de exegese van Joh 1,3.4 in de traditie," *Bijdragen* 16 (1955): 117-35; K. Aland, "Eine Untersuchung zu Joh. 1.3/4 Über die Bedeutung eines Punktes'" ZNW 59 (1968): 174- 209 ; E. L. Miller, *Salvation-History in the Prologue of John: The Significance of John 1:3/4* (SupNT ; LX; Leiden: Brill, 1989).

[54] See Miller, *Prologue of John*, 51-72; Moloney, *John*, 36.

is an act of revelation."⁵⁵ The mention of light, life, and darkness is part of the language of the creation. As Brown argues, it would have been a tautology to have the incarnation appear before and after the appearance of John the Baptist.⁵⁶ Verses leading up to John explain that not only did the Word create (aorist) the world but also life. Light and the futility of darkness are sustained (perfect tense) by the power of the Word.⁵⁷ Here, the reader is informed that revelation (light) and life are intrinsically connected. Later in the Gospel one will see how revelation will produce eternal life: "so that everyone who believes in him may not perish but may have eternal life" (3:16).

The prologue begins now to shift its focus from the Word to the world in order to introduce a witness to testify concerning the Word. After a brief introduction showing how the ineffable beauty of the heavenly Word contributes to the world, the reader leaves divine space and for the first time is on earth with the introduction of John of the Baptism. One immediately notes a literary change of style. Poetry and staircase progressions are replaced with prose. The shift has harbored numerous investigations. Either the prose reflects a later interpolation, the original with the poetic version added later, or the author intended to differentiate the celestial and earthly spheres with varied literary styles. It is not the scope of this study to jump into this particular discussion. It is enough to say that the final

---

⁵⁵ Brown, *John*, 25.

⁵⁶ Ibid., *John*, 26-27.

⁵⁷ The term "overcome" is difficult to translate. Scholars offer four possibilities: (1) to grasp, to comprehend, (2) to welcome, receive, accept, appreciate, (3) to master, (4) to overtake, overcome (grasp in a hostile sense). See Brown, John 8, for a complete overview.

edition reflects two distinct styles to represent two distinct spheres. The text shows that John is of human origins with direct contact with God. The only other person who is described as "from God" is Jesus (1:14; 6:46; 7:29; 9:16, 33; 16:27; 17:8). Like the Word, he is sent on a mission. He also clarifies the differences between himself and the Word, just as the literary style distinguishes the two for the reader. John's mission is to validate the light to the world—i.e., the revelation of God—with his testimony.[58] John's witness is legitimate because he was sent from God. For both the Word and John, the legitimacy of their witness depends on their origin: God.

After the encounter with John on earth, the audience returns to the divine sphere in verse 10 where the first sign of negativity and resistance occurs. He—the Word—entered creation but the world did not know him. This indicates the need for revelation. Its importance cannot be under-estimated because truth is the antidote for ignorance. The problem of obliviousness can be easily remedied by the presence of the Word/truth/revelation. John 1:11-12 represent two responses to revelation: rejection or acceptance. Light is "life" coming into the world and everyone will be exposed. No one can escape decision. All must make the choice.[59] Before John, light overcame darkness. That was a definitive act. No one had a choice in the

---

[58] John is not the light but Jesus calls him a burning and shining lamp in 5:35. He also confirms John's role as a divine messenger who testifies to the truth (32-34). See Peter Borgen, "Logos Was the True Light: Contributions to the Interpretation of the Prologue of John," *NT* 14 (1972): 115-30.

[59] "The revelation brings division, sifting out persons according to how they respond to it. Each of the characters around Jesus represents a type of response to him. By surveying the entire scheme of characterization in the

matter. Now there is a choice. One can prefer darkness and ignorance. Unlike the creation of animated beings before John, the production of children of God requires a positive response: belief. The divine project is beginning to take shape. The Word comes into the world where there is ignorance. Truth appears to all as revelation. One is required to choose, a decision that will end in rejection or acceptance. Those who receive him will be children of God. So the creative Word enters creation to make children of God by revelation of the truth, as light symbolizes truth. Divine power is contingent on human reception, whereas, before John, light and life were not options. John the Baptist represents the watershed.

In 1:14 the terms "flesh" and "Word" are juxtaposed in a unique way. Instead of presenting the terms as bitter rivals, they are contrasted not as odds against each other but highlighting their compatibility. The "Word" has entered the constraints of the flesh and has come among its own things. Why embrace limitation? The answer is visibility or divine glory. The "Word" is now visible, tangible, and audible to humanity because it takes on flesh. Gnostics, of course, would not approve such a downgrade. Flesh is susceptible to restrictions such as instability, emotional flux, contingency, and death. Hellenistic philosophical sensitivities would have been shaken with such a phrase as "the Word became flesh." It would be unthinkable in such circles to encourage anyone to leave the sphere

---

Gospel, we see the whole range of responses to the revelation and the consequences of these responses." Culpepper, "Theology," 426.

of truth, universals, logistics, stability, and permanence.⁶⁰ There is nothing in the text to indicate that this transformation bears limitations, restrictions, or negative consequences on the Word. On the contrary, it offers accessibility and availability by becoming tangible. What was invisible (no one has ever seen God) is now visible for all to see. For this Gospel, the only way to contact truth is it has to appear to humanity from God. Later in the Gospel, the truth of revelation will liberate believers, not from materiality, but death and slavery. Choice is a requirement because God is manifested to the senses. Later in the Gospel, "testimony" produces a stronger bond between the believer and God: "blessed are those who do not see and still believe" (20:29) will be more important than tangible evidence.

The prologue then goes on to use a curious word to describe the Word's presence among us: σκηνόω ("to tabernacle, or "to pitch a tent"). Why use the verb "to tabernacle" (σκηνόω)? A clue may be found in the Gospel at the festival of booths (ἡ σκηνοπηγία), an agricultural feast that requires Jewish males to live in tents for the duration of the feast.⁶¹ The feast is a thanksgiving to God for the gift of light and water that facilitates growth and makes the harvest possible. During the celebration in John 7, Jesus, ironically, will declare that he provides living water and that he is the light of the world, the very metaphors for revelation that offer humans eternal life. Water and light are understood as sources of agricultural growth that contribute to human life. The imagery represents how divine revelation

---

⁶⁰ Chris H. Dodd, *The Interpretation of the Fourth Gospel* (Cambridge: CUP, 1953),15; Brown, *John*, 31.

⁶¹ God abides with his people in the desert in the tent (Sknvn) Exod 25:8-9 (See also Exod 29:46; Sir 24:8, 10; Zech. 2:10).

produces eternal life. The prologue presents the creative ingredient of light that is celebrated at the feast. By stating the Word pitches His tent among the celebrants during the celebration of water and light prepares the reader to understand the role of Christ in the world as a source for living food and provider of light and water.

In verse 15, John once again clarifies the pre-existence of the Word. This informs the reader of the importance of the Word's origin. Establishing origin is necessary in the Gospel because, as I will argue throughout, it authenticates Jesus' revelatory claims. The verse also connects the prologue to the Gospel where the words of the verse are repeated in 1:30: "After me comes a man who ranks ahead of me because he was before me."

The Torah of Moses cannot provide eternal life. Why does God need to send the Word to create children when He has already given the Law through Moses, a covenant in which God becomes a father to the Israelites? Are the people of God not already His children? In John 6, Jesus will show that God provided food, water, and protection in the desert, but the Israelites all died in there. God will now offer eternal life to all who believe.[62] According to the author of John, believing in the one who was sent is the only way to become a child of God with access to eternal life. God gave gifts through Moses but all have died, while Christ produces "grace against grace." This odd expression has been often debated. The preposition that separates the two mentions of grace can be understood in two ways. One grace

---

[62] The expression "life eternal" occurs in John 17 times and "life" 36 times.

complements the other, or one grace replaces the other. The interpretive key to this phrase seems to be located in the next verse. There, the text contrasts the Law of Moses with the truth of Christ.[63] In the Gospel, Jesus says that divine gifts were given through Moses, such as food from heaven, but all have died (6:49). The gift that Jesus offers produces eternal life. Both Moses and Jesus offer divine gifts but one has a clear advantage over the other, as if one gift replaces the other. The prologue also discusses two gifts with unequal advantages in order to promote the power of divine revelation. Revelation can make a distinctive difference for everyone.

In the next and final verse, the reader meets the informant of divine truth and His qualifications. The purpose of this verse is to legitimate the revealer. Here, the prologue expounds on Christ's relationship with the Father. The reader has already encountered the relationship between the Word and God. The prologue now describes it as a Father/Son relationship. Since the incarnation of the Word made flesh, the prologue replaces the term "Word" for "Christ." Christ is like no one else: "no one has ever seen God." In 1:18 the "bosom" of the Father is used as a metaphor to highlight their close connection. Later, the one whom Jesus loved will be reclined next to him at dinner, again describing closeness. Being at the

---

[63] Heil states "For example, whereas the law was given through Moses, the gift of truth came about through the person of Jesus Christ (1:17); the abundant and choice wine that has now arrived with Jesus at Cana (2:10) replaces the water of the Jewish ritual cleansings (2:6); the resurrected body of Jesus replaces the destroyed sanctuary of the temple (2:20-22); the bread of life that Jesus gives surpasses the manna Moses gave (6:32)." John Paul Heil, "Jesus as the Unique High Priest in the Gospel of John," *CBQ* 57 (1995): 745.

bosom is a position of particular notoriety. It is attested in Pliny the Younger's letter: "He spoke no less courageously in the presence of the emperor Nerva, who was dining with a few People. Veiento was next to him, and snuggled up against him (*in sinu recumbebat*, lit., "laid on his chest" [Ep. 4.22.2]).[64] In the parable of Lazarus and the rich man, Lazarus is found in Abraham's bosom. Philip F. Esler maintains that the scene represents a messianic banquet because reclining at the bosom describes a dinner.[65] According to Alexey Somov and Vitaly Voinov, the expression "Abraham's bosom" in the parable means both a close fellowship and a "banquet."[66] It would not be unreasonable if a first century reader were to understand the expression "in the bosom of the Father" as sharing these two features, especially in light of the Last Supper when the beloved disciple and Jesus are reclined together. In 1:18 Christ assumes a reclined position to be at the bosom of the Father: "It is God the only Son, who is close to the Father's bosom, who has made him known."[67] So if one understands the term "bosom" to refer to a seating position at

---

[64] Pliny the Younger, *Complete Letters* (Rans. P. G. Walsh; Oxford World's Classics; Oxford: Oxford
University Press, 2006), 101. Cited from Alexey Somov and Vitaly Voinov, "Abraham's Bosom" (Luke 16:22-23) as a Key Metaphor in the Overall Composition of the Parable of the Rich man and Lazarus," *CBQ* 79 (2017): 627. See also Joachim Jeremias, *Parables of Jesus* (London, S.C.M. Press. 1972), 184.

[65] Philip F. Esler, *Community and Gospel in Luke-Acts: The Social and Political Motivations of Lucan Theology* (SNTSMS 57; Cambridge: Cambridge University Press, 1987), 193.

[66] Somov and Voinov, "Abraham's Bosom," 628.

[67] Jesus is the only one who is referred to as "the Son of God." Believers (children of God) are never called sons of God in the Gospel.

meals and banquets in the ancient world, then it is reasonable to picture a person in the reclined position. One can lean to the side where the head can rest on the chest or bosom of the person. Due to the close proximity, the one leaning back into the chest of the neighbor can hear everything the bosom buddy says, even whispered tones that are not heard by others around the table. Verse 18 offers a portrait of a son leaning against his father with his ear a few inches from his father's mouth and hears everything. Christ's ear is so close to the Father that he hears everything. The Son knows what the Father says, what he is thinking, and what he feels. Due to his privileged position as a Son, the Word has access to the voice of God. This same Word can deliver with existential ramifications. God's Word delivers the same message as if the one hearing is likewise at the same privileged place of the Son at table. The last word of the prologue in Greek is ἐξηγέομαι. It has a prefix. Without the prefix the word, means "to lead," "to think," "to believe," or "to regard as." It is only used once with the prefix by John and six time in the entire New Testament: "to make known," "to describe," or "to explain." Placing the word at the end of the sentence further highlights its significance. Here the prologue ends with a term which begins the process of the Word: revelation. The creative Word now enters to reveal the words of the Father, those who hear it and believe will obtain the same information as the only begotten son, as if they were at the bosom of the Father hearing the voice of God. "Jesus' role is defined from the outset as that of revealing the Father."[68] After all, the divine

---

[68] R. Alan Culpepper, "The Theology of the Gospel of John," *RevExp* 85 (1988): 422.

initiative is to produce children of God by revelation. Accepting the truth offered by Christ metaphorically places that person in the seat of a son at the banquet.

In conclusion, the prologue gives the reader important information about the message of the narrative that is to follow. First, it talks about relationships: a Father, a Son, and soon to be children. The purpose of the incarnation is revelation: "to make known" (1:18). The truth forces a choice: darkness/destruction or children of God. It all depends on how the Word is received. This is very unlike the production of the world, which was not contingent on any factors. What the reader does not know from the prologue is that the term "children of God" means possessing eternal life. One knows, however, that revelation and life are linked together. Implicitly one can conclude that obtaining the truth as a child of God will result in life. It also does not explicitly say that the Father sent the Son, nor that the Son will return to the Father. Still, the preposition in 1:1 already alerted the reader to some kind of gravitational movement with regard to the Word and God. The Gospel will flesh out the skeletal structure of the prologue, expanding on the divine plan, a strategy to send the word in the world to create children of God by revelation. I will now proceed with my interpretation of the Gospel. To my knowledge, no one has ever systematically read the Gospel using the prologue as a roadmap or using intratextuality to seek out interpretive solutions quite like this study.

Part 2

The Books of Signs

(Revelation Accessible to Particular Groups)

Part 2

The Books of Signs

(Revelation Accessible to Particular Groups)

Section 1: Believers

Seven Days (1:19–2:11)

The Gospel of John appears to have two distinct sections. The first comprises of 12 chapters that showcase Jesus offering revelation to individuals and small groups. We begin with the first section. The first 12 chapters are often known as the book of signs. The focus of these chapters is to highlight all of the characteristics of believers and non-believers. The second section is often called the Book of Glory, where Jesus no longer offers revelation to select groups but to everyone. These chapters introduce us to a new category: believers who fear.

After the prologue, the Gospel proper begins with an account that is divided into seven days (1:19–2:11), recalling the seven days of creation.[69] The first four days speak of John the Baptist and the calling of the disciples. Next, the author records an additional three days, the last of which is a wedding: "On the third day there was a

---

[69] Another attractive insight into the matter of the three days that introduces the wedding of Cana is the use of Exodus as a background source. "On the third day" is also a quote from Exodus 19:16 which introduces a report of the presence of God in the camp. God gives instructions to Moses and Aaron before he gave Moses the Decalogue on Mount Sinai in Exodus 20. According to Maloney, the Exodus text provides the necessary background for understanding the wedding of Cana. In addition to literary and thematic links, he claims that the prologue also confirms the Old Testament passage by specifically calling out attention to the Law given to Moses: "The Law was given through Moses; the gift that is the truth came through Jesus Christ" (1:17). See Moloney, *John*, 66.

wedding at Cana." The seven-day creation motif allows the narrative to continue the Genesis 1 theme that began the prologue.[70] However, this motif is not the only detail that connects these two sections. In both the prologue and the seven-day narrative, John the Baptist testifies. The prologue discusses those who accept the Word and those who do not. In the seven-day narrative, those who will not accept Jesus (Jews, religious leaders, Pharisees) are introduced before those who accept Jesus (disciples), the same sequence that is found in the prologue.[71] The prologue discusses the Word's origin. The seven-day narrative likewise focuses on Jesus' origin: We will see the disciple's question to Jesus: "Where do you remain," and the comment by Jesus on angels "ascending" and "descending" on the Son of Man (1:51).[72] The prologue also reports that those who believe will receive

---

[70] See M. Boismard, *Du Baptôme à Cana (Jean 1,19–2,11)* (LeDiv 18. Paris: Cerf., 1956), 14-15; Harold Saxby, "The Time-Scheme in the Gospel of John," *ET* 104 (1992), 9-13. Some scholars maintain that the days bear no interpretive meaning. See Schnackenburg, *John*, 297, 308, 313.

[71] Dorothy A. Lee, understands discipleship in John as "primarily in terms of witnessing and abiding." See her "Abiding in the Fourth Gospel: A Case-study in Feminist Biblical Theology," *Pacifica* 10 (1997): 123-36. See also Rekha Chennattu, "On Becoming Disciples (John 1:35-51): Insights from the Fourth Gospel," *Salesianum* 63 (2001): 465-496; Fernando F. Segovia, "'Peace I Leave with You; My Peace I Give to You': Discipleship in the Fourth Gospel," in *Discipleship in the New Testament* (Philadelphia: Fortress, 1985), 76-102; Mark F. Whitters, "Discipleship in John: Four Profiles," *WW* 18 (1998): 422-427; P. Palatty, "Discipleship in the Fourth Gospel: An Acted Out Message of Disciples as Characters," *Biblebhashyam* 25 (1999): 285-306.

[72] The title "Son of Man" appears thirteen times in John (1.51; 3.13, 14; 5.27; 6.27, 53, 62; 8.28; 9.35; 12.23, 34 a, b; 13.31). Its common usage is understood as a way of emphasizing the incarnation. See Jerome H.

Part 2: The Books of Signs (Section I: Believers)

power to become children of God, since the purpose of the creative "Word" was to come among his own. Finally, at the end of the seven-day narrative, during the wedding feast, it is announced that the disciples believe: "and his disciples believed in him" (2:11). The seven day narrative (1:19–2:11), I will argue, carefully follows the prologue, which was introduced with the opening words from Genesis describing the seven-day creation narrative: "In the beginning."[73]

There is a nice transition from the prologue and the beginning of the body of the Gospel proper. Both texts mention John who is sent to witness and in both texts he states that the one coming after him existed before him (1:15, 30). The entire Gospel never drifts far from the divine plan that was introduced by the prologue. This is especially true when the prologue shifts to treat John the Baptist as a testifier. James Dodd notes that the first three days which discuss John the Baptist match the treatment of John in the prologue.[74] On the first day, John informs the leaders who he is not. On the second day he testifies about Jesus. On the third day, he points out Jesus so

---

Neyrey, "The Noble Shepherd in John 10: Cultural and Rhetorical Background," *JBL* 120 (2001): 267-291; Peter W. Ensor, "The Authenticity of John 4.35," *EvQ* 72 (2000): 13-21.

[73] Although Brown acknowledges a seven-day week after the prologue, he remains reluctant to conclude with certainty that the seven days of creation is in fact the intention of the author or final redactor. However, Brown does not take into account the purpose of the Word's reentry into the world, which according to the prologue is to create children of God through belief in the Word. I will show that at the end of the seven-day cycle, the disciples believe, reflecting the creation theme in the prologue which states that the Word re-enters the world to offer truth which will produce believers.

[74] Dodd, *Interpretation*, 248.

his disciples will follow. Similarly, in the prologue, John is described by what he is not: "he was not the light" (1:8); his role is to testify: "he came to testify to the light" (1:8); and he will lead all to believe: "so that all might believe through him" (1:6). In both texts, it specifies that John is sent to testify. Finally, in the prologue, John witnesses so that all might believe through him: "he came as a witness to testify to the light so that all might believe through him" (1:7). This prediction comes to fruition in the Gospel because it is reported that many came to believe in Jesus because of John's testimony, not because he offered signs: "John performed no sign, but everything that John said about this man was true. And many believed in him there" (10:41).

John is the microcosm of the prologue, the place where heaven and earth meet. Having direct contact from God makes him an authoritative and legal witness. A person's origin validates his testimony. Later, the Gospel makes clear that Christ cannot testify on his own. Christ always has backup for his words and identity, typically from the Father Himself. John the Baptist's role is expressed repeatedly as a witness (1:7, 19). It is John's role to provide the witness that can lead to faith in Jesus: "He came as a witness to testify to the light, so that all might believe through him" (1:7).[75] John the Baptist gives witness and his origin that he comes from God authenticates this testimony on earth. One gains possession of the Word by a witness who can verify its authenticity and validity. Yet, the gift only counts when it is accepted and possessed by the recipient through belief.

---

[75] The verb for witness is used 33 times. The noun is used 14 times.

Part 2: The Books of Signs (Section I: Believers) 55

Even though the testimony gives validity to the Word, still, the recipient must believe in its authenticity. Testimony is the necessary link between the Word that comes from God and the recipient/believer. That is why the "witness" is so essential in this Gospel. Testimony puts the faithful in contact with the Word and provides proof of its authenticity by way of the witness's origins. The one who receives the Word then believes and becomes eligible for eternal life. Later, the Gospel will show that the believer will be required to witness to the truth so that others will be eligible for eternal life. The Word, therefore, passes from one witness to another. As the reader advances through the narrative it becomes more apparent that the purpose of the Gospel is to encourage, support, and ensure this continuing cycle.

John the Baptist begins this cycle. His direct contact with God authenticates the testimony that he offers. Because he is sent from God, he provides a necessary link between the origin of the Word that comes from above and the presence of the Word in the world.

John the Baptist in the Gospel of John is very different from the synoptic versions: he is not Elijah (Mark, Matthew),[76] not a prophet (Luke), and does not promote a baptism for the forgiveness of sin: that is the role of the "lamb of God who takes away the sin of the world" (1:29).[77] Also absent from the Synoptics is John's sole interest

---

[76] Mark 1:2 cites Mal 3:1 to identify John with Elijah and Matthew 11:14 records Jesus' words "If you are willing to accept it, he is Elijah who is to come."

[77] On the relationship between John and the Synoptics, see C. K. Barrett, "John and the Synoptic Gospels," *ExpTim* 85 (1973-74): 228-33; Frans

to witness. Only John refers to Christ as the "Lamb of God." John also adds geographic locations not specified in the other Gospels, such as his ministry in Aenon near Salim (3:23).

There are also a number of similarities between John and the Synoptics. All four confirm John's baptisms in the Jordan, discuss the removal of sin, and cite Isa 40:3. There are many minor discrepancies between the Synoptics which single out each Gospel's treatment of the Baptist. The author of John adopts some of these differences but shows that he does not favor one Gospel over the other. John follows Mark's lead when using the term "stoop" (κύπτω, 1:7), and both do not mention a baptism with fire, unlike Matthew (3:11) and Luke (3:16). John agrees with Matthew's "carry sandals" (Matt 3:11) and both adopt the phrase ἐν ὕδατι ("in water," Matt 3:11; John 1:26), while Mark and Luke prefer ὕδατι (Mark 1:8; Luke 1:16). John and Luke both "unfasten the straps" (Luke 3:16; John 1:27). Both Acts and John use the term "worthy"(ἄξιος, Acts 13:25; John 1:27); both also do not use the expression "mightier than I."[78] Dodd claims

---

Neirynck, "John and the Synoptics," in *L'Évangile de Jean: Sources, Rédaction, Théologie* (ed. Marinus de Jonge; BETL44; Leuven: Leuven University Press, 1977), 73-106; Thomas Brodie, *The Quest for the Origin of John's Gospel: A Source-Oriented Approach* (New York: Oxford University Press, 1993); Paul N. Anderson, *The Christology of the Fourth Gospel: Its Unity and Disunity in the Light of John 6* (Valley Forge, PA: Trinity Press International, 1996); Raymond E. Brown, *The Community of the Beloved Disciple: The Life, Loves, and Hates of an Individual Church in New Testament Times* (New York: Paulist, 1979); John Painter, *The Quest for the Messiah: The History, Literature, and Theology of the Johannine Community* (2nd ed.; Nashville: Abingdon, 1993).

[78] Brown, *John*, 52.

that the diverse treatment of John the Baptist between the four Gospels is probably due to multiple traditions circulating in the early church.[79] I would rather suggest that the different treatments of John has more to do with the theological theme of each Gospel. John the Baptist appears to introduce each Gospel's unique themes. Due to the limitations of this study, I will restrict my findings to John's Gospel. One why of discovering this theme in John is to observe repetition and redundancies in this section.

One notes the number of doublets in this first chapter after the prologue: twice a group arrives to interrogate (19-23 and 24-27), twice John claims the pre-existence of Christ (15, 30), twice he draws attention to the Lamb of God (29, 36), twice it mentions that John the Baptist was baptizing with water (1:26, 31), twice the Baptist "saw" the Spirit (32, 34), twice John "testified" (32, 34), twice he did "not know him" at first (31, 33), and twice the Spirit descends (32, 33). Scholars usually attribute such doubles to a literary evolution, speculating that the final canonical form was a product of editorial stages. Scholars offer reconstructions that reflect this development.[80] Without denying the stages of development, I will argue that the repetition serves the final author by connecting the four separate days with literary and thematic links and establishing theological coherence early on in the narrative. The seven days elaborates on the prologue's creation theme. The Word will enter the world. He will be witnessed by John the Baptist. Those who accept him will believe.

---

[79] Dodd, *Interpretation*, 256.

[80] See D. Moody Smith, *The Composition and Order of the Fourth Gospel: Bultmann's Literary Theory* (New Haven, Yale University Press, 1965); Brown, *John*, 67-71; Boismard, "Les Tradtions," 67-71.

Day one introduces those who will reject revelation (Jews, religious leaders, Pharisees). Day two will introduce Christ. Days three and four introduce those who accept him. The final day realizes the goal of the prologue in creating believers (those who accept the "word"), a fitting conclusion for the "Word" who was sent to create children of God.

The First Day: Introducing the rejecters of the Word (1:19-28)

John the Baptist's role is expressed twice as a witness (1:7, 19). His introduction in 1:6 brings the sublime celestial gaze to earth. As mentioned above, he is the microcosm of the prologue, the place where heaven and earth meet. It is John's role to provide the witness that can lead to faith in the Word: "He came as a witness to testify to the light, so that all might believe through him" (1:7).

Immediately following the prologue, John is introduced as one who gives testimony: "This is the testimony given by John when the Jews sent Priests and Levites" (1:19). John's identity is addressed while informing the first "sent" group that he is a voice crying (1:19). In light of the prologue, that "cry" (κράζω) is meant to give testimony to the Pre-existent One who is to come after him: "John testified to him and cried out" (1:15). John clearly has something to say because the light has arrived: "And I myself have seen and have testified that this is the Son of God" (1:34). The two groups that are "sent," Priest/Levites (1:9) and Pharisees (1:24), provide question-and-answer sessions that explain who John is (1:15, 23, 26) and who he is not (1:8, 20-22, 25).

In the prologue, the reader is introduced to those who would reject the "Word" before any mention of the believers is made. Here the same pattern follows: Jews, religious leaders, and Pharisees, who are mentioned in the two interrogation scenes with John the Baptist (19-23; 24-27), will be linked later on with those who reject Jesus and his testimony. They represent those who do not receive him. After introducing the nonbelievers, the future believers (disciples) are then introduced to Jesus and they begin to follow Him. The nonbelievers are introduced before the believers, reflecting the order of the prologue as stated above. John testifies to both future non-believers and believers, confirming the prologue's description that John came to testify to everyone: "so that all might believe" (1:7). Both the future non-believers and believers ask questions, but those who accept Jesus ask the question, "where." The two disciples ask "Where do you remain?" (1:38), and Nathaniel asks, "Where did you get to know me?" (1:48). Both were invited with the same phrase: "Come and you will see." Both questions receive positive answers while those who represent the rejecters receive negative responses from their interrogations: "I am not the Messiah," "I am not," "No" "You do not know." The purpose of the opening section to the main body of the Gospel is to introduce and begin to distinguish the non-believers from the believers, a distinction that was also made in the prologue.

It is important to remember not to conflate the role of John the Baptist with the other Gospels: "And they asked him, 'What then? Are you Elijah?' He said, 'I am not.' 'Are you the prophet?' He answered, 'No.'" (1:20-21). In John's Gospel, the Baptist does not look like Elijah who in 2 Kings 2:11 is described as a hairy man with a leather belt around his waist (Mark/Matthew), nor is he a prophet who is filled with the Holy Spirit (Luke 1:76). All the fiery passion of John's preaching, his dramatic death, his biographical details, and the comparisons to Jesus with which we have become so familiar in the Synoptics make no appearance in John's Gospel. There is little hope that most people could emulate the lifestyle of John the Baptist portrayed in the Synoptic Gospels – eating locusts, wearing camel hair, and acting as a stand-in for the prophet Elijah. The fourth evangelist's John, however, is the one whom one can imitate because his work is to witness, something that will be expected from other believers. John's role will be imitated by the mother of Jesus, the Samaritan woman, the man born blind, and the beloved disciple at the foot of the cross.

John's baptism is not described as a baptism of repentance for the forgiveness of sin as in the Synoptics. John has one task: testimony. His baptism is a baptism of witness. In the Synoptics, people go out to be baptized for the forgiveness of sin. In the Gospel of John, the Baptist does not offer a baptism of repentance or for the forgiveness of sins. It is solely for the purpose of revealing.[81] Here, people go out to John to ask him who he is. John has little to say about himself because his job is to identify and bear witness to the Son whom the Father sent. John was sent by God to say that Jesus who existed before him came from the Father: "I came baptizing with water for this reason, that he might be revealed to Israel" (1:31). This is

---

[81] See Thompson, "Baptism with Water," 65.

the first hint that water symbolizes revelation.[82] Washing in the baptism of John provides Israel with divine revelation/truth (1:31).

According to the prologue, the Christ event is an extension of creation and not directly tied to any eschatological expectations of the time. The opening scene seems to confirm this by downplaying future hopes: i.e., the return of Elijah, the coming of the Messiah, and the arrival of a prophet.[83]

The first "I am" (Ἐγώ εἰμι) statement comes out of the mouth of John the Baptist to assure priests and Levites from Jerusalem that he is not the Messiah: "I am not the Messiah."[84] His next two denials ("I am not," "no") differ from the first in that they do not include the phrase "I am." Even when Peter denies Jesus, he never uses the "I

---

[82] Sherri Brown states that "Water symbolizes revelation. Giving water points to Jesus as the revelation of new life and the means by which one enters it, the Spirit." See her "Water imagery and the power and presence of God in the Gospel of John," *TT* 72 (2015): 298. See also Culpepper, *Anatomy*, 194.

[83] Howard Merle Teeple argues that there was a general expectation that God would raise a prophet like Moses according to Deut 18:18: "I will raise up for them a prophet like you (Moses) from among their own people; I will put my words in the mouth of the prophet." See his *The Mosiac Eschatological Prophet* (JBL Monograph, X; Philadelphia, Society of Biblical Literature, 1957). A. S. van der Woude suggests that the three eschatological figures associated with John the Baptist in John are linked to the Covenanters' expectations. He draws similarities between John the Baptist and the Essenes, from both locations (desert) and ideology. For example, both John and the Essenes use Isa 40:3 to describe themselves. See his *La secte de Qumran* (recherches Bibliques, IV; Louvain: 1959), 121-34. See also 1QS 9:11.

[84] See Edwin D. Freed, "Egō Eimi in John 1:20 and 4:25," *CBQ* 41 (1979): 288-91.

am" statement (18:17, 25). It is only in reference to the Messiah that the "I am" statement is used. The next time the expression "I am" is employed, it actually affirms Jesus as Messiah: "I know the Messiah is coming. 'I am' (Ἐγώ εἰμι) he, the one who is speaking to you" (4:25-26). The first two "I am" statements appear to be related to the Messiah.[85] The Samaritan woman reveals the role of the Messiah: "When he comes, he will proclaim all things to us" (4:25). That is, she understands the role of the Messiah as one who will reveal everything. Later she reports to the villagers that Jesus told her everything, confirming her job description of the Messiah: "Come and see a man who told me everything I have ever done. He cannot be the Messiah, can he?" (4:29). Her statement confirms the prologue's words that Jesus' role is to reveal (1:18).

The first four days mark a progression of Christological titles. We saw above how, on day one, John refers to the Messiah. On day two, John the Baptist introduces Jesus as the: "Lamb of God" (twice: 1:29, 30) and "Son of God" (1:34). On day three, John's two disciples call Jesus "Rabbi" (1:34) before they "come and see." After staying with Jesus, Andrew upgrades his decision and calls Jesus "the Christ" in 1:41. On day four, Nathanael includes all three of these titles in his address to Jesus: "Rabbi, you are the Son of God, you are the king of Israel" (1:49). Nathanael's final insight that Jesus is the king brings the reader back to John's first words, "I am not the Messiah." If John is not the Messiah then who is? John answers this question before

---

[85] The fourteen ἐγώ εἰμί statements found throughout the Gospel are used to associate Jesus with God the Father. Richard Bauckham, *The Testimony of the Beloved Disciple: Narrative, History, and Theology in the Gospel of John* (Grand Rapids: Baker Academic, 2007), 247.

the wedding at Cana where Jesus reveals himself with a sign. The role of the Messiah is well defined as a revealer: "When he comes, he will proclaim all things to us" (4:25); "Come and see a man who told me everything I have ever done. He cannot be the Messiah can he?" (4:29).

After the initial disclaimers to those who will eventually reject Jesus's words, John describes himself with a citation from Isaiah 40:3. "I am the voice of one crying out in the wilderness, Make straight the way of the Lord" (1:23). One notes a slight difference from the Synoptic Gospels in that the Baptist himself uses the text to witness about himself, further demonstrating his role as a testifier. In the Synoptics, the authors use the citation to characterize John. One also sees that the Isaian citation is an abbreviated version of the Synoptics quote, combining two phrases into one. Here the reader catches a first glimpse at the way the author loosely cites the LXX to pad his own rhetorical agenda.[86]

The geographic reference to "Bethany across the Jordan where John was baptizing" at the end of the passage is not unusual in this Gospel (1:28). The same phrase "across the Jordan" is used to describe Jesus at the end of an argument with the Jews during the festival of the Dedication: "He went away again across the Jordan to the place where John had been baptizing earlier, and he remained there" (10:40). Besides the geographical parallel, there is another link between these same passages with a reference back to the Baptist. At 10:41 it continues: "Many came to him and they were saying John

---

[86] See Charles Harold Dodd, *Historical Tradition in the Fourth Gospel* (London: Cambridge University Press, 1976), 252.

performed no sign, but everything that John said about this man was true. And many believed in him there." Both references to the Jordan refer to John and his work, but the second confirms the singular achievement of John which was to witness about Jesus, producing believers.

The Second Day: Introducing Christ (1:29-31)

Jesus arrives on the scene for the first time in the Gospel in verse 29. John responds by calling him "the Lamb of God who takes away the sins of the world" (1:29). It is important enough for John to proclaim the statement a second time in 1:36. I will show that the "Lamb of God" proclamation is a reference to Jesus' "hour" because it refers to His trial and death. The first pronouncement of the phrase, "Behold, the Lamb of God" (1:29), offers no explanation or reaction by others. It is very hard to understand the phrase by way of the immediate context. However, the second time the line is delivered (1:36), the force of the term can be grasped more readily. Two of John's disciples leave John to follow Jesus. The disciples' transition from John to Jesus is made by the mere uttering of this phrase. The repetition of this phrase along with the disciples' dramatic abandoning of their teacher John demonstrates to the reader that there is an important meaning attached to these words. The reader, however, at this early stage of the Gospel has little access to what the term fully implies. Part of the reason for this difficulty is the fact that this is the first scriptural instance of a lamb taking away sin.[87] There are no Old

---

[87] The Lamb is an apocalyptic figure which will conclusively destroy evil. In Rev 7:17, the lamb leads the people, and brings an end to evil in

Testament references to confirm that the lambs at Passover were considered an expiatory sacrifice.[88] The phrase "Lamb (ἀμνός) of God" is, indeed, difficult to understand.[89] It is not found elsewhere in the New Testament, although it is often pointed out in commentaries that Jesus is referred to as the triumphant Lamb (ἀρνίον—a different word) in Revelation (Rev 5:6, 8, 12, 13; 6:1, 6; 7:14).[90] It has been suggested that the phrase is an allusion to Isa 53:7: "like a lamb that is led to the slaughter, and like a sheep that is before its shearers is silent."[91]

17:14. See Dodd, *Interpretation*, 236, for a more extended presentation. The lamb is also described as a suffering servant in Isaiah 43:1-4; 49:1-6; 52:13–53:1. See Morna Hooker, *Jesus and the Servant* (London: SPCK, 1959), who does not see the suffering servant theme as a pre-Christian eschatological salvific figure. Helmer Ringgren maintains that the Essenes did not see the Suffering Servant figure as an eschatological figure or messianic persona, but rather a figure that represented a community that suffered for the sake of others. Jesus is described in terms of the suffering servant elsewhere in John 12:38 following Isa 53:1. See his *The faith of Qumran: Theology of the Dead Sea Scrolls* (Philadelphia: Fortress, 1963), 196-98. For a more complete presentation see Thomas Stanks, *The Servant of God in John 1:29, 36* (Louvain dissertation, 1963).

[88] The paschal lamb does not remove sin, although its blood causes the angel of death to pass over. Joachim Jeremias, "ἀμνὸς," *TDNT*, 1:339; Haenchen, *John*, 152.

[89] Leon Morris, *The Gospel According to John* (Grand Rapids, MI: Eerdmans, 1995), 126. See also Dodd, *Interpretation*, 231-233.

[90] Schnackenburg, *John*, 155-56; Moloney, *John*, 59.

[91] Raymond Brown argues for the connection between John's 'Lamb of God' and Isaiah's 'Suffering Servant', who is likened to a lamb and who 'bore the sins of many,' See his *John*, 60-61, 72.

Regardless of whether these outside sources contribute any interpretive data to John's proclamation, its meaning seems to imply salvation by a vicarious sacrifice. Indeed, one can find the interpretive key of the phrase within the confines of this Gospel. All of the individual components of the phrase are words or themes that can be found in the trial and death of Jesus. Breaking down the phrase, one word at a time, one will discover many references to Jesus during the passion narrative at the end of the Gospel. The phrase "Behold the Lamb of God who takes away the sins of the world (Ἴδε ὁ ἀμνὸς τοῦ θεοῦ ὁ αἴρων τὴν ἁμαρτίαν τοῦ κόσμου) anticipates other similar proclamations about Jesus at his trial. The "behold" formula which is also found in 1:35-37; 47-51, and 19:24-27 is unique to John and not found in the other Synoptic Gospels. The word "behold" is a significant term used by Pilate to prove Jesus' innocence: "behold the man" (Ἰδοὺ ὁ ἄνθρωπος, 19:5); "behold the king" (Ἴδε ὁ βασιλεὺς, 19:14).[92] Also, the Greek word for "take away" (αἴρω) has a highly charged role during Jesus' trial. The crowds demand that Jesus be taken away: "take, take, crucify him" (ἆρον ἆρον, σταύρωσον αὐτόν, 19:15).[93] The term normally refers to the removal of inanimate objects. But there is one instance where the object of this verb is Jesus, and that is at his trial. It is precisely at this time—

---

[92] Ἴδε ("behold") is used 15 times in the gospel whereas ἰδού is used only four times in John, compared to Matthew (62) times, Mark (7), and Luke (57). All three uses here are followed by the nominative.

[93] John uses this term αἴρω ("take away") 26 times. Sometimes he refers to the removal of stones (11:39, 41, 21:1) a mat (5:9, 10, 11, 12), bodies (20:2), unproductive branches (15:2), and joy (16:22).

the "sixth hour"—when the crowds make this demand, the time the lambs begin to be sacrificed in preparation for the Passover.[94]

The Passover symbolism cannot be ignored at Jesus' final hour. While Jesus was on the cross, a sponge full of wine was raised to him on hyssop; it was with hyssop that the Israelites applied the blood on the doorposts (LXX, Exod 12:22; John 19:29 - ὕσσωπος). None of Jesus' bones were broken (19:31), similar to the Passover lamb of Exodus (Exod 12:22). Raymond Brown puts it this way: "The difference between the lamb's blood smeared on the doorpost as a sign of deliverance and the lamb's blood offered in sacrifice for deliverance is not very great."[95] Even by the mid-first century, Paul compares Jesus to the paschal lamb, in terms of sacrificial language: "Christ our Passover has been sacrificed" (1 Cor 5:7). Thus, Jesus' death can be understood as the paschal lamb that was sacrificed.

The term "sin" (ἁμαρτία) is likewise an important term at Jesus' trial. Jesus identifies sin with those who reject him: "Therefore the one who handed me over to you is guilty of a greater sin" (19:11). The word for "sin" is used twelve times in the singular.[96] In John 8 the word "sin" is used a number of times and provides the evangelist an opportunity to define the meaning of the term. Jesus tells his opponents that they cannot come where he is going. The question of "where" is at the center of Jesus' argument. They cannot come because they are from a different place: "You are from below; I am

---

[94] Brown, *John*, 62

[95] Ibid.

[96] 1:29; 8:21, 34, 46; 9:41 (twice); 15:22 (twice); 15:24; 16:8, 9; 19:11. There are four instances that the word is used in the plural (8:24, [twice]; 9:34; 20:23). The term ἀναμάρτητος is used once in 8:7.

from above" (8:23). The two locations are not compatible. The reason they are irreconcilable locations is because of sin: "I told you that you would die in your sins" (8:24). Access to where Jesus is going is reserved for those who believe: "for you will die in your sins unless you believe that I am he" (8:24). The witness, who knows "where," has access to what is essential for entry. Sin prevents access to eternal life and to the kingdom. Only those who believe will have eternal life. The line of argument nicely pairs two sets of opposites. "Above" and "below" are as opposed to each other as "sin" and "belief."[97] John is a witness from above because he was sent: "No one can receive anything except what has been given from heaven" (3:24). In the prologue, John is a man who was "sent from God" (1:6). Now that sin is clearly defined as the privation of belief in revelation, one can see what role sin plays during Jesus' trial.[98]

After the comment on the Lamb of God, John then reechoes what was stated in the prologue: "This is he whom I said, 'After me comes a man who ranks ahead of me because he was before me.'" (1:30). The phrase that follows differs from the Synoptics: "the one mightier than I" (Mark 1:7; Luke 3:16, Matt 3:11). Instead, the phrase "Among you stands one whom you do not know" (1:26) better complies with what the reader heard from the prologue: "The world came into being through him; yet the world did not know him" (1:10). In the narrative, the "sent" representatives do not know

---

[97] Category are often accentuated by its opposite: good/evil, light/darkness, love/hate, above/below. These merisms reveal the scope of God's absolute rule of power.

[98] "Sin" during the passion narrative represents a refusal to believe in Jesus. Brown, *John*, 350.

"him," nor does John, who twice claimed, "I did not know him" (1:31, 33).[99] The ignorance not only follows the prologue script but also alludes to the fact that the Baptist's knowledge was received from above. Only by an outside source, in this case God, did John receive a revelation to recognize the one who existed before (1:33). That is precisely the line of reasoning here. No one can know Jesus unless it is given from an outside divine source: "No one can receive anything except what has been given from heaven" (3:27). John claims that he has a special kind of knowledge: "The one who sent me to baptize with water said to me, 'He on whom you see the Spirit descend and remain is the one who baptizes with the Holy Spirit.' And I myself have seen and have testified that this is the Son of God" (1:33-34). Special knowledge produces bonds. Later, John will describe his relationship with Jesus as a "friend" (φίλος) of the bridegroom (3:29). Jesus describes friends as those who are given divine information/revelation: "I have called you friends (φίλος), because I have made known to you everything that I have heard from my Father" (15:15). Information from above is given to John. In fact, he was sent from above: "He whom God has sent speaks the words of

---

[99] There are a number of repetitions in the John the Baptist narrative. There are two sets of sent representatives (1:19, 24,) as well as a number of phrase doublets: "They questioned him further" (1:21, 25), "Look, the Lamb of God" (1:29, 36) "I myself did not recognized him" (1:32, 33). John 1:15 and 1:30 are the same. Boismard put out the theory that there were two introductions to Jesus and a final redactor included both Boismard, *"Baptôme à Cana,* 39-44.

God" (3:34). John continues to differentiate his role with that of Jesus. He sees the Holy Spirit descend and remain, so the one who has the Holy Spirit will baptize with the Holy Spirit.

John, however, baptizes with water. We will see that water consistently symbolizes divine truth or revelation in this Gospel. The symbolism begins with John, who makes available the truth to others with his testimony: "I myself have seen and have testified that this is the Son of God" (1:34). John's witness is legitimate because of the origin of his testimony: "The one who sent me to baptize with water said to me he on whom you see the Spirit descend and remain is the one who baptizes with the Holy Spirit" (1:33). One should observe the strong connection between origin and testimony. Origin provides proof that the witness is valid. John's origin is God because he was sent. Jesus' origin is the Father. Later, Jesus will offer the Holy Spirit to future witnesses so that they too will have their origin in God when they testify. The role of the Holy Spirit is essential for witnessing to the truth. When Jesus returns to the Father, others will have to continue to testify to the truth. As witnesses, they will need a connection with the divine and Jesus will offer the Spirit to fulfill this requirement. Once one has the Holy Spirit, their origin is in God. This will legitimate their future witness. The Spirit of truth authenticates the truth. "When the Spirit of truth comes, he will guide you into all the truth; for he will not speak on his own, but will speak whatever he hears" (16:13). All truth needs to be authentic, and the way to demonstrate valid testimony is tracing it back to God. In other words, truth needs to answer the question: "Did this come from God?" The Holy Spirit who reveals truth comes from God: "For he will not speak on his own, but will speak whatever he hears"

(16;13). Origin and testimony are inseparable and these early chapters emphasis this point.

The Third Day: Introducing the believers (1:35-42)

The reader is now introduced to those who will accept the truth. John's witness has been validated with his association with God who sent John. His proclamation will now bear fruit. I have argued above that the full meaning of John's proclamation that Jesus is the "Lamb of God who takes away the sin of the world" appears to make sense in the context of Jesus' final hour when Jesus dies on the cross. Judging from the impact the message had on the two disciples, one can conclude that John's testimony will have some significance later in the Gospel. So John's words are really the first description of what takes place during the hour of glory when everyone will be exposed to revelation. During the reading of the passion narrative, the audience will recall John's words to his disciples. Only in retrospect will the reader understand its full meaning. The reader may comprehend the impact of John's testimony by the departure of John's two followers, but will only understand its full implications at the trial and death of Jesus.

Jesus turns and asks John's disciples what they seek. Here, one sees Jesus taking the initiative. This makes sense in light of what Jesus says later in the Gospel when He tells his disciples that they did not choose Christ but Christ chose them (15:16, 19).[100] The question

---

[100] Brown, *John*, 78.

"where do you stay" (1:38) at first comes as a surprise.[101] One would rather anticipate a question pertaining to Jesus' identity or mission based on John's "Lamb of God" statement. The question is directed, rather, not to vocation, but location. Why is location so important? Where Jesus is from is essential to the Gospel because it is proof of the validity of what Jesus will say and do. His testimony is valid because he is from the Father.

At first, the two address Jesus simply as "Rabbi." It is apparent that they do not know Jesus is from the Father. They are not aware of the prologue which confirms that Christ is from the bosom of the Father. Yet, after they "stay," Andrew recognizes Jesus as the Christ by calling him the Messiah: "'We have found the Messiah' which is translated Anointed" (1:41). Andrew upgrades Jesus' title from rabbi to Messiah. It is apparent that their knowledge of "where" Jesus stays provides Andrew with this new insight. The term Messiah in John's Gospel applies more to location than to vocation.

The reference to "four in the afternoon" is curious.[102] There are no other references to this particular hour in the Gospel. It is possible that the author mentions this detail as a reference to Jesus place

---

[101] The first time that Jesus reveals where he remains is in 6:56: "The one who eats my flesh and drinks my blood remains in me and I in him."

[102] Scholars who understand the hours in the Gospel as marking the time of day: Charles. K. Barrett, *The Gospel According to St. John* (London: SPCK, 1955), 151; Brown, *John*, 1:75; Francis J. Moloney. *Belief in the Word: Reading the Fourth Gospel, John 1–4* (Minneapolis: Fortress, 1993), 68; Lindars, *John*, 114; and Schnackenburg, *John*, 309. Others interpret these specific hours as a reference for Jesus' ministry to be taken in a deeper sense. See Jojko, "Eternity and Time,"245-78; Klaus Wengst, *Das Johannes evangelium* (W. Kohlhammer Verlag, 2007), I, 88.

with the Father. Later in the Gospel, Jesus will tell his disciples that he will return to the Father. Shortly after this revelation, Jesus dies on the cross sometime after Pilate's encounter with the crowd at noon. Perhaps the four in the afternoon reference parallels the afternoon hour when Jesus returns to the Father. At four in the afternoon, the disciples will discover something more about Jesus that causes Andrew to shift the title from Rabbi to Messiah. If one follows the narrative from the initial question of where Jesus remains, the declaration of Messiah must come from an insight on where Jesus is from: the Father. I suggest that the mention of the four o'clock hour is another reference that is intended to confirm the origin of Jesus. Origin will continue to be the main theme when Philip calls Nathanael.

The Fourth Day: Confirming Jesus' Origin (1:43-51)

On the fourth day, Philip calls Nathanael. Philip apparently did not read the prologue because he misinforms Nathaniel that Jesus is from Nazareth, not from the bosom of the Father: "We have found him about whom Moses in the law and also the prophets wrote, Jesus son of Joseph from Nazareth" (1:45). Nathanial, who is misled about Jesus' true origin raises a question about Philip's claim. Nazareth is not on the messianic eschatological radar. How can someone that is known from the writings of Moses and the prophets come from Nazareth? He raises a legitimate theological point. Despite Philip's ambiguous assertion, Nathanial accepts the invitation to come and see (ἔρχου καὶ ἴδε). By accepting the invitation, Nathanial will come to know Jesus' true origin. We know this because John's disciples accepted the same invitation which led them to Jesus' location. Jesus' compliment to Nathanial supports this: "Here is truly an Israelite in whom there is no deceit" (1:47). According to Jesus comment, Nathanial is seeing the truth about Jesus' origin due to the fact that Nathanial is a true Israelite. His answer to Philip "Can anything good come out of Nazareth" (1:46) is not a flippant cultural dig, so the motive behind the statement is not deceit but rather seeking the truth. That is why he accepts Philip's invitation. Jesus recognizes the distinction. The compliment by Jesus is an affirmation of one trying to understand Jesus' true origin: "Here is truly an Israelite in whom there is no deceit" (1:47). Both invitations to "come and you will see" will result in knowing Jesus' true origin.

Nathanial is perplexed by Jesus' insight and asks: "Where did you get to know me?" (1:48). Note that the question is a reference to location: "where." I argue that the purpose of day four is to clarify Jesus' heavenly origin. Jesus' response to the Nathanial's "where" inquiry appears odd. Instead of giving a direct answer about his location, Jesus refers to Nathanial's location: "I saw you under the fig tree before Philip called you." This means that Jesus discovered Philip before Philip approached Nathaniel about Jesus. Not only did Jesus know Nathanial but that he knew him as a true Israelite even before Nathanial accepted Philip's invitation to "come and see." After Nathaniel asks Jesus a question that refers to location ("Where did you get to know me," 1:48), Jesus gives him an answers that centers on location: "under a fig tree" (1:48).

The significance of the fig tree has baffled scholars to the point that many look outside of the Gospel to Old Testament passages for interpretive background. Some cite the passage in Hos 9:10 "Like grapes in the wilderness I found Israel. Like the first fruit on the fig tree...I saw your fathers." There is also a vision that alludes to men under fig trees (1Kgs 4:15; Mic 4:4; Zech 3:10). However, as Koester points out, the image of peace and prosperity is not the issue in John 1:45-51.[103] There are some intriguing parallels with Jacob, later named Israel (Gen 32:28), who was considered guile for his deception to obtain Esau's blessing (27:35), and who saw a vision of angels ascending and descending on a ladder to heaven (28:12). One would suspect that John is borrowing Old Testament phraseology.[104] According to this text one could conclude that, like Jacob, Nathanial is a true Israelite, and will see angels of God ascending and descending upon the son of man (1:51). Yet, unlike Jacob, Nathanial is not a trickster and deceiver. Does John leave the reader with enough references to establish a solid link with these Old Testament texts? Even if it was clear, would the intended audience of the first century be familiar enough with the Old Testament to make such connections. Is one to assume that all readers had conventional knowledge of the Old Testament? What about Jacob's ladder? There is no reference to

---

[103] Craig R. Koester, "Messianic Exegesis and the Call of Nathanael (John 1:45-51)," *JSNT* 39 (1990): 24-25. For understanding Nathanial in the light of Zechariah 3; see his *The Word of Life: A Theology of John's Gospel* (Grand Rapids: Eerdmans, 2008), 92.

[104] J. Gerald Janzen claims that ascending and descending refer to Jacob at Bethel. "I take Jesus to mean that he himself embodies that true Israel - and that true humanity - whose communion with God is deep, true, and uninterrupted amid a world where the darkness of guile is all too prevalent. See his "How Can a Man Be Born When He Is Old?: Jacob/Israel in Genesis and the Gospel Of John," *Encounter* 65 (2004): 336.

a ladder to establish a solid connection with these outside sources.[105] Or rather, can one determine the meaning by way of context, without the use of outside sources? I argue we can.

I maintain that the author provides the interpretive clues to the fig tree within the Gospel to which all readers have access. After Philip tells Nathaniel that Jesus is from Nazareth, he observes the obvious. Nazareth is not a location for greatness, not the kind that Philip is claiming. It is odd that Nathanial does not walk away in doubt but continues to persist by honoring the request to "come and see." He is not like those who reject and walk away (7:15, 27, 41; 9:29, 41). He accepts the invitation to "come to see." What he will come to see is location— that is, Jesus is not from Nazareth but from God. Unlike the Jews who will reject Jesus, Nathaniel seeks the light to see. Jesus calls Nathaniel a true Israelite. Nathaniel wants to know "where" He is from that allowed him access to such information. It is only obvious to Nathanial that he was seeking to glean from Philip what information was valid and what was not valid. Nathanial is wise to ask the "where" question: "Where did you get to know me?" (1:48). Jesus' response was a clue to Nathaniel that Jesus has access to information that would not come from Nazareth.[106] It cannot be

---

[105] William Loader, "John 1:51 and Johannine Christology," in *Historical, Literary, and Theological Readings from the Colloquium Ioanneum 2015 in Ephesus* (Wissenschaftliche Untersuchungen zum Neuen Testament 385; ed. R. Alan Culpepper and Jörg Frey; Tübingen: Mohr Siebeck, 2017), 125.

[106] William T. Pyle also sees the issue of Jesus' origin in this periscope. He writes, "Origins is a major theme in John: Jesus has come from the father, from above. Jesus is the bread which came down out of heaven. The entire controversy of chapter 7 has focused on the origin of Jesus. The

from Nazareth if he is to be a Rabbi, a son of God, and the king of Israel, all the titles given to Jesus by Nathanial.[107]

As I pointed out earlier and as we will see later in the Gospel, Jesus' kingship is not a reference to His vocation but His knowledge. The expression "King of Israel" is not used by Jesus himself or the narrator. It is here used by Nathaniel to confirm Jesus' knowledge that he could only get from God. In the Synoptic Gospels, Jesus is from the line of David. In John, Jesus is the Messiah because he is from God. God is the source of his truth and the revelation he will offer. Later, I will show that the reference to Jesus as king during his trial and execution is also a reference to his origin: "My kingdom is not of this world" (18:36). The scene is about location, because knowing "where" will prove Jesus' authenticity. Jesus informs Nathaniel that he will someday have no question as to Jesus' origin when he sees angels ascending and descending from heaven upon

---

crowd cannot accept Jesus as the Christ because they believe they know His origins (7:26-27). And Nathanael asked in 1:46, "Can any good thing come out of Nazareth?" The Messiah could not have come from Galilee (7:41). Jesus testified that He was from above (ano); the Jews were from below (8:23). Because writers often add their own shade of meaning to words they employ, the author's work should be analyzed to determine his or her usage of a term and to determine the particular shade of meaning the writer is using." See his "Understanding the Misunderstanding Sequences in the Gospel of John," *Faith and Mission* 11 (1994): 40.

[107] Jesus' response demonstrates his supernatural knowledge. For a detailed discussion on this view, see C. F. D. Moule, "A Note on 'under the Fig Tree' in John 1:48. 50f," *JTS* 5 (1954): 210-11; U. C. von Wahlde, *The Latest Version of John's Gospel: Recovering the Gospel of Signs* (Wilmington, Del.: Michael Glazier, 1989), 71 n. 17.

the Son of Man.¹⁰⁸ Knowing "where" (πόθεν – 2:9; 3:8; 7:27; 9:29, 30; 19:9) is very important in John's Gospel, and there are a number of citations to back up this claim: "Where does this man intend to go that we will not find him?" (7:35); "Where do you stay?" (1:38); "Where is he?" (7:10); "Where did you get to know me?" (1:48); "Where are you from?" (19:9); "Where are you going?" (13:36); "Where do I get this water?" (4:11).¹⁰⁹ Later, when Jesus argues with the Jews, the subject of his origin becomes the central issue. They cannot accept Jesus because they do not know that His origin is from God, raising their doubts about his authenticity.

One should also observe that Nathaniel comes after Peter, and that he is the last one who is called. He, not Peter, fulfills the reason for John's witnessing: "The very reason why I came and baptized with water was that He [Jesus] might be revealed to Israel" (1:31).¹¹⁰ One should also note that John the Baptist begins his work with a denial that he is the Messiah. The calling of the disciples ends with a

---

¹⁰⁸ Charles A. Gieschen sees the reference as an obvious allusion to the crucifixion. "Jesus promises Nathaniel a theophany in which the Son of Man is seen as the ladder stretching between heaven and earth rather than being enthroned at the top of the ladder where one would expect to see him." See his "The Death of Jesus in the Gospel of John: Atonement for Sin?" *CTQ* 72 (2008): 249. See also Jerome H. Neyrey, "The Jacob Allusions in John 1:51," *CBQ* 44 (1982): 586-605.

¹⁰⁹ There are three terms that are used in Greek for the word "where." Πόθεν is used 13 times (1:48; 2:9; 3:8; 4:11; 6:5; 7:28, 29; 8:14; 9:29, 30; 19:9), ποῦ 18 times (1:38; 3:8; 7:11, 25; 8:10, 14 [2X], 19; 9:12; 11:34, 57; 12:35; 13:36; 14:5; 16:5; 20:2, 13, 15), and ὅπου 30 times (1:28; 3:8; 4;20, 26; 6:23.62; 7:34, 36, 42; 8:21, 22; 10:40; 11:30, 32; 12:1, 26; 13:33, 36; 14:3, 4; 17:24; 18:1, 20; 19:18, 20, 41; 20:12, 19; 21:18 [2X]).

¹¹⁰ Brown, *John*, 87.

proclamation that Jesus is the King (anointed/Messiah) bringing the narrative to full circle, confirming that John is not the light, but he witnesses to the light.

Verse 51 is further confirmation with regards to location. Again, scholars struggle to understand how the verse fits within the context of the passage.[111] To many, it appears to be an interpolation.[112] Jesus is no longer addressing Nathaniel but a group: "You (plural) will see." The promise to see angels is never fulfilled in the Gospel. To understand the passage some scholars look again to the Old Testament for interpretation: "Intertextuality offers many diverse interpretations of John 1:51."[113] According to David R. Kirk, Jesus is the new Jacob, bringing forth a new Israel.[114] There is a direct reference

---

[111] Peder Borgen, "God's Agent in the Fourth Gospel," In *Religions in Antiquity: Essays in Memory of Erwin Ramsdell Goodenough* (Leiden: Brill, 1968), 137-148; Stephen Smalley, "Joh 1,51 und die Einleitung zum vierten Evangelium" in *Jesus und der Menschensohn* (eds. R. Pesch, R. Shnackenburg, O. Kaiser; Freiburg: Herder, 1975); Seyoon Kim, *The Origins of Paul's Gospel* (WUNT 2/4 Tübingen: Mohr, 1981), 254-255; Christopher Rowland, "John 1.51, Jewish Apocalyptic and Targumic Tradition," *NTS* 30 (1984): 498-507; John Painter, *John, Witness and Theologian* (London: SPCK, 1975), 55-56; J. Harold Ellens, "A Christian Pesher: John 1:51," *Proceedings* 25 (2005): 143-55.

[112] See Jon Cochrane O'Neill, "Son of Man, Stone of Blood (John 1:51)," *NT* 45 (2003): 143-155.

[113] David R. Kirk, "Heaven Opened: Intertextuality and Meaning in John 1:51," *TynBul* 63 (2012): 238.

[114] Kirk, "John 1:51." See also John Herman Conrad Neeb, "Jacob/Jesus typology in John 1:51," *Proceedings* 12 (1992), 83-89; Neyrey, "Jacob Allusions," 586-605; Derek Tovey, "Stone of Witness and Stone of Revelation: An Exploration of Inter-Textual Resonance in John 1:35-51," *Colloquim* 38 (2006): 41-58.

to Jacob in the Genesis account. Perhaps the author is familiar with Jacob's experience, but can he be sure that the audience will make the connection? On the other hand, intratextuality allows the reader to see coherence from the context of the narrative. 1:51 is also the first "amen, amen" formula "Amen, amen I tell you, you will see heaven opened and the angels of God ascending and descending upon the Son of Man." The "amen-amen" formula is employed in the Gospel twenty-five times[115] in order to highlight the key message of a particular discourse.[116] The author has directed the reader to observe the importance of location both in the prologue and in the storyline which follows. I conclude that the dialogue between Jesus and Nathanial is about origin. He first asks Jesus "where," because He has special knowledge about Nathanial's location. Jesus tells Nathanial that he will see the angels ascending and descending because Jesus must correct the misinformation from Philip about Nazareth by showing that He is from above in the image of the movement of angels. Jesus' origin is essential to the Gospel because it authenticates Jesus' words and deeds. He is from the Father so he has Divine knowledge. Witness and origin are never isolated issues; one needs the other.

The first four days successfully follow the plot of the prologue. We can sum up the four days by confirming the prologue themes are very much present: there is a creation theme, John the Baptist witnesses, both those who reject and accept Jesus are introduced, and

---

[115] 1:51; 3:3, 5, 11; 5:19, 24, 25; 6:26, 32, 47, 53; 8:34, 51, 58; 10:1, 7; 12:24; 13:16, 20, 21, 38; 14:12; 16:20, 23; 21:18.

[116] Richard Bauckham, "Historiographical Characteristics of the Gospel of John," *NTS* 53 (2007): 33.

Jesus' origin is well-founded. The only thing left is belief, which comes at the end of the wedding on the seventh day, which will be metaphorically the final day of the new creation when the Word enters the world again.

The Seventh Day, Creating Believers (2:1-12)

The narrative has now reached the final day of what appears to be a reflection of the seven-day creation motif. In the prologue, the goal of the "Word" was to produce believers. In this final day, a wedding feast, disciples turn into believers. Another detail that links this passage with the prologue is "Glory": "The Word became flesh and dwelt among us and we have seen his glory" (1:14). The purpose of the wedding is to reveal his glory (2:11). Finally, from the prologue, the reader learns that the creative "Word" will produce children of God, so it is appropriate to end the creative seven days with a wedding, the traditional path for acquiring a family with children. This wedding produces believers, which, according to the prologue, means children of God.

Along with the prologue, this narrative has parallels with other passages in the Gospel. The author has not spoken of John the Baptist since the third day but there are a few terms that will recall him once more at the wedding. Note the numerous literary connections between 2:1-11 and 3:22-30:

ἐν Κανὰ τῆς Γαλιλαίας (in Cana of Galilee)
    2:1,11 and 3:22

ἐκεῖ (there)
   2:1, 6, 11 and 3:22, 23
καὶ ὁ Ἰησοῦς καὶ οἱ μαθηταὶ αὐτοῦ: (Jesus and his disciples)
   2:2, 12 and 3:22
καθαρισμός (purification)
   2:6 and 3:25
Ἰουδαίων (Jews)
   2:6 and 3:25
ὑδρία (water)
   2:7, 9, 10 and 3:23
νυμφίος (groom)
   2:9 and 3:29

φωνεῖ τὸν νυμφίον voice of the groom: 2:9 and τὴν νύμφην νυμφίος διὰ τὴν φωνὴν τοῦ νυμφίου at the groom's voice 3:29

The word ἐλαττόω ("decrease") which is used to describe John's status in relationship to Jesus in 3:30 is related to the word ἐλάσσων ("inferior," 2:10) which describes the ordinary wine at Cana.[117] In addition, John later portrays his relationship with Jesus as a friend of the bridegroom: "The friend of the bridegroom, who stands and hears him, rejoices greatly at the bridegroom's voice" (3:29). The

---

[117] Numerous scholars see verbal and literary links between 3:22-30 and 2:1-12. See Ardel Caneday, "The Word Made Flesh as Mystery Incarnate: Revealing and Concealing Dramatized by Jesus as Portrayed in John's Gospel," *JETS* 60 (2017): 756; ibid., "John in the Middle: Jews, Purification, and Jesus (John 2:1-11 & 3:22-30)," Johannine Literature Program Unit, annual international meeting of Society of Biblical Literature, University of St. Andrews, Scotland, July 7—11, 2013; Brown, *John,* 153.

only other reference to a bridegroom (νυμφίος) is at the wedding at Cana (2:9), the place where Jesus first reveals his glory (2:11).[118] Finally, the conversation John has with his disciples about Jesus' practice of baptism begins with a discussion about purification (καθαρισμός, 3:25).[119] At the wedding in Cana, there are six stone jars for purification (καθαρισμός, 2:6). Why the connections between John and the wedding at Cana? A new witness is about to be introduced. John provided a witness for Jesus that highlighted his origin from the Father. This time it is the mother of Jesus who exposes him as the divine Word: "do whatever he tells you" (2:5).[120] The qualifications of the witness have been nicely spelled out with John as a model, and they will be reduplicated at Cana by Jesus' mother. The mother, like John, is a servant because she takes the role of the headwaiter. It is the headwaiter's job to inform the groom about the wine. Without the mother of Jesus, the identity of Jesus as a groom would have been unknown to the reader.[121] The author of John provides a nice transition from the witness of the Baptist to the

---

[118] Duncan M. Derrett, "Intoxication, Joy, and Wrath: 1 Cor 11:21 and Jn 2:10," *FN* 2 (1989): 50.

[119] Brown agrees that there are clear parallels between 3:25-30 and the Cana scene that should be considered as theologically significant. See *John*, 1:154

[120] "Mother of Jesus" or "his mother" can be found four times (2:1, 3, 5,12).

[121] "It is almost universally recognized that Mary's role at Cana cannot be understood by itself, but only in relationship to the coming hour of Jesus' death and glorification, of which he spoke (2:4)." Joseph A. Grassi, "The Role of Jesus' Mother in John's Gospel: A Reappraisal," *CBQ* 48 (1986): 67.

Mother of Jesus who now seems to be acting out the role of the head-waiter who is concerned about the lack of wine. This, of course, was part of John's strategy: "He must increase, but I must decrease" (3:30). The Gospel writer can now move to the next witness.

First, at the wedding at Cana, the head-waiter in the story does not act at all like someone in charge.[122] He gives no orders, has no clue about the problem of no wine or its solution, and questions the bridegroom in a way that exposes a flawed work ethic, amounting to a total lack of communication between the supervisor and client. The mother of Jesus seems to do all the work of the head-waiter; she is aware of the problem and seeks the help of Jesus. Jesus, on the other hand, first appears to be a guest: "Jesus and his disciples had also been invited to the wedding" (2:2). Yet, He is acting as if he were the bridegroom at his own wedding. He converses with his mother as if she is the head-waiter and he himself is the groom.[123] Why would John want to allude to the reader that Jesus is the bridegroom?

---

[122] Just from a compositional perspective, the Cana narrative is impressive. Note the detail involved in such a short story: six different characters (disciples, mother of Jesus, servants etc.), the location and timing of the event, measurements (water jars), a dilemma (lack of wine at a wedding banquet), subplots, instruction to the servants, tensions between the main characters, dialogue between the steward and the groom, including information on cultural backgrounds. See Michael J. Thate, "Conditionality in John's Gospel: A Critique and Examination of Time and Reality as Classically Conceived in Conditional Constructions Journal of the Evangelical Theological Society," *JETS* 50 (2007): 502.

[123] Jean-Bosco Matand Bulembat, "Head-Waiter and Bridegroom of the Wedding at Cana: Structure and Meaning of John 2.1-12," JSNT 30 (2007): 60-62.

Because in the next chapter, John the Baptist is going to describe Jesus as the bridegroom: "the friend of the bridegroom, who stands and hears him, rejoices greatly at the bridegroom's voice" (3:29). With all the rhetoric of a wedding feast – "joy," "friend," "voice of the bridegroom"—the Baptist reaffirms his successful role as a witness. John, who came to witness to Jesus ("And they came to John, and said to him, "Rabbi, he who was with you beyond the Jordan, to whom you bore witness [μεμαρτύρηκας]"—3:26), has now turned his own followers into witnesses ("You yourselves bear witness [μαρτυρεῖτε] to me, that I said, I am not the Christ"—4:28). The irony that Jesus is the bridegroom at the wedding at Cana allows the author of John to link the wedding with John's role as witness when he is treated again in the next chapter.

Likewise, at the wedding feast, Jesus is understood to be the living water and the light of the world. In John 2 the mother of Jesus turns to her son for more wine because she knows that he has all the requirements to produce a great wine. He is the vine (15:1)., the light of the world, and the living water.[124] At the feast of Tabernacle in John 8:12, Jesus announces that he is the light of the world. He tells the Samaritan woman in chapter 4 that he provides living water. Looking back to John 2, the reader knows why the mother of Jesus turns to Jesus. She must know him to be the true vine, but she also knows that he is the supplier of light and the water which is necessary for great wine: "But you have kept the good wine until now" (2:10). If it is true that Jesus is the true vine, then the mother of Jesus

---

[124] Wine is used in eschatological feasts (Isa 25:6) and represents the age of salvation (Amos 9:13; Hos 2:24; Joel 4:18; Isa 29:17; Jer 31:5; Enoch 10:19: Apoc Bar Syr 29:5).

will know that winemaking, by its nature, is a fruit-producing endeavor. Pruning the branch is necessary as it produces fruit: "Every branch that bears fruit he prunes to make it bear more fruit... by the word that I have spoken to you" (15:2-3). The "woman" knows what it takes to make vintage grapes. The phrase, "Do whatever he tells you" is advice from a branch that knows how to bear much fruit, that is, "by the word that I have spoken to you." The mother of Jesus will know that the branch will bear fruit if it receives the word of God: "Every branch that bears fruit he prunes to make it bear more fruit" (15:2). She is already familiar with the instructions for bearing much fruit that were given by Jesus in John 15. This should answer Jesus' initial question, "What have you to do with me?" (2:4). The question is reflected in Jesus' words to Peter when he refuses to let his feet be washed, "Unless I wash you, you have no part with me" (13:8). Jesus' mother wastes no time accepting the invitation to answer his question about what part she has with him. She is his witness. She, like John the Baptist, will point Jesus out to the others.

Still, the dialogue between Jesus and his mother is notoriously difficult.[125] Is Jesus' response to his mother an affirmation or refusal?[126] Verbal parallels of the phrase "what to you and me" in Greek and Hebrew texts lead scholars to interpret Jesus words as a

---

[125] John McHugh, *The Mother of Jesus in the New Testament* (London: Darton, Longman & Todd, 1975), 362-67. Brown, *John*, 99.

[126] Christian Ceroke, "The Problem of Ambiguity in John 2:4," *CBQ* 21 (1959): 316.

negative response signifying a rebuke, a protest, or a sign of disassociation, and for good reason.[127] The phrase is well known in Scripture.[128] It is spoken by a harassed king (2 Sam 16:10), an indignant prophet (4 Kgs 3:13), a military commander in the midst of a fray (Jos 22:24), by devils (Matt 8:29; Mark 1:24, Luke 4:34; 8:28), and is used to dissociate oneself from the issue at hand (2 Kgs 3:13; Josh 14:8). Still, despite what the term means from outside sources, one should approach these citations with caution because the author can use outside phrases and terms for his own theological purpose and meaning. According to the meaning of these outside sources, one could easily conclude that Jesus uses this same term to deny and silence his mother. However, the opposite happens. According to the context, the phrase seems to engender a positive response. She acts and speaks as if she was the maidservant encouraged to do so by the groom of his wedding. Jesus' remark is no rebuke but rather a signal that he is aware of the full implications of what is being asked.[129] Whatever negative inferences of distance and disinterest Jesus' words seem to imply, his mother's response interprets the words as

---

[127] Elisabeth Schussler Fiorenza, *In Memory of Her: A Feminist Theological Reconstruction of Christian Origins* (New York: Crossroad, 1984), 327; John McHugh *Mother of Jesus in the New Testament* (Garden City, NY: Doubleday, 1975), 367-69; Barrett, *John,* 159.

[128] "What to me and to you," can be understood as "this is not my concern," Whereby Jesus distances himself from his mother... thus clarifying the autonomous of Jesus work. See Adriana Destro, and Mauro Pesce, "Discipleship, and Movement: An Anthropological Study of John's Gospel," *BibInt* 3 (1995): 272, 271 n. 17.

[129] R. H. Williams, "The Mother of Jesus at Cana: A Social-Science Interpretation of John 2:1-12," *CBQ* 59 (1997): 689.

positive and affirming.¹³⁰ Jesus' words have to be read in the light of the mother's reaction and so the reader's translation has to be context-specific. Jesus' words appear sharp and cutting, like pruning shears to a healthy branch that is about to bear much fruit.

The mother of Jesus points Christ out to the servants because she has pertinent information found in the prologue—that he is the true light. The mother of Jesus simply knows "where" to go if there is a question about bearing much fruit. Jesus later explains to his disciples the means by which to bear much fruit: "the word I have spoken to you" (15:3).¹³¹ In retrospect to this information one understands why the mother of Jesus tells the servants to do "whatever he tells you." Scholars have argued that the mother approaches Jesus to remind him to offer a wedding gift to the groom. I argue that this is not about a mother giving her son a lesson in etiquette.¹³² This is a dialogue that represents a witness who knows Jesus as a groom who

---

¹³⁰ "Jesus responds positively by creative anticipation." J. Miriam Blackwell, "The Hour of Jesus in the Gospel According to John," *Journal of Theta Alpha Kappa* 3 (1980): 16.

¹³¹ Cristos Karakolis contends that "Jesus' Mother has an unparalleled level of Knowledge with regard to Jesus, as well as a unique connection with him....However, the Gospel's readers are at least expected to conclude that she knows and understands Jesus more, and is closer to him than any other narrative character." See his Recurring Characters in John 1:19–2:11" in *The Opening of John's Narrative (John 1:19–2:22): Historical, Literary, and Theological Readings from the Colloquium Ioanneum 2015 in Ephesus* (WUNT 385; eds. R. Alan Culpepper and Jörg Frey; Tübingen: Mohr Siebeck, 2017), 22.

¹³² It has been argued that the wine would have been supplied by the wedding guests, thereby one can understand the mother's comments in light of this local wedding custom.

will produce much fruit by the power of his creative Word; "Do whatever he tells you" (2:5). Her knowledge of her son allows her to take the role of a witness, one who exposes him to others: "Do whatever he tells you" (2:5).[133]

Note that Jesus does not address her as "mother" as this is not a mother and son conversation. Her words reflect that of a witness, not a mother.[134] As pointed out in the introduction, Jesus addresses three females in the Gospel as "woman" (γύναι): his mother (2:40; 19:26), the Samaritan woman (4:21), and Mary Magdalena (20:15).[135] Even the two angels at the Lord's tomb address Mary Magdalena as "woman" (20:13). The term woman is never used as a derogatory greeting in the Gospel. Those called "γύναι" (woman) are believers who testify to others about Jesus. All three women have this common attribute. The mother of Jesus witnesses to the servants of the wedding at Cana, the Samaritan woman brings the Samaritans from the village to believe in him, and Mary witnesses to the disciples after the resurrection. The mother of Jesus certainly plays the

---

[133] "Mary's command to the servants indicates she still expected a miracle. She now also saw a new relationship with her son and she recognized His authority." Stanley D. Toussaint, "The Significance of the First Sign in John's Gospel," *Bibliotheca sacra* 134 (1977): 49.

[134] Jesus' mother is never named. According to Ignace de la Potterie the absence of the name has a symbolic meaning: "the Mother of the incarnated Word." See his *Maria nel Mistero dell'alleanza* (Genova: Mariet, 1988), 95.

[135] There is a fourth female figure addressed by Jesus as γύναι, the woman caught in adultery (8:10). The woman in this narrative, unlike the other females, does not witness to others in the Gospel. Perhaps this is another indication that the passage is not original to the Gospel because it does not fit this pattern.

role of a Johannine witness, that is, she instructs with her special knowledge. "Do whatever he tells you" (2:5). Both Jesus' words and the mother's reaction come as a surprise to the audience. The sharp and pointed dialogue between the pair does not reflect mother and son but rather the "Word" and the revealer.

Jesus tells His witness that his hour has not yet come. The term "hour" (ὥρα) represents both an event in the future and in the present.[136] The hour is coming (4:21, 23; 5:28; 16:21); not yet come (7:30); is here (12:23; 13:1; 17:1). Jesus even prays: "take me from this hour" (12:17). The hour in question is a deadly one and it is divinely appointed. No one or no event will alter or control the timing and outcome of the hour. Jesus' first use of this important term introduces the reader to the first sign (σημεῖον, 2:11). The first sign and the first mention of the hour belong together. After the first sign, the arrival of the hour is now set. Jesus' solemn response to his mother's request for his first divine manifestation proves that nothing is easy, automatic, predictable or routine when it comes to the moment of God's glory.

Jesus' response: "My hour has not yet come" (οὔπω ἥκει ἡ ὥρα μου - 2:40), will be re-echoed in 7:30.[137] In that passage, Jesus' opponents were not able to arrest Jesus because his hour had not yet come

---

[136] The term "hour" occurs 26 times underscoring the words importance in the Gospel.

[137] The number of times the Gospel cites hours and days suggests that the symbolic "hour" plays a major role:

"the next day (1:29.35.43; 6:22; 12:12); the third day (2:1); the first day of the week (20:1.19); after this (2:12; 3:22; 5:1; 6:1.66; 7:1; 11:7; 19:28.38); in the meantime (4:31) the sixth hour (4:6; 19:14); winter time (10:22);

(ὅτι οὔπω ἐληλύθει ἡ ὥρα αὐτοῦ, 7:30). The verbal exchange between Jesus and his opponents focuses on where Jesus is from: "You know me, and you know where I am from?" (7:28). Jesus assures them that they do not know who he is or where he comes from. Jesus' hour is not simply controlled by human hate or zealous motivation.[138] Because his hour had not yet come, no one arrested him, and so Jesus successfully evades the grasp of his opponents. The mother of Jesus hears the same explanation that blocked the action of the opposition in 7:30. Jesus himself tells her: "My hour has not yet come" (οὔπω ἥκει ἡ ὥρα - 2:4). The real difference, however, is that the action she wishes to initiate is not blocked. She is not ignorant of or in opposition to her Son's mission, making her very different from the Jewish opponents of 7:30 because she knows Jesus' origin, unlike the unbelievers. She is one of the Johannine witnesses. For the witness, knowledge of Jesus and his origin presupposes evangelization.

---

early in the morning (8:2; 18:28); by night (3:2; 19:39); it was night (13:30); the Jewish day of Preparation (19:42).

Like, e.g., the next day (1:29.35.43; 6:22; 12:12); the third day (2:1); the first day of the week (20:1.19); after this (2:12; 3:22; 5:1; 6:1.66; 7:1; 11:7; 19:28.38); the sixth hour (4:6; 19:14); winter time (10:22); early in the morning (8:2; 18:28); by night (3:2; 19:39); it was night (13:30); the Jewish day of Preparation (19:42)." Bernadeta Jojko, "Worshiping the Father in Spirit and Truth: An Exegetico-Theological Study" in *4:20-26 in the Light of Relationships Among the Father, the Son and the Holy Spirit* (Tesi Gregoriana 193; Roma: Gregorian & Biblical Press 2012), 258 n. 16.

[138] Another passage that shows that the hour is unaltered by human ambition: "But no one arrested him, because his hour had not yet come" (10:20).

Signs

The wedding, which is not recorded in the other Gospels, highlights the "sign" by announcing that it is the first, meaning others will follow: "Jesus did this, the first of his signs" (σημεῖον, 2:11).[139] What is the meaning and role of a "sign" in this Gospel?[140] A "sign," I will argue, represents divine revelation/truth. In the prologue, the "Word" creates. The "Word" reveals God, not only by communication ("Word") but by deeds (creation): "All things come to being through him" (1:3). In the Gospel, Jesus, likewise reveals through tangible means: words (audible) and deeds (visible). There are seven (deeds) signs before Jesus' hour of Glory on the cross: (1) turning water into wine, (2) healing the royal official's son, (3) curing the invalid at Beth-zatha (4) feeding the five thousand, (5) walking on the sea, (6) healing the blind man and (7) raising Lazarus from the dead. These are not the only deeds Jesus performs, for the author of John confirms the existence of "many other signs" (20:30) and "many other things that Jesus did" (21:25).[141] The purpose of writing

---

[139] For Brown, the sign represents the replacement of Jewish purification with wine, revealing who Jesus is: "the one sent by the Father." See his *John*, 104.

[140] The word "sign" (σημεῖον) appears in 2:11,18,23; 3:2; 4:48,54; 6:2,14,26, 30; 7:31; 9:16; 10:41; 11:47; 12:18, 37; 20:30.

[141] John's σημεία (signs) are generally spectacular in scope and drama: over 150 gallons of water turned into wine towards the end of a wedding (2:6); someone disabled for 38 years (5:5) or born blind (9:1-3) IS healed, or raised after being in the tomb for four days (11:17); 153 fish are caught in a net after a night of fruitless toil (21:11)." Dorothy A. Lee, "Signs and Works: The Miracles in The Gospels of Mark and John," *Colloquium* 47 (2015): 91.

down the signs is so that the reader may come to believe (20:31).[142] This matches the goal of the prologue: "But to all who received him, who believed in his name, he gave power to become children of God" (1:12). So there are two modes of revelation: testimony and deeds.

All revelation, whether by word or deed, offers a choice. Either one accepts or rejects revelation/truth. In the prologue, the "Word" forces choice. Either one accepts the "Word" or does not. Creation is a manifestation of the divine. That is, divine action becomes visible in creation. Because the process involves sight, light becomes an in important metaphor. In the prologue, "light shines in the darkness," (1:5), and the true light enlightens everyone" (1:9). Light or revelation is not accepted by all: "His own people did not accept him (1:11). Yet, others do: "But to all who received him ...believed in his name" (1:12). Deeds are visible (light) manifestations of the divine. One must either receive or reject them. Everyone is exposed when the light of truth comes on. Ignorance can no longer be used as an avoidance tactic. The appearance of the "Word" may not always produce belief, but it does force a decision.

It is not surprising in the Gospel that signs produce belief in some (the disciples believe when they see the water turned into wine in 2:11, the royal official's family believes when the son is healed in 4:53, the crowds believe after Jesus raises Lazarus from the dead in

---

[142] Schneiders defines a sign as "1) a sensible reality 2) which renders present to and 3) involves a person subjectively in 4) a transforming experience 5) of transcendent mystery." Thereby claiming that signs are instruments used to communicate revelation. See her *You May Believe*, 65-69.

11:45, and at other times it does not (the Pharisees refuse to believe after the man born blind gains his sight). In the Gospel, like the prologue, light is also linked with deeds. The works of Jesus are only done in the day (9:4; 11:9). One cannot do anything at night (9:4), and "When Jesus is in the world, he is the light of the world" (9:5). The man who was born blind will receive his sight "so that God's works might be revealed (9:3). Light is revelation. When Jesus performs a sign, all those who witness the sign/deed must decide. Not only must they choose, but their decision is exposed. When Jesus produces a sign he exposes his divinity. Jesus is not the only one who is exposed. All others are exposed as either believers or nonbelievers because the sign forces a decision. The sign acts as an X-ray machine. Everyone associated with the sign is exposed. No one can hide in the light of Jesus' revelation through his deeds. While Jesus is in Jerusalem, the Gospel reports that many believed in him because they saw the signs that he was doing (2:23). If the narration stopped there, one could easily conclude that the purpose of the sign is to produce faith. However, the narrative goes on to say that Jesus did not trust (believe) them because he knew them (2:24-25). Here again we see the role of light in the making of the signs. The people "saw," which concludes that light was available to make such an activity possible, enough light also for Jesus to be able to see deeply into people.

Signs expose people. The disciples' lack of faith was exposed when they saw Jesus walking on the water.[143] In the case of the man

---

[143] John Paul Heil, *Jesus Walking on the Sea: Meaning and Gospel Functions of Matt 14:22-33, Mark 6:45-52 and John 6:15b-21* (AnBib 87; Rome: Biblical Institute, 1981), 155-57.

born blind, not even the parents show any sign of gratitude toward the healer. Their indifference was exposed. When the Pharisees are confronted with the truth about the blind man, they decide to err on the side of disbelief despite the indisputable proof of the man's sight from being born blind. The disciples believe when they see water turned to wine during the wedding at Cana. Jesus' deeds expose the truth. One either receives or rejects. Deeds are visible; all see the deeds, but not all believe.

Jesus is the only revealer of the truth in both words and deeds. The Baptist, who was also sent by God, reveals by words but deeds are exclusive to Jesus: "John performed no sign, but everything that John said about this man was true" (10:41). He needs no miracles to impress his two disciples. John simply points Jesus out to them. The Samaritan woman, another witness who is sent, needs no miracles to assist her; she simply points Jesus out: "He told me everything I did (4:39)." She testifies to the truth. The entire town believes without even a single sign performed by Jesus. Jesus differs from other witnesses because he can provide the truth by way of deeds as well as by his word. Likewise, Jesus gives testimony and witnesses through his works: "The works that I do in my Father's name testify to me; but you do not believe" (10:25), and "The very works that I am doing, testify on my behalf that the Father has sent me. And the Father who sent me has himself testified on my behalf" (5:36-37). Because he is the light of the world, only he can perform deeds that are visual. He is the creative Word. However, not everyone is exposed to Jesus' deeds: "Blessed are those who do not see and still believe" (20:29). Thomas preferred to see rather than hear testimony of the eyewitnesses who were present when the risen Lord appeared.

Yet, both words and deeds are valid because both are two modes of presenting the truth. Both force decision. One should not accept one mode of revelation over the other. Thomas preferred a sign over testimony, and he was called out for it: "Have you believed because you have seen me? (20:29). He should have believed before Jesus appeared a second time in the upper room. Thomas had valid testimony to the truth and he rejected it. The crowd likewise limited their belief to only one mode of manifestation: "What sign are you going to give us then, so that we may see it and believe you?" (6:30). Instead of a sign, Jesus offers verbal testimony: "Very truly I tell you…." (6:32).[144] Jesus' valid testimony to the truth was not accepted: "This teaching is difficult; who can accept it (6:60). Truth, therefore, is presented in two legitimate forms. No matter by what way one receives the truth, they are forced to choose whether to believe or not. "Unless I see the mark of the nails in his hands, and put my finger in the mark of the nails and my hand in his side, I will not believe" (20:25).[145]

To sum up: the "Word" enters the world as light (visibility of the divine through deeds). Light exposes everyone to the truth. One is then forced to accept or reject, and thus the word or the sign will

---

[144] The double use of "amen" is unique to John and appears twenty-four times in the Gospel.

[145] "Jesus is the light of the world which shines forth most clearly on the cross where he is exalted and glorified. All people must choose to accept or reject the light, and in doing so they receive either eternal life or judgment." John W. Romanowsky, "When The Son of Man Is Lifted Up": The Redemptive Power of the Crucifixion in the Gospel of John," *Horizons* 32 (2005): 116.

expose a person to whether they are of the light or the darkness.[146] To conclude, a sign may not always produces faith, but it always forces decision.

We now return to the wedding at Cana. The first sign was water turned to wine. What then is the symbolism of the wine? Why transform purification water, which is meant to clean people and solidify their relationship with God, into wine? The prologue insists that the Word came into the world and those who receive him will believe and become children of God (1:12). In terms of the wedding, this means that the relationship with God that was once managed by purification (water) is now replaced by the revelation of truth which transforms the believer into a child of God. The symbol of the wine is the 'Word" bearing much fruit, creating children of God. This is confirmed when the disciples become believers: "But to all who received him, who believed in his name, he gave power to become children of God" (1:12). The fact that glory was seen means that the word came and made a visible appearance. The creation motif is now complete. The Word has entered the world, made himself manifest and produced believers. The reader is now introduced to the subject of a home for believers.

---

[146] Udo Schnelle contends that the signs are "the divine presence in the world." Udo Schnelle, *Theology of the New Testament* (trans. M. Eugene Boring; Grand Rapids: Baker Academic, 2009), 677. That is, the signs do not only point to Jesus as the source of the divine life; they are also the presence of the divine life. That is to say, signs not only point to Jesus as the source of the divine life; "they are also the presence of the divine life." Gorman, "Missional Gospel," 152.

The Temple (2:13-23)

As the reader has seen throughout the Gospel, the sections are strung together with literary and thematic links. Both the wedding and the temple narratives mention "three days": "After three days there was a wedding" (2:1) and "destroy this temple and in three days I will rebuild it" (2:19). There is also a contrast between the disciples who believe and the "Jews" who respond with doubt and aggression.[147]

The "Jews"

At the Temple, Jesus encounters his first opposition, the "Jews." The Gospel refers to those opposing Jesus as "Jews," a term (*Ioudaios*) that is employed 70 times, which is significant considering that Luke uses the word only five times. The term represents a political group, not an ethnic one, and should not be misunderstood by the contemporary reader as anti-Semitic.[148] Often outsiders classify a small contingent of people with a generic title. The negativity toward the Jews reflects opposition to the legitimacy of Jesus' claims.

---

[147] See H. Van den Bussche, "Le signe du Temple," *BVC* (1957): 92-100.

[148] James H. Charlesworth explains that "the apparent anti-Judaisms in the New Testament are usually additions to the tradition, and reflect the social hostility between two distinct Jewish groups." See his "Exploring Opportunities for Rethinking Relations among Jews and Christians." *Jews and Christians: Exploring the Past, Present, and Future* (New York: Crossroad, 1990), 53.

To do this they have to deny and reject Jewish tradition and sensitivity. That is, the criticism is directed toward religious and political decisions, not ethnicity.[149]

Jesus had friends among the Jews so not every Jew was against Jesus and not every Pharisee was unfavorable toward Him (i.e. Nicodemus). The term represents an organized group within the Jewish tradition that opposes those who profess Jesus. The term appears to target this restricted grouping. The Gospel presents many favorable pro-Jewish values such as the Jewish Scriptures, ritual purification, the Temple, worship in Jerusalem (4:22), and Jewish feasts such as the Sabbath, Passover, Tabernacles, and Dedication. There are many examples of favorable Jews. Jesus is a Jew (4:9). Jews have a special role in God's plan for salvation: "You worship what you do not know; we worship what we know, for salvation is from the Jews" (4:22). Many Jews believed in Jesus (2:23; 7:40; 8:30). The prologue describes the Law as a gift through Moses (1:17). John the Baptist came that Jesus might be revealed to Israel (1:31). Jesus is the servant of God, the apocalyptic lamb (1:29), the Holy one of God (6:69). Nathanael is called a genuine Israelite. The trial of Jesus is less anti-Jewish than the Synoptics. For example, there is the presence of Roman soldiers at Jesus' arrest with no priests or Jewish leaders. There is no Jewish trial. Not all the Jews are present at the Roman trial. The

---

[149] Kysar feels that the term *Ioudaioi* should be seen as pointing to certain Jewish leaders rather than to the entire Jewish people. See his "Anti-Semitism and the Gospel of John," in *Anti-Semitism and Early Christianity* (eds. Craig A. Evans and Donald A. Hagner; Minneapolis: Fortress, 1993), 118.

citation of Psalm 69:9a. "For zeal for your house has consumed me" seems to be a reference only to the opponents who uses the zeal of the Temple to destroy Jesus and bring upon his death. Jesus' response to such a threat is the resurrection: in three days I will raise it up. The word "raise" is not found in the Synoptics. The word can refer to the construction of a building or the body in a resurrection.

Aside from the positive, there are also many times that the term "Jews" have a negative connotation. Jews regard Jesus as a law breaker and blasphemer. The rejection of Jesus brings about condemnation (3:18; 12:48).

To contrast the opposition of the Jews, the disciples are mentioned as a counterpart. Twice the disciples remember: "His disciples remembered that it was written, 'Zeal for your house will consume me'" (2:17), "and his disciples remembered that he had said this; and they believed the scripture and the word that Jesus had spoken" (2:22). The Jews question and doubt while the disciple remember and believe. The Jews often come across as clueless and naive. For example, at the temple in John 2 the Jews claimed that the construction of the temple took forty-six years, pointing out the impossibility of its restoration in three days. The Jews simply missed the metaphorical usage of the Temple and focused on the literal meaning. Once again the disciple will remember this at the triumphal entry into Jerusalem at 12:16. The Gospel makes these literary connections so that these earlier scenes can provide meaning to the events just before and during the hour of glory at the end of the Gospel.[150]

---

[150] Thate, "Conditionality in John's Gospel," 500.

The overturning of tables at the beginning of the Gospel is a surprise since the Synoptic Gospels place the scene at the end of Jesus public ministry.[151] One possible reason for the relocation is to distance the disturbance at the Temple from the trial of Jesus. That way, the resuscitation of Lazarus, not found in the Synoptics, could be the logical source for Jesus' arrest, conviction, and death.

The scene takes place in Jerusalem just before the feast of Passover. This is the first of three mentions of the Passover in the Gospel. The second occurrence of the feast takes place at the beginning of the multiplication of the loaves (6:4) and the last before the passion narrative (13:1). All three demonstrate the fact that Jesus' body is a location for believers. Jesus talks about his own body as the Temple: "he was speaking of the temple of his body" (2:21). Jesus "becomes himself the place of God's presence and God's worship, no longer centered on Mount Zion or Mount Gerizim, but available universally."[152] As one will notice that many of the passages are introduced by a Jewish feast. The passage should be read in the light of these feast days. Jesus will give new meaning and transform Jewish feasts, upgrading them to a new passage toward eternal life. In the original Passover, the Jews commemorate the freeing of the nation from

---

[151] There would have been three Passovers during the public ministry of Jesus, the Synoptic only report one. Scholars are divided as some assert that John is historically reliable (J. Wiess, Lagrange, McNeile, Brooke, J. A. T. Robinson and V. Tayor) and others say the Synopitcs (Bernard, Hoskyns, Dodd, Barrett, Lighfoot).

[152] Richard Bauckham, "Historiographical Characteristics of the Gospel of John," *NTS* 53 (2007): 32.

Egyptian slavery. Jesus will now transform the Passover to commemorate the freeing of people from death to life.

In John 6 he discusses his own body as the locus for eternal life: "Do not work for the food that perishes but for the food that endures for eternal life, which the Son of Man will give you" (6:27). "I am the bread of life; whoever comes to me will never be hungry" (6:35), and "For this reason, I have told you that no one can come to me unless it is granted by the Father" (6:65). During the preparation period of the third Passover, Jesus tells his disciples "to abide in me as I abide in you. Just as the branch cannot bear fruit by itself unless it abides in the vine. Neither can you unless you abide in me" (15:4).

Jesus is a location for the believer when he calls his body a temple.[153] The fury of Jesus is ignited when he discovers that his Father's home (τὸν οἶκον τοῦ πατρός μου) has been turned into a shopping plaza (2:16). There is even a play on the word "house" when he calls it a "house market" (οἶκον ἐμπορίου). During the final discourse, Jesus describes the house of God as a mansion with many rooms. He tells his disciples that he will return and bring the believers back to his Father's house (14:2-3). The fact that Jesus is a locus for believers is confirmed in the prologue by describing the Word becoming flesh to pitch his tent among his own. So the purpose of the "Word" becoming visible (flesh) is indwelling. In the Gospel, indwelling is a major theme. Those who obey dwell in Christ as he dwells in the

---

[153] Time and space is transformed during Jesus' temple presence during feasts. See D. Mollat, *Remarques sur le vocabulaire spatial du quatrième évangile* (Studio Evangelica 1; eds. K. Aland, F. L. Cross, J. Daniélou, H. Riesenfeld and W. C. van Unnik; TU 73; Berlin: Akademie-Verlag, 1959), 321-8.

Father (15:10). Jesus tells his disciples that "those who love me will keep my work and my Father will love them, and we will come to them and make our home with them" (14:23). Also, in the prologue, acceptance of the Word empowers believers to be children of God. The purpose of the Word is to create children. This supports Christ's request from the cross for the disciple to take his mother into the disciple's home (19:26-27). A family is thus created with the death of Jesus. The Gospel appears to be preparing the reader to understand the communal element of accepting the Word, so that the one who believes is a part of a family. The Gospel first treats a wedding, and after the wedding there is discussion of a family home. Then, in chapter three, there will be talk about having children. The Gospel reveals a very sequential process. Once the divine home is secured, the Gospel now turns to a discussion about bearing children.

Nicodemus (3:1-21)

If there is a wedding, eventually there will be talk about children. Children are typically the products of a marriage. It is no surprise that shortly after the wedding of Cana, the groom, Jesus, discusses housing (temple) and birth (born from above). According to the prologue, the first priority of the creative Word is the production of the children of God. In the first chapter, John baptizes in the Jordan River so that Jesus might be made known: "I came baptizing with water, that he might be revealed to Israel." In the story of the wedding at Cana, Jesus is revealed in the changing of the water into wine. Six water jugs were filled with water by the servants. They knew they had to obey the odd request made by Jesus because the mother of Jesus told them to do whatever he says.

All the witnesses to Christ in the Gospel so far, starting with John, have one essential connection with one another: water. The presence of water in the Gospel usually indicates that there is a new witness for Jesus. That is, witnesses need truth/revelation in order to witness and water symbolizes truth.[154] John the Baptist, who was sent to baptize with water, is a witness because he saw the Holy Spirit descend upon the Son of God (1:33-34). The mother of Jesus exposes Jesus as the groom in the wedding at Cana. The Samaritan woman at Jacob's Well is sent by Jesus and testifies to the entire village (4:39). The paralytic at the sheep pool proclaims (ἀναγγέλλω, 5:15) the identity of his healer to the Pharisees. The blind man washes his eyes in the pool of Siloam, and he witnesses to diverse unbelieving groups (9:9-12; 15-17; 25-32). Jesus fills a basin with water and washes the feet of his disciples to initiate the long awaited "hour" (13:1). I will argue later that this gesture suggests to the disciples to become witnesses to others even if it may cost them rejection and death. The beloved disciple witnesses that he saw water flowing from the side of Jesus (19:34-35). Here, there seems to be a link between water containers and the birth of a new witness who will testify on

---

[154] John Paul Jones argues that water symbolizes a call for a decision in John. He concludes that water allows or facilitates an opportunity for characters in the narrative to come to belief, thus the term functions as a call for a decision. See his *The Symbol of Water in the Gospel of John* (Sheffield: Sheffield Academic, 1997). I rather argue that water represents revelation/truth. One who accepts revelation/truth will have access to eternal life.

Christ's behalf. There are water containers because they symbolize that the believer is a water/truth container. As the reader begins to see this connection, the author of John decides to elaborate on the theme of water. Why is water an important symbol in this Gospel?

The encounter with Nicodemus offers us the opportunity to discuss the important role of water in the Gospel of John. Jesus explains to Nicodemus that one must be born of water and the Spirit (3:5). It is a difficult passage to interpret because "water" and "Spirit" can be both understood as either contrastive (two different entities) or as appositional (two ways of saying the same thing). Drawing from the prologue, the reader has already been informed how the children of God are not born through human causes: not of blood or of the will of the flesh or of the will of man but of God" (1:13). Recalling this verse will shed some light on Nicodemus's misunderstanding of Jesus' comment on being born from above. It is obvious that Nicodemus did not read the prologue.[155] The cause for the confusion is the Greek word: ἄνωθεν, which can mean "from above" or "again." Jesus says that one must be born "from above" while Nicodemus thinks that Jesus is saying that one has to be born "again."[156] The

---

[155] See Michael R. Whitenton, "The Dissembler of John 3: A Cognitive and Rhetorical Approach to the Characterization of Nicodemus," *JBL* 135 (2016): 155.

[156] The purpose of Nicodemus' confusion according to Meeks is to provide an opportunity "(a) for the reader to feel superior, and (b) for the sage who is questioned to deliver a discourse." See his "The Man from Heaven in Johannine Sectarianism," *Journal of Biblical Literature* 91 (1972): 54-55.

dialogue never really gets resolved and advances forward as a comedy of errors.[157] Eventually Nicodemus drops from the conversation which allows Jesus to expand on what it means to be born from above by water and spirit.[158]

Spirit and water are sometimes viewed in 3:5 as a hendiadys. L. P. Jones points out that there is only one term for water (3:5) but several for Spirit. Because the copulative conjunction "and" (καί) joins the two terms in 3:5, they can be understood epexegetically, that is, the addition of the second word is used to clarify the meaning of a previous word. In this case, the addition of spirit elucidates the meaning of water.[159] Water has multiple functions including purification, and consumption. If water is symbolic, then it needs clarification. What is the function of water in this Gospel? It symbolizes revelation, the gift that offers eternal life. Spirit likewise means a source for truth. That is, both terms are interchangeable so the

---

[157] William T. Pyle explains that the "misunderstanding sequence" in John's Gospel consists of three basic moves: (1) Jesus used an ambiguous, metaphorical, or a word with double meaning; (2) an interlocutor misunderstood His statement; and (3) the misunderstanding provided an opportunity for Jesus or the narrator to clarify or elaborate on the failure. See his "Understanding the Misunderstanding," 26-27.

[158] According to Andreas Kostenberger misunderstandings by various characters often underscore meaning "inextricably linked to the concept of revelation," See his *A Theology of John's Gospel and Letters* (BTNT; Grand Rapids: Zondervan, 2009), 142.

[159] Tricia Brown insists that the water in 3:5 represents sexual relations. She cites 1:13 which alludes to a natural birth resulting from the will of the flesh. One has to ask the question as to why the terms water and spirit are not contrasted in other Johannine texts (4:10-14; 7:39; 19:34). Tricia Gates Brown, *Spirit in the Writings of John* (London: T &T Clark, 2003), 121.

reader understands both terms as accomplishing the same function.¹⁶⁰ Jones also notes that just as the water can be transformed into wine, so too the birth of water in 3:5 can "provide access to the realm of God."¹⁶¹ Later in John 7:39, water appears to symbolize "the Spirit."¹⁶²

Birth by water and spirit represents the process by which truth/revelation allows one to have access to eternal life.¹⁶³ In order for one to receive eternal life, one must believe in truth. The witness provides the revelation, the object of belief. One needs to have access to revelation and that is provided by the one who testifies. Water and spirit symbolize revelation/truth which produces eternal life. Revelation is a gift just as living water or life is a gift. So both water and spirit represent the life giving revelation, divine knowledge. For revelation to be valid, it must have its origin from the Father: "No one has ascended into heaven except the one who descended from heaven, the Son of Man." (3:13). One must be born from above because the origin of revelation must come from the Father. Revelation has to be received as a gift; it must be delivered by the witness. The one receiving the gift has no control over how it is acquires, as if it can be located and earned: "The spirit (πνεῦμα) blows where it wills, and you hear the sound of it, but you do not know whence (πόθεν)

---

[160] Jones, *Symbol of Water,*" 74.

[161] Ibid.

[162] Wai-yee Ng, *Water Symbolism in John: An Eschatological Interpretation* (New York: Peter Lang, 2001), 72.

[163] "True understanding is a matter of grace, a gift to be granted by God himself, an inward change under the impulse of the Spirit." Marinus de Jonge, "Nicodemus and Jesus: Some Observations on Misunderstanding and Understanding in the Fourth Gospel," *BJRL* 53 (1971): 359.

it comes or whither it goes" (3:8). Then Jesus continues to explain that revelation must be given by way of testimony: "I say to you, we speak of what we know, and bear witness to what we have seen" (3:10).

Nicodemus eventually ceases to talk and the dialogue turns into a monologue.[164] Much of what Jesus says is not supposed to make sense for the reader until we meet Nicodemus again at the preparation for the burial. How is the Son of Man lifted up? "Just as Moses lifted up the serpent in the wilderness, so must the Son of Man be lifted up" (3:14). How does God love by giving his Son to the world? "God so loved the world that he gave his only son" (3:16). How exactly does Jesus save the world? "God did not send the Son into the world to condemn the world, but in order that the world might be saved through him" (3:17). The statements make sense after Jesus' death, right at the time that Nicodemus makes his final appearance. His presence at the burial of Jesus allows the reader to recall the dialogue he had with Jesus when they met at night at an early stage of the Gospel.[165] The word "night" (νύξ) is employed seven times in

---

[164] Michael J. Thate observes that "John is clearly speaking to Nicodemus on Jesus' behalf as his own audience listens on the sidelines; at some point, John's eye shifts from Nicodemus to his own audience, Johannine Christians, to whom he offers his interpretation of these events. See his "Conditionality in John's Gospel," 504.

[165] According to Bruce Chilton, "The terrain is prepared by the mention of Nicodemus in connection with Jesus' burial and with the reminder of Nicodemus's nocturnal visit (19:39). John establishes the parameters of chap. 3 as part of the setting." See his "The Gospel according to John's Rabbi Jesus," *BBR* 25 (2015): 52.

John's Gospel (3:2; 7:50; 9:4; 11:10; 13:30; 19:39; and 21:3), two times with reference to Nicodemus (see also 19:39).[166]

Nicodemus is considered by many to be an ambiguous character.[167] Is he a believer, sympathetic to Jesus, or rather antagonistic?[168] The reader is not given enough information at his cameo appearance

---

[166] "This characteristic description becomes the identifying mark for Nicodemus." Pyle, "Understanding the Misunderstanding," 40. According to Brown "darkness and night symbolize the realm of evil, untruth, and ignorance." Brown, *John*, 130.

[167] See Meeks, "Man from Heaven," 52-57; Raimo Hakola, "Burden of Ambiguity: Nicodemus and the Social Identity of the Johannine Christians," *NTS* 55 (2009): 438-55; Nicolas Farelly, "An Unexpected Ally: Nicodemus's Role within the Plot of the Fourth Gospel," *TJ* 34 (2003): 31-43; Slicia D. Myers, "The Ambiguous Character of Johannine Characterization: An Overview of Recent Contributions and Proposal," *PRST* 39 (2012): 289-98. Susan E. Hylen, *Imperfect Believers: Ambiguous Characters in the Gospel of John* (Louisville: John Knox, 2009), 23.

[168] Meeks defines Nicodemus as a representative of Jews of inadequate faith who evolves in chapter 8 into a "potential Christ-killers." See his "Man from Heaven," 55. Sean Freyne identifies Nicodemus as an unbeliever. See his "Vilifying the Other and Defining the Self: Matthew's and John's Anti-Jewish Polemic in Focus," in "To See Ourselves as Others See Us": Christians, Jews, "Others" in Late Antiquity (ed. J. Neusner and E. S. Frerichs; Chico, CA: Scholars, 1985), 127. M. de Jonge takes him to be a representative of the Crypto-Christians (12:42-43). See his "Nicodemus and Jesus," 30-31. According to Jouette Bassler, "Marginality" is the better category for understanding Nicodemus because he shows no real movement towrd believing in the narrative as he is no more a disciple at the end of the Gospel than at the beginning. He remains throughout a *tertium quid*, which, in this Gospel, is still to be an outsider and is not good enough to be a disciple of Jesus. See his, "Mixed Signals: Nicodemus in the Fourth Gospel," *JBL* 108 (1989): 646.

here, but his second appearance draws some answers to this question. At the death of Jesus, during the hour of glory, Nicodemus in no longer in the dark of the night. It is under the cross that the nebulous statements by Jesus to Nicodemus can be understood by him. Under the cross, one can see the Son of Man was lifted up. It is near the cross where one can see living water and the blood of Christ that provide eternal life: "Who drinks my blood will have eternal life" (6:54). It is at the death of Jesus that both water and spirit are made available by Jesus on the cross. Water flows from Jesus' side (19:34), and He hands over the Spirit (19:30). "He who saw this has testified so that you also may believe" (19:36). These connections are imperative for interpretation. But, while Nicodemus converses at night, in contrast, he fails to understand. The return of Nicodemus at the death of Jesus confirms the connection between the two texts. The later text (the passion narrative) informs the former dialogue with Nicodemus. Jesus ends his speech by returning to a theme from the prologue: light. Both light and water are essential materials in the seven-day creation in Genesis. They make their first appearance together here and will be treated later on during the feast of Tabernacles when Jesus announces the availability of living water and claims to be the light of the world. These two creative elements represent revelation. When one believes, he or she becomes a child of God and can inherit eternal life.

Jesus uses veiled terminology while his conversation partner struggles to understand. His teaching, ironically, is meant to conceal as well as reveal. Meeting Jesus at night is symbolic for darkness. The two accounts of Nicodemus highlight the difference between meeting Christ in the dark (3:1-21) and reappearing in the light during the hour of glory (19:39-42).[169] In the prologue the "Word" is the light that dispels the darkness. However, for Nicodemus, the encounter with truth will appear as a teaching without context similar to the blind man who first encounters Jesus, the light of the world, without eyes to see. Both will progress in sight and understanding with the passage of time. For Nicodemus, context, I will argue, comes later when he assists at Jesus' burial. Unlike the man born blind, the Samaritan woman, and others who encounter Jesus, Nicodemus has three appearances in the Gospel. He has room to progress. So the vague words Jesus uses are situational and can only be understood in context to the divine plan from the prologue or an event such as the hour of glory when Nicodemus re-appears in the narrative. Jesus' teaching is unclear at other passages as well. For example, one sees the crowds struggle to understand the discourse on the body and blood of Christ: "This teaching is difficult; who can accept it?" (6:60). Perhaps this is proof that the author intends the reader to understand through intratextuality.

Still, is Nicodemus a friend or foe? In this first meeting with Jesus, there is not enough information to form a characterization of Nicodemus. Does he align himself with the world of darkness or is he one who moves from darkness to light?[170] Does he reject or accept

---

[169] Whitenton, "Cognitive and Rhetorical Approach," 156.

[170] Nicodemus appears to be a "type" cast who represents a secret believer who remains in the shadows of the Jewish community. This is a faith that Jesus finds inadequate. Yet he overcomes the darkness and emerges as one who proclaims Jesus as King by offering one hundred pounds of myrrh for His burial. His faith progression appears to be similar to the man born blind who begins his encounter with Jesus in the darkness of his

the teaching of Jesus? He disappears in the monologue without any reference to his decision. His response comes in a later appearance. To understand the progression, one must first understand that Nicodemus represents a group when he first meets Jesus. He says, "We know that you are a teacher who has come from God" (3:2). Jesus answers in the plural "Yet you (plural) do not receive our testimony. If I have told you (plural) about earthly things and you (plural) do not believe how can you (plural) believe if I tell you about heavenly things" (3:11-12). One should note that just before Nicodemus was introduced, a group believed in Jesus: "many believed in his name because they saw the signs that he was doing" (2:23). However, Jesus did not trust them because "he knew what was in man" (2:24).[171] Similarly, in the very next line in 3:1, Nicodemus is introduced as a man: "Now there was a man (ἄνθρωπος)." Likewise, he was impressed with Jesus' signs: "for no one can do these signs that you do apart from the presence of God" (3:2). And Jesus has reasons for not trusting the group: "They do not receive our testimony" (3:11), "do not believe" (3:12) and "are condemned already" (3:18). Nicodemus meets Jesus, the light of the world, who tells him that the "light has come into the world, and people loved darkness rather than light because their deeds were evil" (3:19). The reader is left to wonder if

---

blindness, challenges the Pharisees to seek the truth, and then proclaims him Lord.

[171] The purpose of the concluding verses of the temple cleansing (2:23-24) is to introduce the reader to Nicodemus. George R. Blomberg, "The Globalization of Biblical Interpretation: A Test Case—John 3-4," *BBR* 5 (1995): 5; Craig L. Beasley-Murray, *John* (Waco: Word, 1987) 47; Xavier Leon-Dufour, *Lecture de Vévangile selon Jean* (Paris: Editions du Seuil, 1988) 1.284.

Nicodemus is a part of the group that prefers the darkness, seeing that he meets Jesus at night. Nicodemus belongs to a group (Pharisees) that will eventually reject Jesus and prefer blindness to sight in chapter 9. Still, Nicodemus has no record of evil deeds, and no reason to prefer the darkness.[172] Finally, we learn in the first appearance that Nicodemus recognizes Jesus as one who is from God. This is always the sign of a future believer, one who knows where Jesus is from.

In the second appearance, Nicodemus begins to disassociate himself from the Pharisees. He defends Jesus against the opposition of his own in-group: "Nicodemus, who had gone to Jesus before, and who was one of them, asked, 'Our law does not judge people without first giving them a hearing to find out what they are doing, does it?'" (7:50). He seems to adopt a Johannine ideology of a fair hearing. He also shows that he is separating himself from the crowd of non-believers.

In the third appearance, it seems that Nicodemus has chosen light over darkness by appearing with Joseph at the hour of glory to bury Jesus' body in a tomb. Both Joseph who followed Jesus in secret

---

[172] "Nicodemus comes to Jesus with a generous openness, acknowledging that Jesus is credentialed by God. He seems to be guilty of nothing more than befuddlement before a confusing revelation, a befuddlement that the reader can easily understand! At the end, Nicodemus does not argue with Jesus or depart in protest. He simply throws up his hands, asking helplessly, 'How can this be?' (v.9)." Schneiders, *You May Believe*, 118.

and Nicodemus who met Jesus at night appear together in the public forum to bury Jesus.[173]

One must ask whether the burial in 19:39 with one hundred pounds of spices–an astonishing amount–means that Nicodemus understood Jesus' identity as the Messiah/King or that is he preoccupied with the permanence of death.[174] According to Brown, it is debatable whether Nicodemus and Joseph are believers or remain cryptic disciples.[175] One clue that the Gospel writer gives is the burial wrappings that are found by Peter when he first entered the empty tomb. There were two sets. One was described as "a facecloth that was rolled, which was upon his head, not lying with the linen cloths, but rolled up into a place apart" (20:7). The headpiece is rolled up and put to the side. Why are not the other wrappings rolled up and put to the side? The reason the burial wrappings around the body are not rolled up is because they cannot be rolled up or folded as the headpiece. Remember, Nicodemus brings one hundred pounds of aloe and myrrh to bury Jesus. A rolled up cloth does not seem to have had a treatment of myrrh which is a hardener and would have stiffened the burial cloths. This may imply that the burial team did

---

[173] See F. Peter Cotterell, "The Nicodemus Conversation: A Fresh Appraisal," *ExpTim* 96 (1984-85): 238; Jean-Marie Auwers, "La nuit de Nicodème," *RB* 97 (1990): 482; Cornelis Bennema, *Encountering Jesus: Character Studies in the Gospel of John* (Milton Keynes: Paternoster, 2009), 79.

[174] Dennis D. Sylva, "Nicodemus and His Spices (John 19:39)," *NTS* 34 (1988): 148-51. See also Bassler, "Mixed Signals," 635.

[175] Brown, Raymond Edward. *The Death of the Messiah: From Gethsemane to the Grave: A Commentary on the Passion Narratives in the Four Gospels* (2 vols.; New York: Doubleday, 1994), 2:1265-70.

not finish the job. The headpiece with just a hand towel may be evidence enough for the reader that the burial was incomplete. With the extravagant amount of spices, the burial cloth would have been affected by the large amounts of resinous gum; indeed, the excessive amount of myrrh seems to indicate a royal burial.[176] The reader is left with the impression that there were two procedures, one with the use of myrrh and the other without.

The myrrh is meant to signify a royal burial. Remember how, during Jesus' trial before Pilate, Jesus told Pilate that he was a king. Pilate believed him and announced him as a king to the Israelites. Pilate also wrote the inscription that Jesus is king in three languages and placed the placard over his head. So Nicodemus gave Jesus a royal burial. Myrrh is a great product. Not only does aloe and myrrh make the tomb smell nice, it also preserves the body. Myrrh is a hardener; it is a resin. So the wrappings turn into a hardened shell so that they cannot be folded or rolled up.

Why did Nicodemus fail to put aloe and myrrh on the headpiece? Why not finish the job? Was he in a hurry? Not likely. How long does it take to dip the headpiece in a hundred pounds of resin? Nicodemus gave Jesus a royal burial because he was a king. But he left an opening because he believed that, with Christ, death was not permanent. It would have been Nicodemus's personal stamp that he believed that Jesus was God.

How did he know? From the conversation, he had with Jesus in chapter 3. In that first exchange, Jesus told a confused Nicodemus:

---

[176] A vast quantity of spices was used in the burial of Herod the Great. See Josephus *Ant.* 17.199.

"When I am lifted up He will draw all people to myself," and that "God so loved the world that he gave his only Son." These statements made no sense at the time. In fact, Jesus needles him: "Are you a teacher of Israel, and yet you do not understand these things?" (3:10). Finally, at the hour of glory, as Nicodemus was standing under the cross preparing to take him down for his burial, the words that Jesus spoke would have made sense to him: "When I am lifted up I will draw everyone to myself. God so loved the world that he gave his only son." There before him is Jesus, lifted on the cross with a placard translated in every language so anyone in the world could read it. It would make sense why the burial was not left in a permanent state, leaving some room for a belief in the resurrection and the life.[177] This would lead me to conclude that Nicodemus walked from darkness to light and his actions reflect one who openly proclaimed Jesus as King in the manner of his burial.[178] Remember too that Nicodemus first referred to Jesus as a teacher. The two disciples and Philip also called him a teacher before upgrading Him to a king. Likewise, Nicodemus believes that Jesus is the Messiah by way of his royal burial.

He gave Jesus a royal burial because he believed that Jesus was a king. He left an opening because he believed that Jesus would rise.

---

[177] Against this opinion, see Sylva, "Nicodemus and His Spices," 148-151, who suggests that Nicodemus had no belief in the afterlife because the extravagant amount of myrrh was symbolic of the permanence of death. See also David Rensberger, *Johannine Faith and Liberating Community* (Philadelphia: Westminster, 1988), 40; Paul Duke, maintains that Nicodemus did not progress in his believe in Christ after the first encounter with Jesus. See his *Irony in the Fourth Gospel* (Atlanta: John Knox, 1985), 110.

[178] See also Farelly, "Nicodemus's Role," 31-43.

He came to such a conclusion because of the information he was given in the beginning of the Gospel, a conversation he did not understand at the time when it was night, but a conversation he would understand at the hour of glory.

Jesus ends the discourse by emphasizing faith. Revelation is a gift from God but it must be believed, "Those who believe in him are not condemned; but those who do not believe are condemned already, because they have not believed in the name of the only Son of God" (3:18). The verb "believe" (πιστεύω) occurs six times in 3:12-18. A child of God is the result of a choice that must be made post-revelation. Either one believes or one does not believe.

John and Jesus (3:22-30)

The attention now shifts back to John in 3:22-30.[179] Both John and Jesus are reported to be baptizing in different locations along the Jordan. The reader recalls that John baptizes with water. Water is symbolic of truth. John confirms this by saying that he baptizes with water "that he might be revealed to Israel" (1:31). John also reported that Jesus will baptize with the Holy Spirit. This means that

---

[179] This passage has its share of sequential, thematic, and literary difficulties. The sequence is not clear because Jesus was in Jerusalem and, suddenly, he is now in Judea. John is still baptizing long after Jesus begins his public ministry. This is not the sequence of the Synoptics where it is reported that John is arrested prior to his ministry (Mark 1:14; Matt 4:12). If John proclaimed that Jesus is the "Lamb of God" to his disciples, why do his disciples complain that "all are going to him" (3:26). See Brown, *John*, 153-56, who discusses further these issues.

others will be commissioned to bear witness to the truth. Later, during the Last Supper discourse, Jesus promises to send the Spirit of Truth. John delivers the truth through his testimony because he was sent by God. Jesus offers the Spirit of Truth so others can give testimony. They, like John, give it because they are connected to God by way of the Spirit. Both the baptisms of Jesus and John are related to the promulgation of divine truth.

In the next scene, Jesus will discuss "water" and "spirit" with a woman who will testify to others so that they may believe. The theme of the bridegroom is also shared in both of these passages. John calls Jesus the bridegroom and Jesus meets the woman at a well, a place where the patriarchs met their spouses (Abraham's servant meets Rebekah in Genesis 24). John is given one more opportunity to clarify his role as revealer before he fades out of the Gospel narrative. This time, he describes his relationship with the bridegroom in terms of friendship. The depiction of John as a friend (φίλος, 3:29) will be recalled when Jesus defines friendship at the Last Supper discourse: "You are my friends (φίλοι) if you do what I command you" (15:14).[180] Here, the definition of friendship is made known and John the Baptist certainly has fulfilled the requirements of being a "friend": John's disciples confirm that he testified to the one who was with John across the Jordan (3:26). Later in the Gospel, John will

---

[180] Jesus' discourse with his disciples on friendship in John 15 includes joy. Joy and friendship with Jesus go together: "I have said these things to you so that my joy (χαρά) may be in you, and that your joy (χαρά) may be complete" (15:11). That is why John describes his friendship with the bridegroom in terms of joy: "rejoices (χαρά) greatly at the bridegroom's voice" (4:29).

be credited for his witness: "John performed no sign, but everything that John said about this man was true. And many believed in him there" (10:41). Earlier, John proclaimed Jesus as "the Lamb of God" (1:36). As a result of his witness, he successfully decreased the number of his followers by two (1:33-39), fulfilling the goal "He must increase, but I must decrease" (3:30). Jesus will continue to increase by the testimony of others. But why highlight John the Baptist after Jesus' meeting with Nicodemus? I argue that John the Baptist is an example of one who progresses from ignorance to understanding, suggesting that Nicodemus also has a chance to progress from ignorance to understanding. Early on, John declared that he first did not "know him" (1:31, 33). These early chapters seem to underscore the believer as a work in progress, one who meets Jesus in varied backgrounds and situations. The next believer to encounter the bridegroom will be a woman outside the Jewish circle, at a water location (the well) where she will listen to his words. Like John, her understanding will develop in stages, and also like John, she will witness to others, thereby increasing the number of Jesus' believers.

Before the next encounter, however, there is a recap of the prologue (3:31-36).[181] The primary features in this text are origin and choice: Christ is from above (origin), testimony forces a decision (choice). The one who is sent from above speaks the words of God and the one who believes has eternal life: The other option is simply self-destruction: "whoever disobeys the Son will not see life" (3:36).

---

[181] It is not clear who is speaking these verses. It is likely either John the Baptist (Barrett, *John*, 224-25) or Jesus (Schnackenburg, *John*, 1:380-81).

Jesus and the Samaritan Woman (4:1-42)

The reader has just been reminded of the program of the prologue before entering into the narrative of the Samaritan woman. The one who receives the "Word" believes and will be given power to become a child of God. In this scene, the bridegroom, after discussing the birth of children with Nicodemus, now meets a woman considered to be outside of the people of God with multiple husbands and a mysterious acquaintance who is not her husband. Jesus will offer the gift of revelation ("he told me everything I ever did") using the symbol of water, the immediate need of the woman who goes to Jacob's Well. The encounter with the Samaritan woman contrasts with Jesus' encounter with the Nicodemus. Nicodemus meets Jesus at night, the woman at high noon, the brightest time of day. The Pharisee enjoys high status in the religious community, the woman holds low esteem in Jewish circles. The man cannot hold a conversation with Jesus, while the woman carries on with a deep theological exchange. The man appears affable, benign, and congenial at first encounter, while the woman is bellicose, contentious, and defensive. Both the man and the woman reappear as workers on public display on behalf of the Lord. Both narratives discuss water and spirit, both bring up the question of "where," and both narratives make better sense in the light of Jesus' crucifixion and death on the cross.

Jesus meets the woman at a well, the location where the patriarchs would meet their spouses.[182] Here, Jesus, the bridegroom,

---

[182] Abraham's servant finds Rebekah, the future wife of Isaac, at the well of Nahor (Gen 24:10-60; Jacob met Rachel at the well in Haran (Gen

meets a woman with marital issues at a Patriarch's well. Worship is discussed, a topic that is often described with a marriage analogy. And in the end, the woman harvests many believers (children of God). The marital motif, which begins with the wedding at Cana in chapter 2, appears in yet another chapter. Many of the Johannine themes that the reader has assimilated from the text thus far are here: revelation, belief, eternal life, and witness.

The scene begins at Jacob's well. The disciples leave to get provisions, while Jesus "sits" at the well from a long journey. The hour is noon (the sixth hour). As I pointed out in the introduction, it is not the only time the words "sit" and "sixth hour" are found together: "sit" (καθέζομαι, 4:6; καθίζω, 19:13) and "sixth hour" (ὥρα ἦν ὡς ἕκτη, 4:6; 19:14). Note the Greek expression ὥρα ἦν ὡς ἕκτη ("the sixth hour") is repeated verbatim at Pilate's trial. In both instances, sitting at high noon will prove that living water is a gift that will produce eternal life for the believer. The beloved disciple under the cross will see that there is one more water container: the Messianic heart where blood and water will flow. This second mention of sitting and the sixth hour provides an important link connecting the promise of living water at the well to the giving of living water at the

---

29:1-20); and Moses and Zipporah also had ties with the well in Midian (Exod 2:16-22). Robert Alter identifies parallels between "betrothal type-scenes" in Geneses 24 (Rebekka), Geneses 29 (Rachel) and Exodus 2 (Zippora). See his *Biblical Narrative*, 47-62 esp. 51-52. See also Karl Wyer-Menkhoff who provides a compelling verse-by-verse graph comparing betrothal type-scenes with John 4 in "The Response of Jesus: Ethics in John by considering Scripture as Work of God," in *Rethinking the Ethics of John* (eds. Jan G. Der Watt and Ruben Zimmermann; WUNT; Waco: Baylor University Press, 2007), 168.

death of Jesus. I will discuss this parallel in more detail below when I treat the passion narrative.

Why does the Samaritan woman go to Jacob's well at noon? The usual time for women to get water is at low light: early morning and early evening. One can only speculate why this woman goes at noon. The text says the man she is with now is not her husband (4:18). Having five husbands is not necessarily indicative of a misspent life, especially if the husbands have died without an heir.[183] One should also note that Jesus does not talk to her as a whore or a sinner who needs repentance. There is no mention of sin, judgment, or condemnation. Any attempt to describe the woman as a socially ostracized and a despised sinner is conjecture without textual evidence.[184] The

---

[183] This could have been a reference to Levite marriage (Deut 25:5) whereby the closest relative would marry for securing an heir. There is also no reference to support that the woman's past is cast in a favorable light. The unusual behavior of going to the well at noon could be interpreted as an avoidance tactic. Jesus' reference to "Not your husband" would generate an initial negative reaction rather than a positive or neutral one. The low social status of the woman seems to be a consistent quality among the other witnesses in the Gospel.

[184] D.A. Carson describe her as unschooled, without influence, despised, capable only of folk religion. See D. A. Carson, *The Gospel according to John* (Grand Rapids: Eerdmans, 1991), 216. See also Kenneth O. Gangel, *John*, Holman New Testament Commentary Series (Nashville: B&H Publishing, 2000), 74 who states, "About noon the woman came to the well, obviously a social outcast since that hour would have been an unlikely time to lug a heavy water jar back into the city"

text rather highlights her as one who is influential with people, theologically well informed and unafraid to approach society.[185] It is likely that the mention of a noontime visit is not a comment on her social challenges but rather theological. It provides a connection with the passion narrative, the other narrative that mentions the sixth hour. There is also a contrast to Nicodemus; he meets Jesus in the dark of the night, whereas the woman's meeting comes at high noon. The reference to "noon" seems to be used to link the Samaritan passage to other texts in the Gospel.

Jewish men are not to seek favors or receive benefits from Samaritan women.[186] Jesus' request for water is so unexpected, at least to this Samaritan woman, that she even tries to be helpful to this poor Jew who just does not seem to understand social protocol (4:9). This is the only time Jesus is referred to as a "Jew." His request for water is only offered to encourage the woman to ask for help: "You would have asked him, and he would have given you living water" (4:10). The playful reversal of need is easily noted.[187] John is brilliant at shifting the identity of the needy and the provider. Irony is John's

---

[185] Jo Ann Davidson states, "This woman is not ignorant and base, nor is she the town prostitute. Rather, the Samaritan woman is a well-informed, politically savvy person to whom people listen when she speaks. An entire village believed her testimony regarding the identity of the Jewish man at the well and went to find the one who revealed himself to be the promised Messiah." See her "Another Look," 168. See also See also Schneiders, *Encountering Jesus in the Fourth Gospel*, 137-44.

[186] Schnackenburg, *John*, vol. 1, 423-24.

[187] Koester, *Theology of John's Gospel*, 61.

trademark, and he feeds his Gospel with a continuous diet of it.[188] The woman who was asked to be the provider of water will now be the one in need of living water while Jesus will become her provider. This will not be the last time that a thirsty Jesus (I am thirsty, 19:28) will turn into a giver ("He gave up his spirit," 19:30)–once again, another reference that points to the passion narrative. A Jewish man offering a godly gift such as "eternal life" wants to give the ultimate gift to someone with whom he should have nothing to do (4:14). The offer to give her "living water" appears absurd because he doesn't even have a bucket and the well is deep (4:11).[189] She appreciates Jacob's gift, but Jesus' offer is much greater. "Are you greater than our ancestor Jacob, who gave us the well?" (4:12). Such a promise that eliminates the drudgery of fetching water on a daily basis is truly a gift that speaks to this woman. Yet, she is slow to understand the full implications, interpreting his generosity as a plumbing upgrade rather than a relationship with God. She does not immediately grasp the divine gift that is offered to her as eternal life, so Jesus advances the conversation by exposing her secret. He knows all things. Nathaniel wanted to know where Jesus came to know him and he called him the king Israel. This woman will also be impressed because he

---

[188] P. D. Duke describes irony "as a literary device is a double-leveled literary phenomenon in which two tiers of meaning stand in some opposition to each other and in which some degree of unawareness is expressed or implied." See his *Irony in the Fourth Gospel* (Atlanta: John Knox, 1985), 17. On Johannine irony, see also See also Culpepper, *Anatomy of the Fourth Gospel*, 165-69; H. Lausberg, *Handbuch der literarischen Rhetorik: Eine Grundlegung der Literaturwissenschaft* (2d ed.; Munich: Hueber, 1973), 582-85, 902-4.

[189] Ibid, 61, 144.

knew her and she will call begin to ponder whether he may even be the Messiah. Her understanding of Jesus is progressive. The "light of the world" penetrates into the woman's inner secrets, and she begins to see. "I see that you are a prophet" (4:19). Water and light, the creation elements, go hand-in-hand if one is going to bear fruit as this woman is about to do.

It is important to note that she addresses Jesus in a succession of titles that progress in status: "Jew," "Sir," "Prophet," "Messiah." Even in the light, the potential believer begins in ignorance and misunderstanding before she contemplates the possibility that Jesus may be the Messiah, a progression that is similar to Nathaniel who snubs Nazareth only to later call Jesus the king of Israel. Both Nathaniel and the Samaritan woman comment on Jesus' extraordinary knowledge. "Nathaniel asked him, 'Where did you get to know me'" (1:48). The Samaritan woman told Samaritans from the city, "he told me everything I ever done" (4:39). Both claim that from this knowledge, he has satisfied the requirements of a king/messiah: "You are the King of Israel (1:49); "Could he be the Messiah?" (4:29).[190] As she comes to know Jesus through the conversation, she

---

[190] The term μήτι (not) in the phrase "Could this not be the Messiah" is used two other times (8:22; 18:35) to alert the audience that a question expects the answer no. One can assume the same negative answer with the question posed by the Samaritan woman. "Could this not be the Messiah?" It is not at all surprising at mid stage before a mass conversion and transformation of a village to exhibit some lingering doubt before such a gargantuan claim. Her negative question ironically stirs a positive response from the people to see for themselves if this may be the Messiah. Her faith may not be fully developed, like Nicodemus in chapter 3 but it is enough to move forward and expose a village to revelation and transformation.

is able to identify him as the Messiah because he fulfills the essential requirement for a king: he knows everything. Note the the definition of Messiah is different from the Synoptic Gospels where Jesus fulfills the Dividic line. In the Book of Samuel, it is the job of the king to keep the people from wandering away from God. The only way the king can achieve this goal is to become a humble servant by obeying God. In the Synoptics, Jesus is portrayed as the king who keeps brings the people to God by being the suffering servant. One must be careful not to import this role in the Gospel of John. Here the definition of a king is one who knows all things. The reason Jesus

---

For a full treatment on this term see Elizabeth Danna, "A Note on John 4:29," *RB* 106 (1999): 219-223. Similarly, Toan Do concludes that "The character of the Samaritan woman is presented as a catalyst that channels the Samaritans' belief, but that also ambiguously leaves the woman herself in suspense." See her "Revisiting the Woman of Samaria and the Ambiguity of Faith in John 4:4-42," *CBQ* 81 (2019): 252-276. Most Johannine scholars read the particle μήτι (not) in v. 29b as an indication of partial faith on the part of the woman. See also Robert Gordon Maccini, "A Reassessment of the Woman at the well in John 4 in Light of the Samaritan Context," *JSNT* 53 (1994): 46. Others, however, argue that her question is rhetorical and "a way of framing her own belief in a deferential fashion. Harold W. Attridge, "The Samaritan Woman: A Woman Transformed," in Character Studies in the Fourth Gospel: Narrative Approaches to Seventy Figures in John (eds. Steven A. I hint, D. Francois Tolmie, and Ruben Zimmermann; WUNT 314; Tubingen: Mohr Siebeck, 2013), 278-79. See also Teresa Okure, *The Johannine Approach to Mission: A Contextual Study of John 4:1-42* (WUNT, 2; Tübingen: J.C.B. Mohr [Paul Siebeck], 1988),169.

knows all is because he is from the Father. She, like Nathaniel, recognizes Jesus as the Messiah because she knows where Jesus is from. This is how she will know where Jesus is from.

Her inquiry begins by seeking answers to where true worship is found: "Our ancestors worshiped on this mountain but you say the place where people must worship is in Jerusalem" (4:20). The woman is not changing the subject and redirecting the conversation away from herself and her life-style because the dialogue that is about to take place has everything to do with marriage and fidelity. Now that Jesus is equal to or possibly greater than Jacob who gave the well, the Samaritan's theology with its Mosaic-patriarchal tradition can be contrasted with the Davidic-monarchial tradition of the Jews. Jesus, who already broke tradition by asking to share utensils with a Samaritan, will break tradition again: "Woman, believe me, the hour is coming when you will worship the Father neither on this mountain nor in Jerusalem" (4:21). On one hand, the woman sees the two mountains as one excluding the other. Jesus, on the other hand, offers an alternative view whereby both sets of worshipers have access to one location. Jesus successfully communicates himself as the place of worship. The Samaritan knows where Jesus is from: he is from God, because he is the epicenter of worship. The woman, who was just exposed by Jesus, now turns the tables. Her query, in essence, exposes Jesus and his mission. It is here that Jesus uses the first "I am" statement (4:26, cf. Exod 3:14)—the revelation formula of the Gospel.[191] Samaria is no longer outside of the divine

---

[191] The "I am" statement identifies Jesus with God. See Gail R. O'Day, *Revelation in the Fourth Gospel* (Philadelphia: Fortress, 1986) 72; Blomberg, "globalization," 9.

plan. The conversation about worship recalls the prophetic language that condemned idolatry as infidelity and adultery against God.

The marital theme reflects a relationship with God that is founded on worship and fidelity. The woman turns the dialogue to the heart of marital fidelity after she is asked to return to get her husband (4:16). The mountains are now replaced with a worship of spirit and truth. How is she able to testify without possession of the spirit of truth? She is sent by Jesus, the son of God, which means her origin or point of departure connects her to God. This link strengthens her testimony with validity. She then brings them back to Jesus, where her testimony is now superseded by Jesus himself: "It is no longer because of what you said that we believe, for we have heard for ourselves, and we know that this is truly the Savior of the world" (4:42). What is the symbolism of "living water"? According to the prologue, the "Word" is the life of the world. Everything that exists comes from the Word. Having access to truth/revelation allows one to believe and believing leads to eternal life. To gain access to eternal life, one must believe in truth. Divine truth/revelation is a gift like living water, which gives one access to eternal life through belief.

In the Nicodemus narrative, both "water" and "spirit" play an essential role in a birth from above. The reader recalls from chapter 3 that both water and spirit mean revelation, the gift that God offers, yielding eternal life. Marital fidelity leads to fertility: children from above. Upon the return of the disciples, the woman leaves her water jar with Jesus indicating that she knows the location of the "living water" and the answer to her earlier question: "Where do you get this living water" (4:11).[192] When she returns to her village, she invites the people to come and see Jesus. This is the third time the reader hears the expression "come and you will see" (4:29, cf., 1:39, 48). It is an invitation to discover the location, the origin of Jesus. Jesus has the truth because he is from the Father. Jesus, the source of truth, provides the necessary requirement for true worship which results in fertility: fulfilling the prologue goal of creating children of God.

Jesus continues to discuss fertility with the disciples when they return with food, using a harvest analogy.[193] Workers are required at both ends of the growing season. Some sow seeds at the beginning of the season and some reap the fruits at the end of the season. In the analogy, both sower and reaper rejoice because fruit has been gathered for eternal life. With that said, an announcement is made that many Samaritans from the city "believed in him because of the woman's testimony." As Sandra Schneiders points out, "(t)he woman is not simply a 'foil' feeding Jesus cue lines, she is a genuine theological dialogue partner gradually experiencing Jesus' self-revelation even as she reveals herself to him."[194] She is a believer who testified to the truth. From her testimony, many came to believe. Jesus remains with the Samaritans for two days and also testifies to the

---

[192] Schneiders interprets the leaving of the water jar as a symbol of faith similar to the disciples leaving their nets to follow Christ. See Schneiders, *You May Believe*, 40.

[193] The word "harvest" in 4:23, which occurs twice in the verse does not occur outside Jesus' speech in any Gospel.

[194] Sandra Schneiders, *The Revelatory Text: Interpreting the New Testament as Sacred Scripture* (Collegeville, Minn: Liturgical, 1999), 191.

truth: "And many more believed because of his word" (4:41). Once again, this narrative reechoes a consistent message. Fresh analogies further illustrate the main points that God is the origin of truth, truth is offered by witnesses (i.e., Jesus and the Samaritan woman), and those who believe become children of God and have access to eternal life. Water, spirit, and truth are all terms that represent revelation (truth). All provide eternal life for those who believe in truth (the Word). In the next story, life overcomes death through the Word of Jesus.

The Royal Official (4:46-54)

The story of the royal official follows the narrative of the Samaritan woman. And there are several similarities between these back-to-back pericopes: both lack any Jewish lineage, both hear and obey Jesus, and both are responsible for others who are now believers. Jesus now returns to Cana. Since his first visit, there has been a great growth in the number of believers; testimony has produced much fruit. At the wedding in chapter 2, the Jewish disciples believe. Just before the encounter with the royal official, the Samaritans become believers; finally, in the second Cana story, the royal official and his Gentile family (and his whole household) become believers.

Before arriving in Cana for the second time, Jesus departs from Samaria and enters Galilee. After the travel itinerary, the Gospel reports a claim made by Jesus that a prophet has no honor in his own country (4:44). Yet, the passage goes on to report that Jesus is welcomed into Galilee because the folks there have seen what Jesus did in Jerusalem. Is the reader to assume that Jesus is from Galilee?

There is no explicit reference that Jesus is from Galilee.[195] His origin has consistently been from above. If not, the coherence between these last two statements is not at all apparent. Another place that juxtaposes non-receivers and receivers in a similar manner is the prologue. Again, the prologue provides logistical background. There the "Word" comes among his own and the people did not receive him. Still, it is reported in the prologue that some received the "Word." In the Gospel, Jesus is also from the Father and he comes among his own. The reader knows that Jesus was rejected in Jerusalem at the Temple (2:13-22). He also had to move away from Judea into Samaria because of the Pharisees (4:1). Finally, it was reported that those in Jerusalem believed Jesus but could not be trusted. Jesus was also well received by the Samaritans and now the Galileans. So the prologue continues to support the Gospel record. The reader is reminded of the original divine plan that was explicated in the prologue, and to use it as a background for understanding the dynamic of the narrative of the royal official.

The author reminds the reader of the first sign at Cana where Jesus turned the water into wine, giving the reader permission to contrast the two narratives: both stories report a request, an apparent refusal, a counter by the conversation partner, and a granted request. The two stories are connected. In the first Cana story the intended audience learns what brought about the sign: "Do whatever he tells you." The royal official, like the servants who served the wa-

---

[195] The Gospel never states that Jesus is from Judea. See Brown, *John*, 187.

ter made wine, will do what Jesus asked. The Samaritan woman likewise does what Jesus tells her to do: "go," "call," and "come back" (4:16). The official predictably obeys: "The man believed the word that Jesus spoke to him and went his way" (4:50). It is the word of Jesus that brings life to the dying child. One recalls the analogy of "living water" which symbolizes the Word. Simply, the divine Word offers life. All three stories about believers are connected through obedience to Jesus' word. This is consistent with the message of the prologue which states that those who receive the "Word" are given power (1:12). The life-giving power of the Word is again emphasized when the official asked what time the boy began to get better. When he found out that the recovery matched the time when Jesus gave his Word, the family believed. Life is not just given to the son, but extended through the gift of the word to all the members of the family: "whoever believes in him will have eternal life" (3:15). Belief in the Word gives one the ability to share by testifying to others. Like the Samaritan woman, the royal official testifies to others about the truth so others will believe.

Now that we have seen how various texts reflect similar themes, we will look at the text in more detail. After hearing a report about Jesus, the official seeks help from Jesus to save his son. The testimony of the Galileans brings Jesus and the official together. The request, which is made by one man, is followed by a rebuke by Jesus to a multitude of people: "Unless you (plural) see signs and wonders you (plural) will not believe" (4:48). One recalls the meeting with Nicodemus. Jesus rebukes a group, not the individual: "You (plural) do not receive our testimony. If I have told you (plural) about earthly things and you (plural) do not believe, how can you (plural) believe if I tell you (plural) about heavenly things" (3:11-12). Eventually, Nicodemus will withdraw himself apart from the group and appear in public view when he buries Jesus' body. Whether or not the official is addressed as a part of this collective representation of sign seekers is still to be seen. One will see that he will emerge as one who puts his faith in Jesus' words before the sign is given. Who makes up this group? The text does not specify. What are important to the reader are the two groups that are represented in the prologue: receivers and non-receivers. The narrative ends with a last reminder of the first sign in Cana where the mother believed in the word of her son, leading to a miracle that brings others to believe, and the official likewise believes in the words of Jesus which leads others to believe.[196]

The reader perceives a natural break with the end of this pericope: Cana to Cana. Many of the stories between the Cana narratives discussed the progress of believers in the word of God: the Cana servants, disciples, Nicodemus, the Samaritan woman and the city

---

[196] Note how John's narratives are longer and fewer than the miracle stories found in the Synoptics. Also note that the locations of events are more detailed in John i.e. Cana or Capernaum; pool of Bethesda near the Sheep Gate; Solomon's Portico. Compare John with the Synoptics where the mention of locations is not as precise such as in Galilee or Peraea or Samaria, or given the vaguest of settings, such as 'a certain village' (Luke 10.38; 11.1), 'a certain place' (Luke 11.1), in 'the grain fields' (Mark 2.23; Matt 12.1; Luke 6.1), a synagogue (Luke 6.6; Matt 12.9) that could be anywhere in Galilee, several unnamed mountains or hills (Mark 3.13; 9.2; Matt 5.1; 8.1; 15.29; 17.1, 9; 28.16; Luke 6.12; 9.28, 37). See Bauckham, "Historiographical Characteristics," 23. Bauckham concludes that "By comparison it is unmistakable that John's Gospel has topographical precision as a consistent characteristic." Ibid.

inhabitance, and the Centurion. One has observed a number of characteristics that they all share. They know where Jesus is from, they progress from ignorance to belief so they are each a work in progress, they upgrade their title of Jesus as a sign of this progression, and their response is obedience to Jesus. Now the focus shifts to the non-believers: the Jews in the Sheep pool, the crowds at the breaking of the bread discourse, doubters at the festival of Booths, Pharisees questioning the man born blind. One also should note that the next series of pericopes are associated to Jewish festivals.[197] The Gospel writer introduces the first of many narratives with the announcement of a feast.

---

[197] The Passover (2:13; 6:4; 12:1; 13:1); the Feast of Booths (7:2); the Feast of Dedication (10:22). Apart from these annual feasts, there are weekly events like the Sabbath (5:9; 9:14; 19:31) and the Feast of the Jews (5:1). See Bernadeta Jojko, "Worshiping the Father in Spirit and Truth: An Exegetico-Theological Study" in *4:20-26 in the Light of Relationships Among the Father, the Son and the Holy Spirit* (Tesi Gregoriana 193; Roma: Gregorian & Biblical Press 2012), 253 n. 19.

Section II: Non-Believers

The Sign at Sheep Pool (5:1-47)

Jesus is back in Jerusalem for a feast, which remains unnamed. At this point in the narrative the reader continues to notice coherence between the texts. Going forward, the healing of the paralytic in this chapter will closely resembles the healing of the man born blind in chapter 9. Both stories involve pools of water, and take place during the Sabbath. Both involve men who suffer from long-term disabilities, give witness by naming their healer, and listen to and obey Jesus' instruction: one picks up his mat, the other washes at the pool of Siloam. Obedience stood out in the episode of the royal official and once again it is a game-changer here. Obedience is the necessary condition for receiving the Word, the proof of belief. This is not clarified in the prologue, but as the reader advances through the narrative it is becoming clearer that the Gospel provides the details of the main themes described in the opening verses. Also in this passage, Jesus once again "knows." He knew Nathanael, the marital history of the Samaritan woman, and now the long illness of this man. Water once again represents the divine word. Here, Jesus replaces the healing waters of the Sheep Pool with his word: "Pick up your mat and go home" (5:7). Jesus' healing words replace the need of moving waters. The Sabbath represents the seventh day of creation, a theme that was introduced in the prologue. It was on the seventh day that the water was made wine at Cana and his sign produced believers. The stories continue to show a consistent theme. Jesus is revealed through the testimony of others and as Christ himself through his words and deeds. Those who accept the truth/revelation become believers. However, this is the first story that exposes those who do not accept testimony or deeds. Their rejection is expressed by violence: "Therefore the Jews started persecuting Jesus (5:16); "the Jews were seeking all the more to kill him" (5:18). Once the sign has been given and the words of Jesus are shared, all those exposed have to make a decision to accept or reject. In this chapter, the reader sees both.

The story begins around a pool of water at the Sheep Gate. A paralytic tells Jesus that he seeks healing waters. Jesus replaces the water with his "Word": "stand," "take," and "walk." All impossible tasks for a paralytic, yet he gets up, takes his mat, and goes. The story recalls the living water that Jesus offers the Samaritan woman. Water is symbolic of truth and revelation. The man must have known it was the Sabbath, that walking in public with his mat was going to be challenged by the local Jews. Still, he follows his healer's directives. Besides, one has to wonder where all these critical Jews were over the last thirty-eight years who did not help the paralytic into the water to heal: "I have no one to put me into the pool when the water is stirred up" (5:7). The healed man does not know the identity of the man who cured him and confesses his ignorance to the Jews who confront him. Later, he will learn his name in a second encounter, and he will testify to others once he knows. Like Nicodemus and the Samaritan woman, belief is a progressive process.

In the second encounter, Jesus warns him not to sin or something greater will happen (5:14). There are not many situations that could be considered worse than paralysis, but sin in this Gospel always leads to death; later, Jesus will tell the Jews that they will die in their sins (8:21). Jesus has completely immersed himself in the man's life. He knows his past, ameliorates his present, and gives advice for the future: "See you have been made well. Do not sin anymore, so that nothing worse happens to you" (5:14). The man carrying the mat truthfully reports what had happened to him to the Jews. He was cured by a man who gave instructions which he carefully followed. The Jews are now exposed to the full truth. They know he was cured by Jesus. The Jews reject the sign. Jesus, who cured the man and warned him of sin, is now facing the threat of death himself: "For this reason the Jews were seeking all the more to kill him" (5:18). When confronted, Jesus responds by confirming his relationship with the Father, a bond which gives him the power to give life to anyone (5:21). Eternal life is available to all who believe. In the prologue, those who believe are given power. This now means that the children of God which the "Word" produces have access to eternal life according to the Gospel. The reader can see how the Gospel narrative slowly amplifies the meaning of terms in the prologue.

I argue that the paralytic became a believer by his obedience and goes on to confess Jesus to others. Schneiders disagrees and sees the paralyzed man as one who never fully recovers from the moral paralysis due to sin. She claims that Jesus' warning of future sin is a reflection on his past. Against Schneiders's assertion, the text does not specifically state that the paralysis was caused by sin. There is a reason to warn the paralytic of future sin because he was just exposed to a sign. He will have to choose because the "Word" came to him. Again, the prologue already suggests the decision that is required after the Word appears. Rejecting truth/revelation is a sin that was not possible before the paralyzed man's personal encounter with Jesus. In John, sin is consistently described as one who rejects the truth. Sin is described as such later in the man who was born blind. The Pharisees refuse to accept the truth, and they remain in sin because of their choice.

Schneiders also blames the paralyzed man's long term illness on a lack of will to be cured: "surely in thirty-eight years he could have figured out how to get into the pool!"[198] Again, the text does not offer any motive, reasons, or judgments on why the man was paralyzed for a "long time." Finally, she maintains that reporting Jesus to the authorities is a treasonous gesture exposing further his moral and spiritual collapse.[199] Again the narrative does not make this clear. It is similarly possible that the man was witnessing what had happened to him, just as the blind man will do a few chapters later. He is certainly not a crypto follower who refuses to acknowledge the sign: "The man went away and told the Jews that it was Jesus that made him well' (5:15). We have already seen characters in the Gospel who progress in their belief. The reader sees the cured paralytic following a similar pattern of obedience and witnessing. From this we can deduce that the author is referring to sin as one who rejects the revelation of Jesus, which could lead to future death: "something far greater."

---

[198] Scheinders, *Written That You May Believe*, 163

[199] Ibid. For another negative appraisal of the paralytic, see Craig Koester who states: "Since the Fourth Evangelist understands sin as unbelief and the actions that proceed from it, Jesus apparently was warning him not to persist in unbelief. His words had no visible effect on the man, who reported Jesus to the authorities." See his "Hearing, Seeing, and Believing in the Gospel of John" *Bib* 70 (1989): 338.

After learning the identity of the man who cured the paralytic, the Jews confront Jesus. Jesus' words to the Jews provide a rich resource for the reader. This is a gathering pool of information that will assist the reader with the interpretation of narratives to come. From Jesus' remarks, one finds that he is a judge: "The Father judges no one but has given all judgment to the Son" (5:22). When Jesus is tried by Pilate, Jesus asks questions; he is a King from above, and the narrative hints that he sits on the judgment seat (19:13). The purpose of a judge is to produce evidence to establish the truth. That is why Jesus is described as a judge, one who exposes the truth with evidence. Jesus provides evidence for the truth that he offers to others by citing His Father: "he has given him authority to execute judgment, because he is the Son of Man" (5:27). Jewish law requires forensic evidence. Truth is established when two witnesses agree. That is why Jesus always refers to the Father, the second witness. Thus, Jesus' words and deeds are indisputable evidence. Life is the evidence of his revelation: Do not be astonished at this…when all who are in their graves will hear his voice and will come out" (5:28-29). The reader will recall these words when Jesus calls Lazarus from the tomb. This is Jesus' mission, to expose others to the truth so they may believe and have eternal life; "Amen, amen I tell you, anyone who hears my word and believes him who sent me has eternal life, and does not come under judgment, but has passed from death to life" (5:24). At the hour during his glorification on the cross when he is lifted up, one will recall this passage when Jesus reports that he is a judge: "As I hear, I judge; and my judgment is just" (5:30).[200]

Finally, Jesus continues to connect the source of his word to the Father: "If I testify about myself, my testimony is not true."[201] John the Baptist testified to the truth about Christ. Yet Jesus distinguishes himself from the Baptist through the use of both words of truth and signs (deeds). John has no deeds. This is because there is a difference between "a lamp" and the "light" of the world who creates (deeds). Before Jesus is finished, he brings up Moses. Both Moses and John the Baptist are mentioned in the prologue. Here they are together in Jesus' discourse, assuring the reader that the prologue is still relevant. Moses will also provide the author with literary and thematic links that lead into the next narrative.

In this passage, we are introduced to non-believers who reject the truth. They deny Jesus' origin, that he comes from the Father. One also notes that the activity for non-believers is violence. These are the two characteristics that are consistently at play when the Gospel exposes those who reject revelation. Still, there are more features that characterize the non-believer.

---

[200] Jesus is true accuser and judge. Carroll and Green, *The Death of Jesus in Early Christianity* (Peabody, MA: Hendrickson, 1995), 82-109.

[201] "In witnessing to God. Jesus also bears witness about himself, and in testifying about himself, he bears witness to God." Andrew T. Lincoln, *The Gospel according to St. John* (BNTC 4; Peabody, M A: Hendrickson, 2005), 61.

The Bread of Life (6:1-71)

The purpose of chapter 6 is to reconfirm Jesus' origin from above. Why is this so important? Jesus' origin authenticates his revelation, providing eternal life for those who believe. In this chapter, Jesus reveals by both deed and testimony, respectively. First, he multiplies the loaves and the fish. Then, he instructs. If Jesus is from the Father, then his deeds and testimony are true. The fact that Jesus is from the Father is announced in the prologue and confirmed throughout the Gospel. To summarize chapter 6, the reader is reminded that the Father sent bread into the desert to sustain the Israelites with life. Now the Father sends the Son, as true bread, to offer the people of God eternal life. According to the prologue, Christ is the Word of God. Those who receive the word are given power. In this chapter, I will show how consuming bread, flesh, and blood are metaphorical for accepting the divine truth which gives life eternal. We have already seen water used as a metaphor for revelation in chapter four. There, Jesus offers living water: "The water that I will give will become in them a spring of water gushing up to eternal life" (4:14). Now He is food and drink. Those who eat and drink will never hunger or thirst again. In the prologue and chapter 6, truth and revelation, which come from God, appears in the world. By choosing to receive and consume the truth, one will become a child of God. In addition to making clear the origin of the "Word," the prologue distinguishes Moses from Jesus. This chapter will do the same in greater detail. Thus, the prologue again provides a background for another narrative.

The chapter begins with the multiplication of the loaves. The story is told in all four Gospels.[202] In John, Jesus goes up a mountain with the disciples with the crowd following. Another feast is mentioned: "Now, the Passover, the festival of the Jews, was near" (6:4).[203] The Passover recalls the liberation of the people of God from slavery in Egypt. The feast celebrates the life to the Israelites because the angel of death passes by them. In light of this past action, God is now about to free the people from death by sending the true bread that offers eternal life. One can think of this meal as an upgraded Passover. Later, Jesus will die during the preparation of the Passover, the act that will give eternal life where both living water and his blood are offered from the lanced side of Jesus: the two fluids that have symbolized eternal life. Jesus is also the Lamb of God according to John the Baptist. Some scholars read chapter 6 in the light of the Last Supper, where Jesus takes bread and wine and tells them to eat his body and drink his blood. However, John does not have a Passover meal in his Gospel. I suggest that this passage be read in the light of Jesus' death on the cross where his body, blood, and water, all the symbols that offer eternal life to those who believe, are present. For this reason, I read the entire chapter as an illustration of what happens when truth appears in the world symbolically in flesh

---

[202] Many scholars contrast John's multiplication of the loaves passage with the Synoptic tradition. There are similarities and differences. No consensus is made as to whether John copied the synoptic accounts, used an independent source, or a mixture from both to produce his multiplication narrative.

[203] Brown contends that "the mention of Passover, certainly fits the whole theological outlook of the chapter." See his *John*, 245.

and blood. Some will accept divine revelation, and some will reject it, as foreshadowed in the prologue.

The drama begins with a challenge from Jesus to his disciples: "Where are we to buy bread for these people to eat?" (6:5). Note the word "where." The sign begins with a question of origin: "where." Philip has a history of unfamiliarity with origins. One recalls that it was Philip who misinformed Nathanial that Jesus was from Nazareth (1:45). Later, when Jesus discusses the "way" to the Father in the Final Discourse, Philip asks Jesus to show them the Father (14:8). In chapter 6, Philip ignores where true food is found and turns Jesus' question into a mathematical problem: "Six months' wages would not buy enough bread for each of them to get a little" (6:7). However, he could have answered the question correctly because Jesus gave them the answer in chapter 4. He is the source of food. In chapter 4, when the disciples returned from purchasing food, they offer Jesus something to eat. He refused because he had food that they did not know about (4:32). Each of the disciples knew from this passage where they could get enough food: "My food is to do the will of him who sent me and to complete his work" (4:35). That is, of course, the work of revelation. According to the prologue his work is to reveal (see 1:18). In light of the prologue, food in chapter 6 symbolizes revelation because Jesus' work is to reveal. The word of God and food are really synonymous. The reader recalls the dialogue between Jesus and the disciples (4:31-38), so the sign that is about to unfold is read in the light of Jesus who is sent by the Father to complete his work. The purpose of the feeding of the multitude is to introduce the idea that Jesus is fulfilling his work by offering eternal life. He is the source of food that represents revelation/truth, the real source for eternal life. The reader also recalls that in John 4 living water symbolized revelation which offers eternal life. John 6 now parallels chapter 4. This time, food, not water, represents revelation. The feeding of the multitude signifies a new version of the Passover whereby the people are no longer bound by death because they will be given food (revelation) for eternal life. The Father sends the Son as the living bread (revelation) come down from heaven. Jesus' work will go beyond Moses who offered bread that did not sustain life permanently.

Later, when Jesus tells his disciples that he is the good shepherd, the intended reader will recall Jesus telling the disciples to have the people recline on a "great deal of grass." Abundant grass for sheep parallels abundant bread and fish for the people. Jesus' sheep never die because they possess eternal life. They follow him (accept truth) because they hear his voice (revelation): "My sheep hear my voice, I know them, and they follow me. I give them eternal life, and they will never perish" (10:27-28). Another allusion to eternal life.

It is important to note that Jesus is the one who distributes the food to those who are reclined, not the disciples: "Then Jesus took the loaves, and when he had given thanks, he distributed them to those who were seated" (6:11). Food comes from the Father who sent the Son. There is so much food that twelve baskets are filled. The crowd recognizes Jesus as a prophet. Recall that the Samaritan woman also called Jesus a prophet only to upgrade Jesus' title to Messiah. The blind man in chapter 9 will likewise tell his neighbors that Jesus is a prophet. Later in the narrative, the blind man will raise his claim and worship Jesus. Calling Jesus a prophet is a sign of progression. Perhaps this is an indication that the crowd is on a progressive path to accept Jesus' testimony as the former blind man in chapter 9 and the Samaritan woman. They call him a prophet but then they seek to take him by force to make him king (6:15). Once the sign of the multiplication of the loaves and fish is complete, everyone must make a decision because everyone had contact with revelation (symbolized by the food). One must accept or reject this revelation. One has to wonder if the crowd will accept Jesus' transformative revelation as the townsfolk from the Samaritan town.

Why would anyone reject revelation that offers eternal life? The root of the problem is location. Those who do not acknowledge Jesus' origin reject revelation. Note that this next section underscores Jesus' location. Where is Jesus from? Soon after the multiplication of the loaves and fish, the Jews try to locate Jesus. They first go where they had eaten the bread, and he is not there. The cat and mouse chase ends when they locate Jesus with the disciples on the other side of the lake. They ask him how he got there because he did not get into the boat with the disciples. The irony that is about to unfold reinforces the importance of accepting Jesus' origin with the Father. First, the Jews do not know where he comes from when they find him with the disciples: "Rabbi, when did you come here?" (6:25). Then they claim to be experts with regard to where He comes from: "How can he now say, 'I have come down from heaven" (6:42). One recalls in 3:8 where Jesus tells Nicodemus "The wind blows where it chooses, and you hear the sound of it, but you do not know where it comes from or where it goes. Revelation is a gift and cannot be obtained by human control. Note how the crowd downgrades Jesus' status. He is no longer a prophet or a king. He is addressed as

"Rabbi." This is a sign that they are not progressing as Nathaniel, the Samaritan woman, and the blind man in John 9.

This scene introduces the obstacle that prevents people from accepting Jesus: the refusal to accept his origin. They are looking for Jesus not for revelation that can give them eternal life, but for food that will only sustain them for a short time: "Amen, amen I tell you, you are looking for me, not because you saw signs, but because you ate your fill of the loaves" (6:26). They are not seeking his location for revelation but for perishable food. They ask what they need to do, and Jesus tells them they must believe in the one who God sent (6:29). This requires that they acknowledge that Jesus is from the Father: location. The irony is bold and striking. They want to see works, not to hear words. So Jesus tells them that the work (sign) is food sent by God (which is metaphorical for Jesus who is sent to sustain them in life). Jesus points out that it was not Moses but the Father who sent bread from heaven, now Jesus is the new source of life for them who is sent. Just as water was symbolic for revelation in John 4, bread is now symbolic for revelation. Both offer eternal life if it is received. Ironically, the Jews began to "grumble" (γογγύζω, 6:41) the same word that is used in the LXX (Nu14:29) when the people complained to God about the lack of food in the desert. Ironically, the crowd complains while they are offered food that can give them eternal life. They object to Jesus' requirement to believe because he claims to come from above, not that he is "bread": "Is not this Jesus, the son of Joseph, whose father and mother we know: How can he now say, 'I have come down from heaven?'" (6:42).

This is the start of their regression. Instead of progressing, the Jews are starting to regress into doubt due to the fact that they do not know where He is from.[204] As they are exposed to the truth/revelation they are forced either to accept or to reject it. Jesus tells them that he is the bread that comes down from heaven. The reason the Father sent the Son into the world is to provide eternal life: "This is indeed the will of my Father, that all who see the Son and believe in him may have eternal life; and I will raise them up on the last day" (6:40). Since the Jews had already received a sign (the multiplication of the loaves and fish), what they really wanted was proof of Jesus' origin from the Father. Jesus provided them with both a sign and his word that his origin is the Father. That is the proof they need. He tells them that true bread comes from heaven and gives life to the world. They know from the multiplication of the loaves that Jesus is a source of food. He is the source that sustains life because he is from God just as manna was sent by God to sustain the Israelites in the desert: "For the bread of God is that which comes down from heaven and gives life to the world" (6:33). Nonetheless, they continue to claim that they know his father and mother and, therefore, they know where he is from. There seem to be striking parallels between the Jews in John 6 and the Samaritan woman in chapter 4, such as the discussion of eternal life and the consumption of sustenance (bread/water).

---

[204] "Again and again in different ways the Fourth Gospel asks: Who is he (Jesus) and where did he come from? John provides the key in the prologue with the comment, "No one has ever seen God; the only Son, who is in the bosom of the Father, he has made him known (1:18)." Mary Ellen Dolan. "Irony in The Gospel of John Part II: Specific Uses of Irony in the Fourth Gospel," *Journal of Theta Alpha Kappa* 11 (1987): 5-6.

The parallel between the crowd ("Sir give us this bread," 6:34) and the Samaritan woman ("Sir give me this water," 4:15) seems indisputable. One of these parallels has to do with origin. The Samaritan woman knows Jesus as someone from God: "Come and see a man who told me everything I have ever done. He cannot be the Messiah, can he? (4:29). The people of the Samaritan village believe the woman and then Jesus himself after they encounter him: "And many more believed because of his word" (4:41). On the other hand, the crowd in John 6 begins to reject him because they fail to know his origin. Jesus again insists that they need to know he is from the Father so they will believe and have eternal life: "He has seen the Father. Very truly, I tell you, whoever believes has eternal life" (6:47). He alludes to the analogy of the manna in the desert once again. Now, Jesus is the bread that comes down from heaven. Yet, without certitude of Jesus' origin, the analogy seems too far-fetched to believe: "How can this man give us his flesh to eat?" (6:51).

Unlike the Jews, the disciples advance because they are aware of Jesus' origin. They are first terrified when they see Jesus walking on the water: "they saw Jesus walking on the sea and coming near the boat, and they were terrified" (6:19). It is the typical reaction to a theophany. They receive Jesus in the boat when he is revealed: "I am; do not be afraid" (6:20). Jesus uses the "I am" statement to reassure them that He is from God.

Throughout 35-50, belief is the proper response to bread (35, 37, 44, 45). One would expect the emphasis to be on eating.[205] Yet, because bread symbolizes revelation, to believe is the proper task at hand. "Hearing," "accepting," and "believing" are activities that lead one to eternal life: "whoever comes to me, whoever believes in me" (35), "all who believe in him may have eternal life" (40), "they shall be taught by God (45)," "everyone who has heard and learned, from the Father comes to me" (45) "…whoever believes has eternal life" (48). One responds to the bread of life with the same verbs that are used to describe the reception of revelation. Therefore, bread appears to be symbolic for the word of God.[206]

The analogy of the bread of life shifts from believing to eating in 6:51-58. One must now accept Jesus' revelation unequivocally with the symbolic action of chewing flesh and drinking blood. The flesh and blood discourse continues to represent what the bread of life symbolized: The word sent down from heaven.

Many scholars read the flesh and blood discourse in 6:51-58 with a Eucharistic optic.[207] They argue that the intended reader would

---

[205] There is only one time that the people eat during the bread of life discourse (35-50): "This is the bread that comes down from heaven, so that one may eat of it and not die" (6:50). The verb "eat" comes at the end of one section and serves to introduce the next section where the term appears numerous times in 51-58

[206] See Brown, *John*, 272-75.

[207] Here are the various positions on the sacramental question regarding John's Gospel: sacramental approach, A. Schweitzer, O. Cullmann, L. Bouyer, and A. Corell; moderate approach, J. H. Bernard, C. H. Dodd, C. K. Barrett, and R. E. Brown; non-sacramental approach, G. Bornkamm, E.

have understood the text from the familiarity of communal Eucharistic celebrations which were common among Christian gatherings and from literary sources that express Eucharistic features from the Synoptic Gospels, Paul, and the Church Fathers. They conclude that the meaning of the Johannine text on eating and drinking the body and blood of Christ reflects an instruction that will generate eternal life. This would be a requirement, in addition to accepting revelation as a means for acquiring life everlasting.[208] According to Brown, verse 51-58 offers a new path to eternal life over the acceptance of revelation: "There are two impressive indications that the Eucharist is in mind. The first indication is the stress on eating (feeding on) Jesus' flesh and drinking his blood. This cannot possibly be a metaphor for accepting his revelation."[209] He notes that there is an obvious shift from "believing" in 35-50 to "eating" in 51-58.[210] One can recognize Eucharistic themes from sources outside of the Gospel. Charles A. Gieschen notes:

Käsemann, E. Lohse; anti-sacramental approach, R. Bultmann, E. F. Scott, G. H. C. Macgregor, W. F. Howard, P. Gardner, J. D. G. Dunn.

Edwyn Clement Hoskyns, *The Fourth Gospel* (2nd ed.; London: Faber and Faber, 1947), 533. Moloney, however, admits that "There is no overtly sacramental teaching in the Johannine story." See his *Love in the Gospel of John: An Exegetical, Theological, and Literary Study* (Grand Rapids, MI: Baker Academic, 2013), 44.

[208] See Brown, *John,* 284-85.

[209] Ibid.

[210] Many maintain that 51-58 is a later addition, which explains the change in focus. There are various interpretive approaches. The entire discourse of 6:35-58 can refer to revelation, the Eucharist, or half-and-half: (revelation in 35-50 then Eucharist in 51-58). For a more extensive discussion, see Brown, *John,* 272-275.

What is present in John, therefore, are not texts that record the institution of Baptism or the Lord's Supper, but the words and works of Jesus that are to be understood in fuller ways after his resurrection when the church is gathered in worship, where Baptism and the Lord's Supper are central to how Jesus continues to abide in us and we in him, bringing us the life given in his death.[211]

Raymond Brown maintains that a Eucharistic interpretation is not consistent with the narrative prior to 51-58:

It seems impossible that the words of 51-58 which refer exclusively to the Eucharist could have been understood by the crowd or even by the disciples. They are really out of place anywhere during the ministry except at the Last Supper. Even such a usually conservative critic as Lagrange has recognized this, and he has been followed by many scholars who otherwise show no facile tendency to dismantle the Johannine discourses. We suggest that 35-50 and 51-58 are two different forms of the Discourse on the Bread of Life, both Johannine in the sense that they are made up of sayings passed down in the Johannine preaching tradition.[212]

Brown admits that a Eucharistic interpretation of the passage cannot be gleaned from the Gospel of John alone. Such an interpretation has to be based on outside sources. According to Charles A. Gieschen, "John's intended readers of his Gospel to see a relationship between this discourse and their participation in the Lord's Supper is made even more apparent by observing that he does not teach about the Lord's Supper through an institution account in his

---

[211] Charles A. Gieschen, "Baptism and the Lord's Supper in the Gospel of John," *CTQ* 78 (2014): 45.

[212] Brown, *John*, 287.

passion narrative."²¹³ James W. Voelz claims that the bread of life discourse was "written for the *cognoscendi*, for those who already know the faith, not for outsiders, for those with no knowledge or who need to be convinced to believe."²¹⁴ Still, as Craig R. Koester points out, "we simply do not know if the Lord's Supper was familiar to Johannine Christians or, if it was, how it was perceived.²¹⁵ There is no explicit sacramental reference in the prologue, nor is there a Last Supper discourse where Jesus explicitly offers bread as his body and the cup as his blood in John's Gospel. Without a Last Supper, the reader would have to obtain Eucharistic familiarity based on previous knowledge from outside the Gospel text. Why would the final redactor/author place a text with a meaning that cannot be understood in its present context? Are not scholars forcing an interpretation without adequate support from the Gospel narrative, forcing them to look beyond the Gospel narrative? There is always a risk for using outside sources to verify an interpretation of a text. One can only speculate if the author/redactor intended a Eucharistic interpretation. Robert Kysar has correctly observed that "it is a misfortunate error of the sacramental interpreters that they assume the widespread popularity of the sacraments in the early church. Only such a popularity could possibly justify the claim that almost any use of

---

[213] Gieschen, "Baptism and the Lord's Supper," 38.

[214] See his "The Discourse on the Bread of Life in John 6: Is It Eucharistic?," *Concordia Journal* 15 (1989): 33.

[215] "John Six and The Lord's Supper," *Lutheran Quarterly* 4 (1990): 433.

one of the standard terms associated with the celebration of the sacraments indicates sacramental meaning."[216] The reader would not get a Eucharistic perspective directly from reading the Gospel of John if Eucharistic texts or Eucharistic gatherings never existed.[217] My point here is to show one example of how scholars interrupt the theological flow of the overall purpose of the Gospel. They isolate units and use background from outside sources for interpretation. The text can have numerous interpretations when they are seen in context to diverse backgrounds. If one wants to understand the intention of the author it is best to read the text in light of the context of the Gospel itself, using outside sources only to verify and confirm what the reader already has learned from the author. I will contend that the 6:51-58 discourse is metaphorical in nature, expressing the need to accept the divine revelation of God represented in the person of Jesus.

To support this argument, I simply point out the numerous terms and symbols that are used to represent divine revelation. Before the flesh and blood analogy, the Gospel uses living water and light to symbolize revelation/truth. The reader is informed, prior to chapter 6, that the welcomed reception of revelation (i.e., living water, light) generates eternal life. One has to accept revelation to receive eternal life, just as one drinks living water to live or uses light to perform the works of God. Analogies, metaphors, and symbols (in the Gospel text) exhibit a theological pattern with a consistent

---

[216] See his *The Fourth Evangelist and His Gospel: The Examination of Contemporary Scholarship* (Minneapolis: Augsburg Publishing House, 1975), 256.

[217] Brown, *John*, 287.

message; there is a consistency by which the reader perceives coherence in the narrative flow and so can interpret individual stories in light of the context of the Gospel without resorting to outside sources. That is why I, as a reader, can understand that eating the body and drinking the blood of Christ is analogous to accepting and receiving revelation which can bring one eternal life because I have seen this before with other metaphors (light and living water). This interpretation is consistent with the theological argument of the Gospel, and also coheres with the mission of the prologue, where acceptance of the Word generates power to be a child of God (1:12). At the same time, I do not run the risk of importing information from outside sources that can alter or add to the meaning that was originally intended. The author, I argue, communicates his intention by way of coherence.

Certainly, in the second century, Christians would have been familiar with the Eucharistic formula from the institution of the Eucharist in the Last Supper discourse of the Synoptics. One could argue that there was a conventional knowledge of the Eucharist at the time the intended audience had access to the final canonical form. One would have read the eating of Christ's body and blood and drawn conclusions from what they know outside of the text. However, a Eucharistic reading does not cohere well with the rest of the Gospel. Without a Eucharistic theme in the prologue or any explicit reference to the Eucharist during the final discourse at the Last Supper, the intention of the author cannot be adequately demonstrated in terms of a sacramental theology. However, the theme of revelation does resonate throughout the prologue and Gospel. It is more likely in light of the overall argument to read the eating of Jesus' body and blood as a metaphor for revelation. Eating and drinking is symbolic for receiving revelation which gives eternal life. The reader has seen this in chapters 4 and 6. Access to living water is also associated to revelation in chapter 7. Even after the body and blood discourse, Jesus returns to the theme of his word that gives eternal life: "The words that I have spoken to you are spirit and life" (6:63). Peter tells Jesus that he has "the words of eternal life. We come to believe and know that you are the Holy One of God" (6:69). The unit as a whole, therefore, reflects the prologue. The word came: some rejected it, while others received and believed. In chapter 6 Jesus' origin is manifested. A sign was performed. Those exposed had to choose based on Jesus' origin. Some rejected and others accepted and believed.

The reader notes that there are numerous repetitions between 6:35-50 and 6:51-58:[218]

- "I myself am the living bread" (35), "I myself am the living bread" (51).
- "I have come down from heaven" (38): "…that comes down from heaven" (51).
- "…should have eternal life and I shall raise him up on the last day" (40); "…has eternal life. And I shall raise him up on the last day" (54).

---

[218] The passage could be read as a non-Johannine sacramental theme that was later added by an ecclesiastical redactor as proposed by Bultmann. See Brown's summary in *John*, 286. However, with so many repetitions, it is apparent that the author/redactor ties the two sections together with the emphasis on origin and eternal life.

- "Let me firmly assure you" (46, 52).
- "Only the one who is from God has seen the Father" (46); "just as the father who has life sent me and I have life because of the Father" (57).
- "Your ancestors ate manna in the desert" (49); "Unlike those ancestors who ate and yet died" (58).[219]

In order to believe in Jesus' word, one must know that he is from the Father. That is proof that his word is true. If one does not acknowledge his origin, then belief, the prerequisite to eternal life, is no longer an option. The whole dialogue that takes place in this scene is an argument about Jesus' origin, because without it no one can inherit eternal life through belief. This is the heart of the argument: if the Father can send bread in the desert to sustain the Israelites, He can likewise send "bread" that will sustain life eternally. The stakes are now much higher since the desert: "Not like that which your ancestors ate, and they died" (6:58). If the Israelites wanted to live, they had to eat. So too, if the children of God want to live eternally, they have to eat what bread God sends them, metaphorically speaking. That is, one has to receive the divine Word through belief, as stated in the prologue. Jesus represents the food that was sent by God.

---

[219] Repetition between 6:35-50 and 6:51-58 suggests to scholars that the two passages have separate origins. See Brown, *John*, 287-91 who offers a detailed report. He maintains that 51-58 has a much "clearer Eucharistic reference than the rest of the chapter" despite the fact that there is no institution of the Eucharist in the Last Supper narrative.

According to the divine project reflected in the prologue, God sent the Word into the world so that he might produce Children of God. The Nicodemus dialogue informed the reader that children are born from above. Then in the next scene the bridegroom meets a woman who produces believers from her testimony. In this chapter, Jesus is sent to provide eternal life. Jesus' flesh is true food and his blood is true drink that can provide eternal life. He was sent by the Father to sustain the children with eternal life, just as the Father sent food in the desert to sustain the children in the wilderness. The new Passover reaches beyond the old. It is no longer a commemoration to celebrate the past freedom from slavery; it is a new freedom from death: "Just as the living Father sent me, and I live because of the Father, so whoever eats me will live because of me." (6:57). Jesus is from the Father. After the crowd rejects Jesus' teaching because it is too hard to accept, He turns to the disciples offering them an easy way to accept his teaching: "What if you were to see the Son of Man ascending to where he was before? (6:62). Again, this passage reminds the disciples of Jesus' origin, providing authenticity to Jesus' words. Belief is only possible when one knows that Jesus is from God. Revelation has its origin in God. Jesus who comes from the bosom of the Father possesses and can share the knowledge of God: "The words I have spoken to you are spirit and life" (6:53). Yet not all believe. First it was the crowd that left Jesus. Since the Jews had already received a sign (the multiplication of the loaves and fish), what they really wanted was proof of Jesus' origin from the Father. Now, the disciples also leave him. The last group to remain is the twelve. Peter's confession of belief ("You have the words of eternal life, 6:68) was intended to be a representation of the entire group's belief in Jesus, but even the small band is fractured: "One of you is a devil" (6:70).[220] Judas is possessed. The role of the devil in the Gospel of John is to contrast Jesus, who represents the truth, to a spirit who represents lies.

It is on this sober note that a new feast is introduced—the festival of booths—and a new line of argumentation to clarify the origin of Jesus. The Gospel is careful to mention the places where Jesus taught as either the synagogue at Capernaum (6:59) or the Temple at Jerusalem (7:14, 28; 8:20; 10:23). The next feast represents the central section of the Gospel where Jesus brings revelation to the center of the Jewish people: the Temple.

Festival of Booths (7:1–8:59)

The Feast of Tabernacle was originally a pagan feast celebrating the ingathering of grapes, olives, first fruits of the winter barley crop, and the end of the wheat harvest. Tents or temporary dwellings were erected in which farmers could live while they were harvesting the crop. Such close proximity to the fields allowed the harvesters to collect the grapes off the vines before the winter rains. With the abundance of food came celebration. The Israelites probably adopted the feast from the Canaanites when they became sedentary dwellers in Palestine. The feast evolved from an agricultural harvest thanksgiving, celebrated by locals, to a full scale national cultic holiday. In fact,

---

[220] He also points out that the phrase "The flesh is of no avail" (6:63) cannot be understood as pro-gnostic because of the prologue: "The word became flesh" (1:14). Viviano, "Prologue." 184.

Zechariah 14 predicts the feast will be celebrated globally, which indicates that the feast has room to expand and evolve even further. At first, the timing of the feast depended on the harvest. Later the celebration was fixed on the fifteenth day of the seventh month (Lev 23:39), becoming a permanent feast in the Israelite calendar. Leviticus seems to have added an extra eighth day. The feast also evolved in meaning. The earlier calendar in Exodus 13:16 and 34:22 refers to this agricultural feast as the "ingathering," which was intended as a joyous agricultural feast to celebrate the fall harvest. One can find the description of the Feast of Tabernacle or Booths in Deut 16:13, 16; Lev 23:34. Here, the meaning shifts from an agricultural feast to a remembrance of God's protection in the desert after the escape from Egypt. The feast day according to Leviticus was to remind the people that God protected them during and after their escape from Egypt: "You shall dwell in booths… that you… may know that I made your people of Israel dwell in booths. I brought them out of the land of Egypt: I am the Lord your God" (Lev 23:42-43). Hosea called this the honeymoon between God and his wife Israel, "…On that day, says the LORD, you will call me, 'My husband…'" (Hos 2:12-23). As one can see from these details, the celebration of the feast was evolving as the need and situation changed.

When the feast is celebrated in Jerusalem, each day the priest goes to the pool of Siloam, gathers water in a golden container, and processes to the Temple area. Arriving at the south gate at the Temple recalls for the people the passage in Ezek 47:1-5 where it states that the waters from the temple will bring life throughout the world.

In addition to the water ritual there was a small ceremony. Four menorahs were set up in the center of the court of the women. Levites sang Psalms 120-134 while men danced under the lights.

It is during this feast that Jesus declares that he is the light of the world and the source of living water. One recalls in the prologue how the Word became flesh and "pitched his tent" in order to become visible "in his glory" (1:14). I argue that the prologue anticipates the festival of booths in chapters seven and eight. Note that in the prologue, the glory of the Word made flesh is never separate from the glory of the Father: "the glory as of a Father's only Son, full of grace and truth" (1:14). According to the prologue, the purpose of God's presence with his people is to give the gift of truth/revelation. Jesus comes to the feast as one who was sent by God to offer the divine gift of truth, revelation, which will give others eternal life. In the festival of booths, the Jews praise God for his gift of water and light, the sources that bring about a rich harvest. The feast will now evolve with the presence of God's Word. Jesus, who is the Word, offers eternal life with divine revelation. Water and light symbolize revelation/truth, which provides eternal life: "Let anyone who is thirsty come to me and let the one who believes in me drink" (7:37-38), and "I am the light of the world," (8:12). The chapter narrates the dialogue of Jesus with the Jewish people at three stages of the feast: just prior to the start of the feast, the middle of the feast, and on the last day of the feast. I will treat each of these three phases of the feast.

Before the Feast (7:1-9)

Jerusalem and Judea have become hostile to Jesus. He tells the brothers, his disciples, to go to Jerusalem and attend the feast without him, informing them that his testimony exposes darkness and sin: "it (the world) hates me because I testify against it that its works are evil" (7:7). The brothers, like the crowd in the previous chapter, do not believe in Jesus. They attempt to lead him to Judea so that they may see his mighty works and display Him to the world. However, Jesus is not performing acts for his own glory, but his actions are done to reveal the truth of the Father. In both Matthew and Luke, Jesus is tempted by the devil to provide bread (Matt 4:3; Luke 4:3), perform marvelous feats of greatness (Matt 4:6; Luke 4:9-10), and become a king (Matt 4:8-9; Luke 4:5-6). In John's Gospel, all three temptations are made by the people: the crowd wants to make him King in 6:15; they look for Jesus because they ate their fill of the loaves in 6:26, and the brothers want Jesus to "show himself to the world" with his works in 7:3-4. Unlike in Matthew and Luke, where the devil is the tempter, the people do the tempting, and Jesus is accused of being the demon: "you have a demon" (7:20). A demon in John's Gospel is one who seeks to prevent revelation. Jesus, of course, is the opposite of this. Jesus is the provider of revelation. It is ironic that the people confuse Jesus, the very one who offers the truth, as one who tries to prevent the truth. In the Synoptics, Jesus casts out demons, but not in John. Non-believers prevent revelation by their violent resistance to those who offer the truth.

When Jesus arrives in Jerusalem in secret, the Jews are looking for him. They ask, "Where is he?" (7:11). At first, Jesus tells the brothers that he is not going to Jerusalem, then he goes in secret. Once again, Jesus is like the wind. No one can know where he comes or where he goes (3:8). The issue again has to do with Jesus' origins. Jesus' testimony is only valid if his source is God. His place at God's bosom, according to the prologue, authenticates His testimony. Jesus' presence in Jerusalem causes a split between those who believe he is a good man, and those who think he is spurious (7:12-13). Yet, neither of the two groups is remotely close to conceding to his divine mission. No one in the group seems to know where he is from, and everyone has fear ("No one would speak openly about him for fear of the Jews," 7:13). Fear and not knowing "where" are appearing more often as the two obstacles preventing belief. They will be treated with more consistency as the narrative leads up to the resurrection.

The author of John uses the term "world" as a location of for those without revelation. There are two ways one can be deprived of the Truth. One way is by rejecting the truth after it is offered. The second is that the truth has not been given. Without revelation, there is no access to eternal life so the world represents a place where there is certain death. Once Jesus makes revelation to everyone, there will only be one why to stay in the world, and that is by rejection. So, Jesus states, "The world cannot hate you, but it hates me because I testify against it that its works are evil" (7:7). The evil of non-believers' violence against Jesus: "the Jews were looking for an opportunity to kill him" (7:1).

Middle of the Feast (7:14-36)

Jesus' origin continues to be a problem for the Jews in the middle of the feast when Jesus begins to teach at the Temple. Predictably, the source of Jesus' teaching is questioned: "How does this man have such learning, when he has never been taught" (7:15). One can rephrase the question as where did he get his knowledge?" Jesus once again discusses his teaching in terms of origin: "My teaching is not mine, but his who sent me" (7:16). Recall in the prologue how the Word pitches its tent to reveal his glory: "And we have seen his glory, the glory as of a Father's only son, full of grace and truth" (1:14). The prologue continues to guide the direction of the Gospel narrative. Here at the feast of the booths, Jesus discusses God's glory: "Those who speak on their own seek their own glory; but the one who seeks the glory of him who sent him is true" (7:18).[221] When Jesus testifies, he always claims that the origin of his words is the Father. Testimony cannot be verified if it only has one source. Jesus teams with the Father for this reason. He then exposes the inconsistency of his opponents' argument by pointing out that a murderous plot is a violation against the very Law that they claim had come from God through Moses (7:19). Once again, this recalls for the reader the contrast between Moses and the Word in the prologue: "The law indeed was given through Moses; grace and truth came through Jesus Christ" (1:17). Jesus continues to beat them and their erroneous logic with

---

[221] Glory is divine manifestation to humans (see Num 16:19, 42; Ps 102:16; Ezek 10:14). This is what Christ does in the Prologue: he is to reveal the divine (1:18).

yet another discrepancy. If circumcision is permitted on the Sabbath, why would healing on the Sabbath be considered a violation against God? (7:23).

The issue of location presents itself again: "Yet we know where this man is from; but when the Messiah comes, no one will know where he is from" (7:27). The irony is striking. They just demonstrated that they do not know where he is from, thus proving, from their own preconceptions, that Jesus is the Messiah. He tells them that He is returning to the one who sent him (7:33), once again indicating his origin: "Where I am, you cannot come" (7:34). The issue of "where" Jesus is from persists until the end of this section. The Jews continue to inquire "where": "Where does this man intend to go that we will not find him" (7:35).

There are no exorcisms in John's Gospel, but there are references to demons. The crowd accuses Jesus of having a demon (7:20) because they deny their evil intention to seek His death. This theme carries over to 7:25 when the people of Jerusalem were enquiring if Jesus is not the man "whom they are trying to kill?" This statement confirms the denial of the crowd who call Jesus a demon. The demon is one who offers lies ("But I know him; if I would say that I do not know him, I would be a liar like you" [8:55]) so it is ironic that they call the one who offers truth a devil. There seems to be a spilt of opinion as to whether some believe that Jesus is the Messiah and some who do not.

Once again there is another division. This is going to be a consistent theme when the Gospel treats unbelievers. This group often appears to be divided in opinion. The reader has already seen divisions of opinion over Jesus, and the text will continue to underscore this point, especially in the upcoming story of the man born blind.

The section ends with the crowd muttering (7:32), and the Jews babbling about where they think Jesus is going. It all sums up the irony that the Jews are confident that they know Jesus is not from God but have no idea where he is going: Where does this man intend to go that we will not find him?" (7:35).

The Last Day of the Feast (part 1): Living Water (7:37ff)

The previous section (7:25-36) shares a number of thematic links with the last day of the feast (37-52): both narratives occur during the feast of booths, report on a crowd that passes judgment on Jesus (25, 40), raise the issue of the Messiah (26-27, 41-42), show the failure of an attempted arrest (30, 44), and describe people who are impressed with Jesus' words (31, 46).[222] Jesus' origin continues to be an obstacle for recipients of God's revelation, this time for those who want Jesus arrested. Jesus' announcement that he is the source of living water sets off the dispute. He tells the crowd that if anyone is thirsty, they should come to him and drink. Ironically, the people pray on the final day of the feast that God will send water to hydrate their fields for a successful and abundant harvest. They did not expect their prayer to be answered in quite this fashion.[223] The announcement comes with mixed opinions. Some call Jesus a prophet, some the Messiah, while others want to arrest him for making false

---

[222] These parallels are found in Brown, *John*, 331.
[223] Brown, *John*, 327.

claims about his origin: "Surely the Messiah does not come from Galilee" (7:41). Once again there is a division among those receiving revelation from Jesus. The opponents to Jesus argue that a Messiah must come from Bethlehem, and Jesus is from Galilee, not Bethlehem: "Has not the scripture said that the Messiah is descended from David and comes from Bethlehem?" (7:42).

The Pharisees and chief priests send for the temple police, but they are unable to fulfill the task: "Why did you not arrest him" (7:45). Despite the fact that no one has ever spoken as Jesus (7:26), the authorities discredit the crowd as being deceived and Nicodemus for suggesting a fair trial. The Pharisees and Jewish authority continue to claim that Jesus is from Galilee (7:45). Just previously in 7:35, the Jews state: "Where does this man intend to go that we will not find him?" They refuse to acknowledge that Jesus is from the God. Thus, Jesus' proclamation on "living water" (37-38) is framed around the issue of his origin. I want to examine the meaning of this proclamation because it comes at the highpoint of the feast. I will show that this statement signifies that Christ offers revelation to the one who believes. Because of Christ, the believer also has access to the wellspring of truth, and like Christ can offer truth to others.[224] I will argue that the author is using irony to make his case, that is, both Jesus and the believer are sources of revelation.

To do this I will examine the citation from Scripture: "Out of the believer's belly shall flow rivers of living water" (7:38). Then I will offer a solution to the identification of the "belly" (κοιλία, 7:38).[225]

---

[224] "Jesus is the giver of the life-giving water and drinking is a symbolic description of believing (6.35). Painter, "Fourth Gospel," 45.

[225] The NRSV translates this term as "heart."

The divine invitation to drink is reserved for believers: "and let the one who believes in me drink" (7:38). The reader recalls the words Jesus spoke to the Samaritan woman: "Those who drink of the water that I will give them will never be thirsty. The water that I will give will become in them a spring of water gushing up to eternal life" (4:14). Jesus' gift of living water is so abundant that the believer possesses an overflowing spring. Again, a similar abundance was offered in the multiplication of the loaves and fish in chapter 6. Christ has access to both food and water because he comes from God. God sends living bread (divine truth). Now, God offers living water.

The passage from Scripture that Jesus cites has been greatly debated: "Out of the belly of the believer shall flow rivers of living water" (7:38). The term "belly" could be either a synonym for "heart" or for the "womb. The word is employed one other time in 3:4: "Can a man enter a second time into his mother's womb (κοιλία) and be born?" How does the term used by Nicodemus help one understand how the same term is used in the citation from Scripture? It appears that the Pharisee is actually stating something profound for those who are familiar with Johannine imagery. The seed that will generate new birth is revelation. Out of the womb will be water/revelation. "Given the prominence of rebirth imagery in John starting with the prologue; and given the 'living water' theme in Jesus' meeting with the Samaritan woman, we may read κοιλία (womb) the same way here, referring to rebirth as a 'child of God' for those who believe in Jesus."[226]

---

[226] J. Gerald Janzen, "How Can a Man Be Born When He Is Old?: Jacob/Israel in Genesis and the Gospel Of John," *Encounter* 65 (2004): 339-40.

The Scripture verse is highly debated due to its complexity and the fact that the citation does not match anything from the Septuagint. It appears that John paraphrased an earlier text. This was not an uncommon practice in the first century. Maarten Menken in his work *Old Testament Quotations in the Fourth Gospel* maintains that John is not governed by any set rules of citation, which reflects a common Jewish practice.[227] Editing Scripture was a legitimate method of interpretation based on *pesher* exegesis. John also may be citing Palestinian Targums.

Due to the fact that the verse is problematic among scholars, it may be helpful to summarize the citation practices in this Gospel.[228] There are between seventeen and nineteen Scripture quotes that are cited.[229] John's citations are generally concise, (9 words on average). He regularly quotes from the LXX, three of which are verbatim (10:34; 12:38; 19:24). For all other Scripture quotations, it is not always easy to identify the source.[230] Sometimes he substitutes a word from the Hebrew text (12:40 and 13:18). At times, the author/redactor seems to change verb tenses (2:17, 7:38). He often adds and omits words to fit the theological pattern of his argument (6:31; 7:38; 12:15, 40, 13:18; 19:36). Sometimes he omits superfluous material (12:15, 40). John's inaccurate citations may be the result of committing the

---

[227] Martinus J. J. Menken, *Old Testament Quotations in the Fourth Gospel: Studies in Textual Form* (Kampen, Netherlands: Kok Pharos, 1996), 14-19.

[228] Ibid., 194-202. Moloney, *John*, 256. Schnackenburg, *John*, 155-56.

[229] 1:23; 2:17; 6:31, 45; 7:37f., 42; 10:34; 12:13 ,15, 34, 38,40; 13:18; 15:25; 19:24, 28, 36, 37.

[230] Joel Marcus, "Rivers of Living Water from Jesus' Belly (John 7:38)," *JBL* 117 (1998): 328.

written text to memory or "collecting its sense rather than quoting." In the first half of the Gospel, the citations proclaim Jesus as lord, temple, living bread, son of God, and king. The second half undeniably shows that Jesus' work, death, and resurrection were "according to the Scripture." The selection of citations is almost exclusively from the later prophets and psalms.

There are a number of worthy candidates from which the author may draw from for his citation in 7:38: LXX Isa 55:1, "Let everyone who thirsts, come to the waters"; LXX Prov 18:4, "The words of the mouth are deep waters; "the fountain of wisdom is a gushing stream"; Psa 104:41, "and water flowed, rivers went through the dry land"; Psa 77:16, 20, "And he brought down water like rivers … As he smote the rock and water flowed and streams overflowed…". However, the most logical source for the quote in 7:38 appears to be Zechariah 14.[231] First, the eschatological tone of Zechariah 14 matches up well with the future tense in the quote "out of his belly will flow rivers of living water." Second, the text of Zechariah is set in context to "the feast of Tabernacles" (τὴν ἑορτὴν τῆς σκηνοπηγίας, Zech 14:16), as is the case in John 7:2 (ἡ ἑορτὴ τῶν Ἰουδαίων ἡ σκηνοπηγία). Third, Zechariah is the only text that refers to rain which would have been an important subject for the celebration of this feast: "If any of the families of the earth do not go up to Jerusalem to worship the 'King' (βασιλεύς), the Lord of hosts, there will be no rain upon them" (14:17).[232] Fourth, Zech 14 uses both terms "light" and "living water": "And in that day there will be no

---

[231] Ibid., 155.

[232] Gale A. Yee, *Jewish Feasts and the Gospel of John* (Wilmington, Del: Michael Glazier, 1989), 73.

light" (14:6); and "in that day there will go forth living water" (14:8).²³³ Jesus makes reference to both living water and the light of the world during the feast as well. Fifth, the phrase "go to Jerusalem to worship your king" (βασιλεύς, 14:17) would have been significant in the mind of the real audience of John's Gospel. John will quote another passage from Zechariah 9:9 which makes reference to Jesus' entrance into Jerusalem: "Do not fear, daughter Zion; behold, your king (βασιλεύς) is coming, sitting on a donkey's colt." Sixth, Zechariah refers specifically to Jerusalem as the location of this living water. John substitutes Zechariah's word for Ἰερουσαλήμ ("Jerusalem") with κοιλία (belly). For Ezekiel, it is the interior of the temple (47:1). Some scholars suggest that John wants also to make reference to Ezekiel 47:1-5 which locates the water source (ποταμός–47:6,7, 12) at the Temple: "water was flowing from below the threshold of the temple" (Ezek 47:1).²³⁴ Ezekiel's location for the living water is more precise because he narrows the site to a building within the larger city. If John does have Ezekiel in mind, he, like Ezekiel, may be looking to give an even more precise location for the water source.

Jesus' presence at the feast of Tabernacles (σκηνοπηγία) harkens back to the prologue which announces that the "Word" pitches his tent (σκηνόω). In John, Jesus is the temple (2:21). Yes, Zechariah locates the living water to a city and Ezekiel locates it more precisely to the interior of the Temple in that city. John's location is even more defined. The source of living water is now personified because since

---

²³³ It may be helpful to see these citations together:
ἐξελεύσεται ὕδωρ ζῶν ἐξ Ιερουσαλημ (Zech 14:8).
ποταμοὶ ἐκ τῆς κοιλίας αὐτοῦ ῥεύσουσιν ὕδατος ζῶντος (John 7:38).
²³⁴ Yee, *Jewish Feasts*, 73.

the announcement in John 2, Jesus is understood to be the temple: "Destroy this temple, and in three days I will raise it up... he was speaking of the temple of his body" (2:19, 21). The "belly" is the personified temple from which the water was prophesized to flow. In conclusion, John seems to use Zechariah but uses Ezekiel as Midrash in the background.[235] By using the citation from Zechariah, the author confirms that Jesus is the belly, the location, from which living water flows. However, that is information that is imported. Even though the author of John may be using the text from Zechariah, he may be employing the refrain for his own purpose, and not as intended by Zechariah. One needs to read the citation from the context of the Gospel narrative, not from the book of Zechariah and Ezekiel.

The difficulty surrounding the interpretation of the quote from Scripture is the antecedent for αὐτοῦ: "his belly." To whom does the "belly" in 7:38 belong: believer (traditional reading) or Jesus (Christological reading)? Below I underscored the punctuation differences.

> **Traditional reading** Ἐάν τις διψᾷ ἐρχέσθω πρός με καὶ <u>πινέτω.</u> ὁ πιστεύων <u>εἰς ἐμέ,</u> καθὼς εἶπεν ἡ γραφή, ποταμοὶ ἐκ τῆς κοιλίας αὐτοῦ ῥεύσουσιν ὕδατος ζῶντος. (If anyone thirsts, let him come to me and drink. He who believes in me, drinks, as scripture says, 'Out of the believer's (his) belly shall flow rivers of living water.'").[236]

---

[235] Keener, *John*, 1:728.
[236] Scholars who opt for the traditional punctuation are Barrett, *Gospel According to St John*, 326-27; J. B. Cortes, "Yet Another Look at John 7:37-

Christological reading Ἐάν τις διψᾷ ἐρχέσθω <u>πρός με,</u> καὶ πινέτω ὁ πιστεύων <u>εἰς ἐμέ</u>. καθὼς εἶπεν ἡ γραφή, ποταμοὶ ἐκ τῆς κοιλίας αὐτοῦ ῥεύσουσιν ὕδατος ζῶντος (Let anyone who is thirsty come to me, and let the one who believes in me drink. As scripture says…).[237]

The traditional reading is preferred by the majority of scholars because it is largely supported by the Greek Fathers.[238] Still, there are irresolvable textual issues that make such a decision inconclusive. One must take the participle "he who believes" as the subject of a new sentence rather than tagging it at the end of the previous conditional sentence. Menken, for example, reads the passage with a stop after πινέτω ("thirst").[239] This, however, is not a typical Johannine construction.[240] Menken's lengthy explanation draws examples from Xenophon JG 4.1.14 and Philostratus VA 2.24 to establish a

---

38," *CBQ* 29 (1967): 75-87; E. C. Hoskyns, *The Fourth Gospel* (ed. F. N. Davey; London: Faber & Faber, 1947), 231; Goppelt, "ὕδωρ," *TDNT*, 8:326. B. Lindars, *The Gospel of John* (London: Faber & Faber, 1992), 301; J. Marsh, *St John* (Philadelphia: Westminster, 1968), 342.

[237] Scholars who opt for the Christological punctuation are, Bultmann, *John*, 303; Brown, *John*, 2:320-23; Keener, *John*, 1:729; Leon Morris, *Reflections on the Gospel of John. II. The Bread of Life, John 6-10* (Grand Rapids: Baker, 1987), 279; Barrett, *John*, 328; Gieschen, "Baptism and the Lord's Supper," 23-45.23, n. 30.

[238] See Schnackenburg, *John*, 2.153 for a complete history of the exegesis of this passage. See also Glen Balfour, "The Jewishness of John's use of the Scriptures in John 6:31 and 7:37-38," *TynBul* 46 (1995): 370.

[239] Menken, *Old Testament Quotations,* 189-91.

[240] G. D. Kilpatrick, "The Punctuation of John vii 37-38," *JTS* 11 (1960): 340-42.

literary connection between a pendent nominative and an accusative pronoun.[241] The argument, however, appears forced by importing extra-biblical sources to justify his cause. It is also easier to argue that Jesus is the source of living water (cf. 19:34), and not a believer. One can argue that the author is claiming that Jesus is the life source, fulfilling the Temple prophecy of Ezekiel 47:1-11 from where life-giving waters flow: "everything will live where the river goes" (Ez 47:9).[242] Still, one has to put the full stop just before καθὼς εἶπεν ἡ γραφή in order for Jesus to be the belly from which the water flows, which is not a preferable alternative.[243] The literary difficulties on both sides of the argument seem to cancel out each other. The literary options are not conclusive, so the decision is typically based on exegetical grounds.

From reading the Gospel, one is likely to assume that Jesus is the better candidate to be the "belly," the source of living water, over believers. He is at the Temple and has described himself as the Temple that will be rebuilt in three days. Jesus' offering living water at the Temple also fulfills Ezekiel's vision of living water flowing from the Temple. Water throughout the Gospel has been a metaphor for revelation, and Jesus is the one sent from the Father to reveal. Still, it is possible that the "believer" drinks and becomes a source of revelation for others. Scholars including Brown, Schnackenburg, and Moloney agree that the believer cannot be linguistically ruled out completely as to whom the belly belongs, but they argue that there is no clear evidence that the believer has access to living water in the

---

[241] Menken, *Quotations*, 193.

[242] See Barrett, *John*, 328.

[243] Schnackenburg, *John*, 2.153.

Gospel.²⁴⁴ Exegetically, the choice should be Jesus and not the believer. However, they fail to point out the frequency of water in the Gospel in relation to the believer. Many believers, who act as a witness to Jesus, have access or reference to water, including John the Baptist, (Jordan river), the mother of Jesus (six water jars), the Samaritan woman (Jacob's well), the paralytic (Sheep pool), and later, the man born blind (pool of Siloam). It is not farfetched to argue the case that the believer is also a source for living water (revelation). In fact, it seems to be the intention of the author to turn cryptic Christians who fear confessing Christ into those who witness to the truth. If this is the case, then it is no surprise that at some point, the Gospel will suggest the role of the believer is to witness to the truth. I suggest that the ambiguity is intended because it allows the reader to pause and reflect on both Christ and the believer as a source of revelation to others. This is not the first time John uses equivocal meanings to suggest two possible scenarios. Later, during Jesus' trial, Pilate and Jesus arrive outside of the Praetorium and one of them sits on the judgment chair. It is not clear from the grammar who is sitting. I will argue that the ambiguity suggests that both Pilate and Jesus are engaged in judging. I propose therefore to read 7:37-38 as another example of Johannine irony.²⁴⁵

---

[244] "He is to drink from Jesus, and when waters flow ἐκ τῆς κοιλίας αὐτοῦ, their source, in the mind of the evangelist, is surely Jesus. Otherwise, we should have to suppose (with the early exegetes) that the image is disjointed: the believer drinks and becomes in turn a source for others. That is not impossible, but unlikely" Ibid., 2.154; See also Brown, *John*, 320; Moloney, *John*, 252.

[245] R. Culpepper defines irony as a double meaning that requires the reader to "decide about the author's knowledge or beliefs; and choose a

As concluded above, the grammar in John 7:37-38 is vague so the reader is unable to reach a conclusion as to who owns the "belly." This, as I suggested above, is perhaps a rhetorical move. The lack of clarity suggests that the author's intention here is to engage the reader by directing the attention back to John 4 which first introduced the idea of drinking "living water." There are a number of literary and thematic parallels to support this linkage. Both 7:37-38 and John 4 share key-words: thirst (διψάω, 7:37; 4:7, 9), drink (πίνω, 7:37; 4:10, 13), believers (πιστεύω πιστεύσαντες), and living water (ὕδωρ ζάω, 7:38; 4:13). There are also important thematic ties. In 7:37 Jesus invites the thirsty to "come to me" (ἐρχέσθω πρός με); in 4:40 they came to him (ἦλθον πρὸς αὐτὸν οἱ Σαμαρῖται). In 7:38, worship is accentuated as the high point of a great feast, the "last day of the feast" (Εν δὲ τῇ ἐσχάτῃ ἡμέρᾳ τῇ μεγάλῃ τῆς ἑορτῆς); in 4:20-27 there is a long discussion about worship. In 7:39, believers will worship in spirit (πνεῦμα) and truth; in 4:39 believers will receive the spirit (πνεῦμα). The terminology in 7:37-38 appears to have already been theologically developed and defined in John 4. One needs to take a closer look at this shared terminology as it is used in John 4 because it seems to provide the interpretive key for 7:37-38. What did the reader learn in John 4 that could help the reader to understand and interpret John 7:37-38?

According to 4:14 the water that is possessed by the believer is a divine gift to those who believe in Jesus. So the reader has already been informed that believers will be given living water: "The water

---

new meaning which is in harmony with the (implied) author's position. Culpepper, *Anatomy*, 167.

that I will give will become in them a spring of water gushing up to eternal life" (4:14). What can the believer do with such abundance? Water, as the reader has seen, represents the gift of revelation, and in light of the prologue, the truth/revelation has transformative power (produces children of God). Truth/revelation from the Gospel narrative offers eternal life. With such a revelatory resource, the believer can become a witness to others. I will argue that the author uses the citation in 7:38 to suggest that those who possess the truth, whether it is Christ or the believer, can testify, thus offering eternal life to another. One must appreciate the radical nature of such a teaching. No other text from the Old Testament, the Dead Sea Scrolls, Pseudopigrahic/Jewish texts or ancient secular sources suggest that a human can offer eternal life to another through a revelation of divine truth. The author of John may borrow familiar expressions, terminology, and phrases from other sources, but the idea itself is not copied from any source. John the Baptist, the mother of Jesus, the Samaritan woman put others in contact with Jesus. The reader has seen the Samarian woman produce other believers. Yet those believers encountered Christ: "And many more believed because of his word. They said to the woman, 'it is no longer because of what you said that we believe, for we have heard for ourselves, and we know that this is truly the Savior of the world'" (4:40-41). So too, the disciples became believers at the wedding of Cana because of the witness of the mother of Jesus and the servants who knew from "where" the wine came. They too were in the presence of Jesus. Yet, there will come a time when Christ is no longer present and others will be needed to witness to the truth: "I will send to you from the Father, the Spirit of truth who comes from the Father, he will testify on my behalf. You also are to testify because you have been with me from the beginning" (15:26-27), "As you have sent me into the world, so I have sent them into the world" (17:18). Not everyone will have direct access to Christ: "Blessed are those who have not seen and yet believe." (20:29). As L. P. Jones states: "The living water believers receive becomes 'life-giving water' as it flows through them to others."[246]

The gift of water and the spirit are available in the future when Jesus is glorified at his hour: "As of yet, there was no Spirit, because Jesus was not yet glorified" (7:39). Later when Jesus is on the cross both water and the Spirit will leave the body of Jesus when he dies on the cross: "Then he bowed his head and handed over his Spirit…the soldiers pierced his side with a spear, and at once blood and water came out" (19:30, 34). The reader has already seen the two terms "water" and "spirit" paired in both the stories of Nicodemus ("no one can enter the kingdom of God without being born of water and Spirit, 3:5), and the Samaritan woman. ("Sir give me this water," and "True worshipers will worship the Father in spirit and truth" 4:15, 23). Spirit and water are the two terms Jesus used to describe to Nicodemus how one is born from above. I showed above how birth by water and spirit means that one has access to revelation which produces eternal life. In the narrative of the Samaritan woman, I argued that water and spirit are once again terms that symbolize revelation (truth). Once again, the appearance of both water and spirit are found together in Jesus' announcement of a future gift "which believers in him were to receive" (7:39). All three texts show

---

[246] Jones, *Symbol of Water,"* 155, 161.

that water and spirit represent the divine gift of revelation that provides eternal life. Later in the final discourse, Jesus will promise the Spirit of Truth: "When the Spirit of truth comes, he will guide you into all the truth" 16:13). The purpose of the Spirit is to supply the believer with truth so that they can testify: "When the Advocate comes, whom I will send to you from the Father, the Spirit of truth who comes from the Father he will testify on my behalf. You also are to testify because you have been with me" (15:26). Do to the frequency of the terms and the consistency of its meaning, the reader is able to connect the symbolism to Jesus' announcement at the end of the feast. The Spirit, therefore, connects the believer with God. This connection allows the believer to give authentic witness to others. Just as Christ was sent from the Father, so too, the believer is sent to witness to others. Just as Jesus could draw from his origin to authenticate his witness, so now with the Spirit the believer has a divine origin because he was sent by Christ with the gift of the Spirit. That is, the believer, like Christ, also has divine origin which authenticates the witness.

The announcement on the last day of the feast is a turning point of the narrative suggesting that believers will be able to give witness to Christ in his absence when he returns to the Father at the hour of Glory: "Now he said this about the Spirit, which believers in him were to receive; for as yet there was no Spirit, because Jesus was not yet glorified" (7:39). The role of the Spirit provides authenticity to the believer's witness to others. An example of this is the Apostles' witness to Thomas after the first appearance. When Jesus first appeared to the Apostles in Thomas's absence, they were given the Spirit. Thomas should have believed their testimony because they were valid witnesses who were sent and given the Holy Spirit, meaning they have their origin in God: "As the Father has sent me, so I send you...Receive the Holy Spirit" (20:21, 22). Jesus confirms the authentic witness of his apostles by telling Thomas: "Blessed are those who have not seen and yet have come to believe." It is during this discourse that Jesus tells His disciples that he is no longer going to be with them. He does promise them the Holy Spirit. The purpose, therefore of the Spirit is to provide the believer with "origin," that is, they are from God. By being establishing their location, their witness to others will appear authentic. Who does the author mean when he writes "his belly?" In light of role of water (revelation) and its relationship to the believer, and the role of the Spirit that will also be given to the believer, one could understand how the believer would be a source of revelation to others, just as it has its source in Christ. The text seems to be preparing the reader for the fact that the Spirit will provide authenticity, allowing the believer to become a witness in the absence of Christ.

In addition, one has to remember that the issue of Jesus' origin plays a significant role both before and after Jesus' announcement is introduced and concludes with the topic of the origin of Jesus. It seems that the "belly" refers to all those who witness to the truth, believers included, who will have the spirit authenticate their testimony. All witnesses are sent and have their place in God.

(Due to the fact that the account of Jesus and the woman taken in adultery (7:53-8:11) is likely an interpolation, I will not treat the narrative here because it is not a part of the author/redactor's theological insights.[247] My goal in this commentary is to analyze the dynamic of the Johannine narrative as it would have appeared in the final form of the author.)

The Last Day of the Feast (part 2): Light of the World

The origin of Jesus is once again the central issue in this section. Its importance is clear. Once again, Jesus needs to validate His testimony. According to Jewish juridical law, truth is established by the testimony of two witnesses: "In your law it is written that the testimony of two witnesses is valid" (8:17). Those who reject Jesus claim that His testimony is invalid because he is alone, and His claims cannot be verified without a second witness: "You are testifying on your own behalf; your testimony is not valid" (8:13). However, Jesus is not alone; He comes from the Father. Jesus claims that the Father is the second voice. The words of Jesus are not His own, but they are the words of the Father: "I am not alone who judge, but I and the Father who sent me" (8:16; cf. 14:10). Once again, Jesus' words expose the obstacle that prevents the rejecters from believing.[248] They

---

[247] The canonical status of the woman caught in adultery passage was universally recognized when Jerome added the passage into the Vulgate in 382. Bultmann, Dodd.

[248] "What is at stake here is not whether Jesus is from Galilee, but whether he is from God. The Jews alternately know and don't know 'where Jesus is from' (1:46; 6:42; 7:26; 7:41; 7:52). They have to admit finally that they 'do not know where he comes from' (9:29). But the reader knows! The reader knows not only that Jesus is from God, but also that he is the Son of God." Dolan, "Irony Part II," 6.

do not know "where." They ask, "Where is your Father?" (8:19). Later, Philip will ask the same question, "show us the Father" (14:8). When both the Pharisees and Philip inquire about the Father's location, Jesus uses the occasion to show that his words are not his own but they have their origin in the Father. He tells Philip, "I am in the Father and the Father is in me; the words that I say to you I do not speak on my own; but the Father who dwells in me" (14:10).

On the last day of the feast he tells the Pharisees twice "Where I am going, you cannot come." His place is with the Father because he is sent and he will return. They cannot come because they have sin: "you will die in your sin" (8:21; c.f., 24). Later, he tells the disciples that they too cannot follow but they will be able to follow Jesus because they believe: "Where I am going, you cannot follow me now; but you will follow afterward" (13:36). Here, the Gospel defines Jesus' death as the return, another proof that his origin is with the Father. The Pharisees cannot come because their death is defined as sin. Sin is rejection of the truth; by rejecting truth they do not believe and thus refuse access to eternal life. In essence, there are two types of death: temporary and permanent. One is a reunion or rejoining with God, the other comes about by rejection or disassociation: sin. That is, belief unites and rejection divides. Death is understood in the Gospel in terms of these behaviors. If one believes, he will be reunited with God. If one rejects the truth, he is separated from God. Later, sin will be demonstrated at the trial of Jesus when he is rejected and handed over by Judas, the high priests, the crowd, and Pilate. If death is a door to reunite with God, then logically anyone who believes cannot die. Later, Jesus will use the occasion of Lazarus's death to expand on this principle: "whoever believes in me will never die" (11:26).

So far, there has not been much discussion about producing children of God. The focus has been on the validity of the Word by way of origin. The reader knows from the prologue that the purpose of the Word sent into the world is to create children of God. So far in the Gospel, there have been a number of themes related to the making of children. There was a wedding, a best man (John the Baptist), a woman with marital issues discussing fidelity with a groom at a common place where married couples meet (Samaritan woman). There was also a dialogue between Jesus and Nicodemus about birth from above. In this section, the argument progresses to how the Word is productive. The shift begins when Jesus tells the Jews how the truth will make them free.[249] This appears strikingly odd to them because they are already free. They maintain that proof of their freedom is their status as children of Abraham. In a household, one is either a slave or a child. The Jews believe they are free because they are children of Abraham. The focus now shifts to children: "The slave does not have a permanent place in the household; the son has a place there forever" (8:35). Father and Son share distinctive qualities. The child adopts and learns the skills of the father. "If you were Abraham's children you would be doing what Abraham did" (8:39).

---

[249] "Jesus is contrasted not only with Caesar but also, albeit more lightly, with Barabbas, the λῃστής, the "freedom fighter." For John, freedom comes from knowing the truth, that is, from abiding in the word of Jesus (8:31- 32)." Rensberger, "Politics of John," 410.

The murderous plot of the Jews and their aversion to the truth reveals that their father is the devil: "You are from your father the devil, and you choose to do your father's desires. He was a murderer from the beginning and does not stand in the truth" (8:44). The opposition to Jesus shares the same skill set as the devil, which exposes their true father. Remember, the role of the devil in this Gospel is to prevent revelation. Jesus' words and works also expose Him as one who comes from God. One can judge that Jesus is God by his works. Later, the blind man will say, "never since the world began has it been heard that anyone opened the eyes of a person born blind. If this man were not from God, He would do nothing" (9:33). Jesus shares the same words and skills as God.

The opposition respond by calling Jesus a demon ("you have a demon," 8:48), but offer no support to back up the claim. The opponents plot the death of Jesus, which confirms that their father is a murderer: a murderer begets murderers. Hostility is raised to its highest level.[250] Jesus offers them a remedy. Twice Jesus says, "whoever keeps my word will never taste death" (8:51, 52). For those who believe in God's Word and keep it, death is a passage to reunite with God because the children are always part of the household. The Jews see death as a permanent state even for the good: "Abraham died. The prophets also died" (8:53). They fail to recognize that God sent his Word to create children who will inherit eternal life. The creative Word, which the reader knows is spirit and life, has been sent into the world to create. "Your ancestor Abraham rejoiced that he would see my day; he saw it and was glad" (8:56).

---

[250] Culpepper, "Theology," 278.

Jesus declares that he is the light of the world: "Again Jesus spoke to them, saying, "I am the light of the world" (8:12). Light means visibility, truth/revelation. The "I am" statement once again confirms His origin in God. This is true since the Jews recognize the implication of the phrase and respond: "they picked up stones to throw at him (8:59).[251] People see deeds. So "light" and Jesus' works are synonymous. People hear words. This also confirms what the reader knows so far about believers. They offer testimony (words) but they do not perform deeds.

I argued above that in addition to Jesus, believers can also be a source of living water. Yet, only Jesus is the light of the world, and so he performs deeds to reveal: "We must work the works of him who sent me while it is day; night is coming when no one can work. As long as I am in the world, I am the light of the world" (9:4-6). When Jesus performs deeds, his origin is authenticated. Only if He is from God can He perform such deeds as healing the man born blind or raising the dead. Both words and deeds are modes of revelation. Thus, in addition to living water and bread, light symbolizes revelation/truth. Brown explains: "Previously we have heard Jesus speak of water that is life-giving and of bread that is life-giving; now he speaks of life-giving light. Since the first two metaphors referred basically to his revelation, we may well suspect that that is what is meant here too."[252] This discussion will play itself out when Jesus, the light of the world, performs the sign on the man born blind. After he speaks, Jesus is violently forced out of the temple, a preview of

---

[251] Brown, *John*, 367.
[252] Brown, *John*, 344.

what is about to come when the Pharisees (9:13) and the Jews (9:22) reject the light. The next chapter underscores Jesus' work when words are now shifted to deeds.

The Man Born Blind: First Words (Water, Light), Now Deeds

During the festival of Booths, Jesus passes by a blind man and stops to cure him. His disciples ask him who sinned to cause the man's blindness. The question gives Jesus the opportunity to instruct them on the work of God that will bring light into a dark world. Here, the man's world is dark. The reader can now observe what happens when light (revelation) comes into the world. Jesus just had a long discussion as the light of the world. Now we are seeing Jesus words actualized into deeds.

So far we have seen a number of examples of believers in the early chapters and examples of non-believers in these most recent passages. Now we are able to see the believer and the non-believer together for the first time. The contrast will show what happens when indisputable evidence is accepted by one party and rejected by another. Here the non-believer works hard to find indisputable truth only to reject it. It makes no sense especially knowing the risk of forfeiting eternal life.

After the man's sight is restored, there is a disagreement about his identity, his blindness from birth, and in what role God played in the man's regaining his sight. The narrative focuses on the characters' pursuit of the facts. What actually happened, and who was responsible? The whole story resembles a court trial with an effort to compile forensic evidence.[253] There are no details about emotion, joy, gratitude, praise to God, or celebration, on the part of the blind man, the neighbors, acquaintances, religious leaders, or even the parents. The focus is judicial and legal. This is a cerebral quest for raw facts. Truth is sought by legalistic measures and found because of the numerous testimonies, all of which agree to the fact that the man born blind now sees. Also, Jesus' origin is once again irrefutably revealed. Why so much attention to finding out what had happened? The author of the Gospel intends to show that those who reject Jesus have been given indisputable evidence pointing to the proven fact that Jesus is from God, exposing them of their willful rejection of truth. That is why Jesus exposes their blindness.

Before addressing the plot in greater detail, it is important to highlight a few of the narrative features. Moloney calls the account a masterpiece of "Johannine storytelling."[254] There are fourteen questions in the story. The first and last are addressed to Jesus ("Who sinned?" 9:2; "Surely we are not blind are we?" 9:40). One concerns Jesus ("How can a man who is a sinner perform such signs?" 9:16). All others are directed toward or about the blind man. There are multiple scene-changes, and each division is composed of two parties: Jesus and the disciples, Jesus and the blind Man, the blind man and the neighbors, the blind man and the Pharisees, the parents and the Pharisees, the blind man and Pharisees (second time), the blind man and Jesus, Jesus and the Pharisees. There is much repetition of phrases and terms such as "mud," "light," "see,"

---

[253] Schneiders, *You May Believe*, 158-59.
[254] Moloney, *John*, 290.

"washed," etc. This is due to the process of establishing the truth by matching testimony. When testimony is not consistent, truth cannot be established. The blind man must state multiple times to various groups what happened to him. His witness is always consistent; it never varies or wavers. His parents also witness about the son and their witness is likewise compatible with each other. No one differs from the other. The story is consistent, and so there is much repetition. Repetition is forensic evidence.

The miracle takes place during the festival of Booths. During the feast, water and light are used as liturgical symbols of worship because they are recognized as gifts from God producing a successful harvest. The entire pericope shows how Jesus is the light of the world. Those who were born in darkness are now able to see, while those who refuse to accept the light (Pharisees, Jews) remain in their darkness. At this stage of the narrative the audience is aware of the theological implications of the prologue and how it is reflected at each turn. The same is true with chapter 9. The prologue discusses a light that comes into the world as a creative power. So, too, the Word of God is transformative revelation, having an effect in the world. Truth originates from the Father and is shared with the Son at his bosom. Its creative power produces children of God. In this narrative, Christ is the light of the world. All who are blind are able to see God by way of Jesus' word.

The disciples are wrong to think that the blindness was caused by sin. The blindness represents the lack of revelation, not sin. In this case, darkness means a world deprived of revelation. Christ was sent to provide revelation, bringing light (truth) into the world.[255] Sin is the rejection and violent opposition of revelation. Sin comes after revelation. Before revelation, however, no one has ever seen God. That is why Jesus states "We must work the works of him who sent me while it is day; night is coming when no one can work" (9:4). Jesus seems to anticipate collaborators with the first person plural "we." Back in 6:29 Jesus tells the crowd what he means by work: "This is the work of God, that you believe in him whom he has sent." The work of revelation is only possible in the light, because it is light.[256] One can see that the details of the prologue (i.e., light comes

---

[255] Meeks writes "The 'accomplishment of the work' is a theme that recurs throughout the gospel (4.34; 5.36; 9.3f.; 10.25, 32-8; 14.10,12; 15.24), culminating in the cry from the cross, τετέλεσται! (19.30). The crucifixion is the completion of the work; the summary in chapter 17 of course presupposes the crucifixion as accomplished." See his *The Prophet-King: Moses Traditions and the Johannine Christology* (Leiden: E. J. Brill, 1967), 304 n. 2.

[256] One could ask if it possible that the disciples cannot work after Jesus returns to the Father. Such an interpretation is not consistent with a later passage which reads, "Amen, amen I say to you, the one believing in me—even that one will do the works that I am doing; and he/she will do greater works than these, because I am going to the Father (14:12). Schneiders identifies the night as "the dark hour of the passion" See her "John 20:11-18: The Encounter of the Easter Jesus with Mary Magdalene—A Transformative Feminist Reading," in *What is John?: Readers and Readings of the Fourth Gospel* (ed. Fernando F. Segovia; SBLSymS 3; Atlanta: Scholars Press, 1996), 157-58. Thomas Knoppler identifies the night as the moment which Judas ends Jesus' work. See his *Die theologia crucis des Johannesevangelium* (WMANT 69; Neukirchen-Vluyn: Neukirchener Verlag,

into the world, the word is rejected, those who accept and believe will be given power to be children of God), provide the thematic outline of this story. Christ, the light of the world comes to a man born blind (one who is deprived of revelation), After Jesus gives sight (light), the Pharisees reject Jesus and act violently by casting the blind man out of the synagogue. The blind man, however, sees by accepting light (revelation) when Jesus reveals "I am." Prior to sight, the blind man did not know the Son of Man: "No one has ever seen God." Yet, after Jesus reveals, the man who was blind now sees God: "He said, 'Lord I believe' and worshiped him" (9:38).

Jesus will speak to the man born blind and he will accept the Word by his obedience: "he told me…I did." In the narrative, the light of the world spat on the ground and made mud with the saliva (9:6). He then "anointed" the mud on the man's eyes. Jesus tells the man to "go, wash in the pool of Siloam" (9:7). Although the literal meaning of Siloam is a "discharge" of water, the text draws on the etymology and defines it as "one who has been sent." It is the same perfect passive participle (ἀπεσταλμένος) that was used in the prologue to describe John the Baptist, who was sent (ἀπεσταλμένος) by God to testify. Jesus, likewise, is one who has been sent. The man who is blind is also one who has been sent by divine authority (go, wash in the pool of Siloam"), and he too will soon begin to testify. Once again, the prologue is very much featured in the story of the blind man with the use of the term "one who was sent" (1:1:6; 9:7). The reader is now going to witness the birth of a believer (child of

---

1994), 178-79. See also Otto Schwankl, *Licht und Finsternis: Ein metaphorisches Paradigma in den johanneischen, Schriften* (Herders Biblische Studien 5; Freiburg: Herder, 1995), 233-34.

God) by water and the spirit (revelation). For the transformative action to take hold, the Word has to be accepted. One must believe in the Word. Belief is always executed by way of obedience to the Word. Jesus will later describe this process in the example of the vine and the branches where the branches bear much fruit when they are clean by the Word (i.e. 15:3). For Jesus, the imagery of the vine and the branches is played out when the believer accepts the Word through obedience: "If you keep my commandments, you will abide in my love" (15:10). The blind man does exactly what Jesus asked him to do. "Then he went and washed and came back able to see (βλέπω)."[257] Jesus' command and the activity of the man create verbal redundancy. This highlights the obedience of the man, the necessary requisite for the creative act. That is, one must accept the Word.

The euphoria of a man seeing for the first time, when his whole body fills with light, color, depth, and height, can only be imagined because the emotion is not recorded in the Gospel. Feelings and reactions are not discussed. The entire episode is told as if one is in a courtroom where the only goal is to determine the truth. Only the obedient acceptance of the Word is mentioned. There are no crowds to witness the event. His washing and seeing is in isolation from the

---

[257] "Throughout John 9, βλέπω, which normally refers to physical sight, is used. But by linking sight and blindness with light and darkness the evangelist shows that he is using βλέπω in a double sense, of physical sight and the seeing of faith, suggesting that the seeing of faith is rooted in physical sight and that there is an inseparable link between the world, with its observable events, and faith. All seeing, rightly understood, points to the seeing of faith." John Painter, "John 9 and the Interpretation of the Fourth Gospel," *JSNT* 9 (1986): 43.

rest of the community. Jesus is not even present. This is not the only time that Jesus, the disciples, and the crowds are not present. The servants at the wedding of Cana go and fill the water jars, the royal official returns to his home and finds his son alive, the paralyzed man picks up his mat and walks away. Obedience means acceptance of the revelation, "Do whatever he tells you." Obedience also produces belief in others. The disciples believe at the wedding. The entire household of the royal official become believers. The obedience of the blind man will likewise lead to his own belief: "He said, 'Lord, I believe.' And he worshiped him" (9:38). He will also offer truth to others, but it will be rejected.

The next scene introduces the neighbors and those who know the blind man because of his activity as a beggar. Once again the Gospel discloses another division (9:16).[258] They cannot agree if this is the same man who they know or someone different: "Some were saying 'It is he.' Others were saying, 'No, but it is someone like him'" (9:9). Note the division between the neighbors. One will also observe a disagreement between the Pharisees. Some claim he may be from God, the others do not. This is another important characteristic among the non-believers. They are divided. One will see this more as the narrative advances toward the second section of the book: the Book of Glory.

The neighbors' questions implies that the blind man had to make more than one attempt to convince them that he was the "beggar," "He kept saying, "I am the man" (9:9). He is asked for the first

---

[258] See other instances of division during the festival: cf. 7:12, 25-27, 31, 40-41.

time to give an account of what happened. He repeats what the reader already has read and knows. The purpose is to show consistency with each witness. Repetition and consistency are necessary to meet the rigorous juridical standards to establish truth. During the testimony, he mentions Jesus by name. He is given sole credit for the sign. It will now be up to the religious authorities to figure out if the activity was backed by divine power. Before the neighbors lead them to the Pharisees, they want to know where he is. This again recalls the prologue in which the reader is first informed where Jesus is from. He comes from the bosom of the Father. There, Christ gains divine truth, having full knowledge of God because of his close relationship to the divine. The blind man does not yet know where he is from, but he will know by the end of the religious leaders' trial that is about to take place. His knowledge is progressive like the Samaritan woman who becomes more aware of the identity of Jesus as the conversation advances forward. As her understanding grows, so do the titles with which he is addressed.

The next scene introduces the Pharisees with a mention that Jesus made mud on a Sabbath. Once again, the reader will recall the seven-day creation narrative. The prologue introduced the idea of the creative power of the word by citing the first words of the creation narrative in Gen 1:1, where God created light. The reader knows that the Word is in the world to create by offering light, and the signs are manifestations of the creative power of the Word. The curing of the paralytic is another sign that took place on a Sabbath. It seems that some of the Pharisees confuse the making of mud with pottery manufacturing, an explicit violation of the Sabbath. The confusion is almost laughable to the reading audience. The fuss they make does not persuade the reader into believing that spitting on the ground and anointing eyes to cure a man is an offence against God. The Pharisees rejected the truth and drawn conclusions before their investigation: "Some of the Pharisees said, 'This man is not from God, for he does not observe the Sabbath'" (9:16). Once again, the blind man must testify: "He put mud on my eyes. Then I washed, and now I see" (9:15). The testimony again matches his previous statement. The man is asked to say something about Jesus. He tells them he is a prophet. The prophet Elijah cured the blind and Elisha sent a leper to wash in the Jordan River. The statement indicates that the man knows Scripture and that he confesses that Jesus represents God through the power of his Word: "and said to me, 'Go to Siloam and wash'" (9:11)."

The Pharisees needed to prove that the man was first blind. They sought after witnesses: the man's parents. The two witnesses testified that the man was indeed born blind. They offer no further testimony as to why he can see. There is no mention of Jesus, nor a hint of gratitude toward the healer. They tell the Pharisees to ask their son about the healer because he is of legitimate age to testify for himself. They cut short their testimony because they were afraid by the threat of expulsion from the synagogue: "they were afraid of the Jews; for the Jews had already agreed that anyone who confessed Jesus to be the Messiah would be put out of the synagogue" (9:22).[259] Perhaps

---

[259] Many scholars view the story as a window into the historical setting. The blind man who receives his sight represents a community of believers that faces expulsion from the synagogue. Schneiders, *John*, 150. Brown maintains that there is a group of believers who fear repercussions from

the intended reader may have understood that same fear. They too may have felt the same threat of expulsion from the protective blanket of Jewish liberties, exposing them to the legal Roman authority if they testify about Jesus. It is likely that the fear of the parents was real and understood by primitive church Christians.[260] Now, the parents seem to be on trial. They are asked a question that could incriminate them: "How then does he now see?" (9:19). Could they even know the answer to such a question? They refuse to answer, referring them to their son.[261]

The blind man now stands alone against the hostility of the religious authority. His own parents put him on the witness stand. The Pharisees have no other choice than to put him on trial, for they are

---

the Jews if they confess Christ (cf. 12:42-43). The Gospel attempts to embolden these "crypto-Christians" to step forward and witness to the truth. See Brown, *Community,* 71-73; J. Louis Martyn maintains that the story reflects the late first-century experience of the Johannine community being excommunicated from the synagogue worship. See his *History and Theology in the Fourth Gospel* (Nashville: Abingdon, 1979).

[260] For a summary of the issue surrounding Christian expulsion see Schnackenburg, *John,* 2.248-50; Brown, *John,* LXXIII-LXXV.

[261] If anyone accepts Jesus they will be rejected by Jewish authorities. A rejection of Jesus means an approval and acceptance. See Philip Tire, "A Community in Conflict: A Literary and Historical Reading of John 9," *Religious Studies and Theology* 15 (1996): 77-100. Threats and retaliation produce fear and the authorities know they can control those who fear. The text makes it plain that the parents have been threatened: "His parents said this because they were afraid of the Jews; for the Jews had already agreed that anyone who confessed Jesus to be the Messiah would be put out of the synagogue" (9:22).

determined to get to the truth. The entire scene is a long trail in which different witnesses are called and interrogated."[262]

The star witness will confirm everything about Jesus and the Pharisees. The next scene provides the climactic drama with the second encounter between the Pharisees and the blind man. They ask him to give glory to God. To do this, the blind man will have to state the truth, something he has been doing all along. Yet, now he is under oath (See Josh 6:19; 1 Esdras 9:8 as an oath formula before taking testimony). The irony is that the Pharisees suggest a different route for glorifying God by rejecting the truth that they themselves researched and acquired: "Why do you want to hear it again? Do you also want to become his disciples?" (9:27). This question pressures the Pharisees to make a decision. The author sets the scene whereby the reader has been exposed to the effects of the sign. Once there is a sign, one must make a decision either to believe or reject. The Pharisees tell the man that they know Jesus is a sinner. Yet, they offer no evidence for their claim, and for that, they are not convincing, at least to the blind man: "He answered, 'I do not know if he is a sinner'" (9:25). They ask him to tell them how is able to see. The man already gave them his testimony, yet he knows how to expose their duplicity, by asking if they want to be his disciple. For those who read Greek, the blind man provides the answer to his own question. He knows that they do not want to follow Jesus. The question gives the Pharisees an opportunity to hide under the banner of Moses:

---

[262] Schneiders, *John*, 158.

"We are disciples of Moses" (9:28).²⁶³ They refuse to follow Jesus because they do not know where he is from. This is the second time there is a concern about "where" Jesus is from (9:12, 30). Not knowing where Jesus is from is the obvious problem that leads the Pharisees to reject the very truth that they gleaned from their involved inquiry. The blind man, instead, knows where Jesus is from: "'Here is an astonishing thing! You do not know where he comes from, and yet he opened my eyes.'" (9:30). When the blind man hears that they do not know where he is from, they are exposed. They took the bait, so to speak, and they are trapped with their own inconsistency. They reject truth which is the same as rejecting the Word that gives light. Light is in the world through testimony, and they reject it. Fear is another obstacle. The parents miss an opportunity to bask in the light of truth due to fear. This is the first presentation in the Gospel of fear as an obstacle for accepting the truth. Later, Pilate will fear the Jews; even though he argued for Jesus' innocence, yet he rejected him by handing him over to be condemned to death. One learns in this narrative that there are two reasons why people reject the truth: (1) fear and (2) not grasping "where" Jesus is from. The prologue provides the intended reader with the necessary resources to address and overcome these two obstacles. It states where Jesus is from and

---

[263] "Although Jesus' opponents attempt to divide Moses and Jesus, setting them on either side of the theological fence, John makes every effort to unite them, not dismissing Moses and all that he stands for but, on the contrary, securing him for the cause of the Johannine Jesus and the believing community which gathers around him. There is contrast." Dorothy A. Lee, "The Significance of Moses in The Gospel of John," *ABR* 63 (2015): 66.

assures that Jesus' coming is part of the creative plan to offer eternal life to all.

The man now testifies about Jesus by recalling to them the biblical fact that no one has ever cured a blind person from birth. Apparently, the blind man knows the Scriptures to acquire this fact. According to the logic of the cured man, this extraordinary event must have its origin in God. His testimony, however, has consequences. He is expelled from the synagogue. The parents' worst fear is now a reality for their son. The son is cut off from everyone from the expulsion. Jesus finds him and completes his visual abilities by introducing himself: "You have seen him and the one speaking with you is he" (9:37). The man born blind now believes.

Note that each time the blind man witnesses to others, his sight progresses. He first knows the name of the man who healed him: Jesus (9:11). He calls Jesus a prophet (9:17), he defends him against the Pharisees (9:25), invites them to become Jesus' disciples (9:27), tells them he is from God (9:33), corrects the Pharisees' theology (9:34), and confesses Jesus as his Lord, and worships him (9:38). As the blind man gains insight, the Pharisees, in contrast, become divided (9:16), suspicious (9:18), angry (9:28),[264] and finally make a judgment not based on the legal testimony they heard from their trial (9:34).[265] Their rejection of the facts produced by their own investigation proves their incompetence. The blind man's sight,

---

[264] This is the only time the term λοιδορέω is used in the four gospels. There are only three other times the term is used in the New Testament (Acts 23;4; 1 Cor 4:12; 1 Pet 2:3)

[265] They set up a trial by telling the blind man to take an oath: "Give glory to God (9:24). "Give praise to God" is an oath formula used before

thereby, recalls the two announcements of Jesus at the Feast of Tabernacles. That Jesus calls himself the light of the world and the source of living water. Both light and water play a role in the narrative of the blind man. The obedient response to Jesus' words by the blind man and his experience of the purification and restoration of his sight are in contrast to the Pharisees who do not believe Jesus and thus their "sin remains."

The journey to full sight is contrasted to the journey to full blindness of the Pharisees. This demonstrates that once the truth has been testified, there are only two options: rejection or acceptance (belief). Note also that neither the blind man nor the Pharisees remain undecided. They both make a choice once they were exposed to the revelatory sign. Sin is defined as the rejection of the truth after it has been revealed by legitimate testimony: "Now that you say 'We see,' your sin remains."[266] The narrative also highlights the two obstacles to belief: fear and not knowing where Jesus is from. The Pharisees refuse to believe Jesus is from God, and the parents refuse to witness because of their fear. The blind man gains his sight by accepting and

---

testimony or a confession of guilt (Josh 7:19; Jer 13:16; 1 Chron 30:6-9; 1 Esdr 9:8). Moloney, *John*, 294. There will be no conflicting stories for the Pharisees because the two parents, according to biblical protocol, satisfy courtroom protocol that requires two witnesses (Num 35:30; Deut 17:6; 19:15). Their make-shift trial produces two agreeing witnesses (his parents), physical evidence, and truth without a reasonable doubt. The case successfully produces the undeniable truth. Their verdict, however, proves them incompetent. They were obviously blind to the evidence and to the truth they so carefully gleaned.

[266] Culpepper, "Theology," 419.

obeying the words of Jesus which recalls the words of an earlier witness: "Do whatever he tells you" (2:5).

The story of the restoration of the sight of the blind man from birth enables the author to confirm what was said in the prologue. Light triumphs over darkness and Jesus is from God because of the work that he does.[267] He was sent to testify to the truth. He knows the truth because he is from the Father. The episode confirms the role of the witness for providing truth and the two obstacles that cause one to reject the testimony. The Pharisees have successfully obtained the truth by way of valid testimony. They know indisputably through a series of witnesses that the man was born blind, and that he now sees because he obeyed Jesus' Word. It is a Word that brings light into the world. Once the truth has been revealed by legitimate testimony there are only two options: accept the Word or reject it. They have the truth in their grasp, and they reject it by expelling the man from the synagogue.

In the next chapter, the author of the Gospel illustrates how those who reject valid testimony turn themselves into a destructive force against the testifier. I will demonstrate that violence is the response of those who reject the truth. Jesus, however, is the life of the world, the good shepherd, disarming the weapons of violent rejecters. The reader is now introduced to the contrast between a good shepherd and wolves/thieves.[268]

---

[267] "In John 9 the symbol of light focuses attention on man's failure to perceive the truth in the revealer." Painter, "John 9," 53.

[268] Johannes Quasten claims that the shepherd "discourse is connected with the healing of the man born blind and thus is clearly characterized as

The Good Shepherd

The purpose of the good shepherd narrative is to address what to do with violent rejecters of the truth/revelation.[269] It also picks up on a third category of responders to Jesus' revelation: believers who fear. There is a reason believers fear. Non-believers are violent against believers who reveal.

The story of the man who was born blind ends with the judgment of those who reject indisputable truth. They are sinners. Sinners not only reject, but they also oppose the truth by means of violence. They drove out the man born blind (9:34), picked up stones to throw at Jesus (8:59), wanted to arrest him (7:44), and wanted to kill him (5:18). They threaten with violence to silence witnesses. Jesus offers a remedy for believers who are threatened. He will take out the opponents' most lethal weapon: death. For Jesus, death is no longer a threat because it is no longer permanent. That is why Jesus

---

the conclusion of a speech rebuking the Pharisee." See his "Parable of the Good Shepherd (Jn. 10:1-21)," *CBQ* 10 (1948): 153.

[269] See the following works for detailed studies on John 10: Theodor Konrad Kempf, *Christus der Hirt Ursprung und Deutung einer altchristhchen Symbolgestalt* (Rome Officium Libri Catholici, 1942); Ferdmand Hahn, "Die Hirtenrede m Joh 10," in *Theologia Crucis - Signus Crucis. Festschrift tür Erich Dinkler zum 70. Geburtstag. Herausgegeben von Carl Andresen und Günter Klein* (eds. Carl Andresen and G Klem; Tubmgen Mohr-Siebeck, 1979), 185-200; Odo Kiefer, *Die Hirtenrede Analyse und Deutung von Johannes 10,1-18* (Stuttgart Katholisches Bibelwerk, 1967); A J Simonis, *Die Hirtenrede im Johannes-Evangelium Versuch einer Analyse von Johannes 10,1-18 nach Entstehung, Hintergrund und Inhalt* (AnBib 29, Rome Pontifical Biblical Institute, 1967).

takes the role of a good shepherd who protects his sheep from violent opposition so that they will never die.

This next passage presents Jesus in various metaphorical roles. He is a door for the sheep (10:7), and a shepherd (10:11). Earlier, according to John the Baptist, He was described as a lamb. Although there appears to be a conflation of metaphors, they all serve a purpose: to illustrate a comprehensive Christology. The door is used to allow entry for the shepherd: "The gatekeeper opens the gate for him" (10:3). It is noted that thieves and predators do not use the door because their intention is to harm the sheep: "The thief comes only to steal and kill and destroy" (10:10). The door is also an exit for the sheep: "He calls his own sheep by name and leads them out" (10:3). The door metaphor is best understood when applying these same details to the next narrative, the raising of Lazarus. Jesus orders the rock in front of the tomb to be moved creating an opening, as if it were a door: "take away the stone" (11:41). Jesus calls out his name: "Lazarus, come out" (11:43). Lazarus hears the voice and exits of the tomb: "The dead man came out" (11:44). The good shepherd calls the sheep by its name and leads the sheep out the door of death.[270] It is as if the resuscitation of Lazarus acts as a dramatization of the door/shepherd metaphor in the previous chapter. I argue that the

---

[270] According to Christopher W. Skinner it seems highly plausible that a person, acting as a shepherd's assistance, managed the opening of the sheep pen in the absence of a door or gate. See his "'The Good Shepherd Lays Down His Life of the Sheep' (John 10:11, 15, 17): Questioning the Limits of a Johannine Metaphor," *CBQ* 80 (2018): 105, n.30. He concludes that Jesus acting as a door means that He is the "locus" of salvation as opposed to others who seek to kill and rob.

role of shepherd imagery prepares for what Jesus is about to do in the next chapter when he calls the dead man out of the tomb. So the gate represents death. Death is no longer permanent but now has a door that can be opened.

The author has done this before: first a teaching which is followed by a sign. The intended audience saw this pattern when Jesus declared that he is the light of the world before he cured the blind man with sight. Here, Jesus declares that he offers eternal life ("My sheep hear my voice, I know them and they follow me. I give them eternal life and they will never perish" 10:27-28) before he raises Lazarus from the dead. Death for those who believe is not an end; it is a door that allows passage to be reunited with divinity. When Jesus talks about his own death later in the Final Discourse, he tells his disciples that he is returning to the Father. He tells them that he will come back again "I will come again and will take you to myself, so that where I am, there you may be also" (14:3). That is why Jesus can say anyone who believes will never die. The Shepherd theme allows the author to introduce death with new meaning for the believer, that is, the one who hears Jesus' voice. The reader just saw what happened when the blind man heard and obeyed the voice of Jesus. Jesus is now the door (death with an exit). He calls the believer by name; the believer hears the voice and exits the door (passage from death), just as it plays out in the story of Lazarus. Jesus' tomb, likewise, has an open door with a body that had exited. For Jesus, death is now a door, a passage to a life with God: "Do not hold on to me, because I have not yet ascended to the Father" (20:17). Jesus gives us the image of a shepherd who lays down his life to save the sheep. At the door

He calls the sheep by name, and they leave through the door to follow him: "When he has brought out all his own, He goes ahead of them, and the sheep follow him because they know his voice" (10:4). The reader is introduced to another symbol for revelation: the voice of the shepherd. Once again, accepting truth is symbolized this time by one who listens and follows the good shepherd.

The voice unites the shepherd with the sheep. The good shepherd has unique characteristics unlike other shepherds of the first century. The good shepherd is different because he offers the sheep life. This is uncharacteristic of herdsmen who raise sheep for the slaughter. Many Palestinian flocks prepare for the feast of Passover. Once a year unblemished lambs are in high demand during the preparation of Passover. However, sheep in Jesus' flock do not die: "I give them eternal life, and they will never perish" (10:28).[271] The good shepherd does what no other shepherd will do. Instead, Jesus lays down his own life, which is also unusual in first-century practice.[272] Death is not just a risk; it is the very job of the good shepherd: "I lay down my life" (17, 18).[273] Note that the phrase is repeated for emphasis with the use of the "I am" sayings (10: 7, 11). That is why he will risk His life to protect the sheep from robbers and thieves—rejecters of the truth who answer with violence: "The good shepherd

---

[271] The phrase "they shall not be lost or perish (ου μη ἀπόλωνται) for eternity (10:28) presents a middle voice verb ἀπόλλυμι which can mean both to be lost and to be destroyed or perish. See BDAG, 95; A. Kretzer, "ἀπόλλυμι," EDNT 1. 135-36.

[272] Skinner, "Good Shepherd," 113.

[273] The expression "laying down one's life" (τὴν ψυχὴν αὐτοί τιθησιν) appears only in the Johannine literature (10:11, 17; 13:37-38; 15:13; 1 John 3:16).

lays down his life for the sheep" (10:11, cf. 15,17).[274] So the analogy of the good shepherd is not reflective of first-century practices but is intended to be Christological.

So, this passage presents a good shepherd (Revealer of the truth that produces eternal life), thieves and robbers (preventing revelation), yet there is a third category to consider: the hired hand: "The hired hand, who is not the shepherd and does not own the sheep, sees the wolf coming and leaves the sheep and runs away" (10:12). Fear of danger scatters the shepherd, forcing him to abandon the sheep to thieves and robbers. The gospel represents three possibilities with respect to revelation: One who offers revelation to others so they may have access to eternal life (the good shepherd), those who are violent and wish to destroy believers who reveal the truth (non-believers), and believers who will not offer revelation to others due to fear, (believers who fear).

Three responses after revelation:

1. Believer: One who reveals
2. Believer: One who fears
3. Non-Believer   One who is violent

Later we will see the disciples abandoning Christ in the garden. Also, Peter, who is inside the gate will deny Christ due to fear.

---

[274] Susan E. Hylen argues that the expression "lays down his life" means a mortal risk and not necessarily death. See "The Shepherd's Risk: Thinking Metaphorically with John's Gospel," *BibInt* 24 (2016): 382-99.

The focus, however, remains on the good shepherd throughout the discourse. Jesus says that the sheep listen only to the voice of the good shepherd and will not listen to other voices: "They will not follow a stranger, but they will run from him because they do not know the voice of strangers" (10:5). The analogy is obvious to the attentive reader. The good shepherd represents the Word sent by God to offer revelation: the means to eternal life. In the previous episode, the blind man refused to listen to the Pharisees or cave under the pressure of their threats. There were other voices, but he listened to the voice of truth. The others offered no proof for their claims and only by threats did they try to persuade. Therefore, the good shepherd narrative can be read in the light of the previous story of the man born blind as well as a preparation for the resuscitation of Lazarus in the next chapter. There, Jesus' voice at the open tomb will reflect the voice of the shepherd calling out his sheep at the gate. Other voices cried out in despair and argued against moving the tombstone. With both signs, Jesus can point to his work as the light of the world who is sent by the Father: "Even though you do not believe me, believe the works, so that you may know and understand that the Father is in me and I am in the Father" (10:38). The discourse is interrupted with a report of more division among the Jews. The revelation always presents a choice: some believe and some do not. So division typically follows testimony of truth. After stating that sheep listen to the voice of the shepherd, many Jews offer a reason not to listen: "He has a demon and is out of his mind" (10:20). Others authenticate Jesus words by way of his work with the blind man: "Can a demon open the eyes of the blind?" (10:21). The reference to the blind man confirms that the good shepherd analogy should be read with reference to the man born blind.[275] The shepherd theme carries over to the next feast that takes place three months later.

The Feast of Dedication

The Feast of Dedication celebrates the re-consecration and re-dedication of the Temple after the pagan altar was built over the altar of holocausts by Antiochus IV to offer a pig sacrifice to Zeus Olympios.[276] The desecration of the Temple (1 Macc 1:59; cf. Dan 11:31) led to a guerrilla-style revolt initiated by the priest Mattathias. Judas, his son, successfully defeated the Syrian forces in 164 BCE (see 1 Macc 2:1-4:35). The altar used for the sacrilegious offering was destroyed, the temple was rebuilt, and lamps were set up to represent the return of the presence of God in the Temple. The Temple was re-consecrated on the twenty-fifth of Chislev, 164 BCE and the event was commemorated each year as the celebration of the feast of the Dedication. In the story, to counter against the blasphemy, God had the temple consecrated or sanctified. The lamp was lit which was symbolic of God's presence. All of these features are well represented while Jesus is in the Temple during the feast. Again, God consecrates and sanctifies the Temple, his Son. The opponents think that Jesus is blaspheming but in reality, God is in the act sanctifying the Tem-

---

[275] Despite the fact that there is a shift in the imagery, there is no sudden change of audience or mention of a different feast or location from chapter 9 leading into chapter 10.

[276] The feast of Dedication is not a feast that required Jews to come to Jerusalem as other feasts did.

ple with His presence: "Do you say of him whom the Father consecrated and sent into the world, 'You are blaspheming'" (10:36). The reader knows that Jesus is the new Temple from chapter 2: "He was speaking of the temple of his body" (2:21). This new Temple, who is also the light of the world, represents the presence of God; "The Father and I are one" (10:29). Once again, like the feast of Booths, a celebration is transformed into Christological meaning. Jesus is now the new Temple that embodies the presence of God. The festival serves as an interpretive background for understanding the words of Jesus and the actions of his opponents. The opponents reject Jesus, causing him to leave the Temple.[277] This recalls the blasphemous service that forced the divine presence from the Temple that required its re-consecration at the time of the dedication. The opponents ironically force the divine presence out of the temple when they attempt to arrest Jesus for blasphemy. God instead consecrates as the place of divine presence: "the one whom the Father has consecrated and sent into the world."

Jesus retreats across the Jordan. John the Baptist is once again remembered: "Everything he said about the man is true" (10:41). The reader recalls the one statement that John made about Jesus: "Behold, the Lamb of God who takes away the sins of the world." After dealing with the opposition and those who reject God and remain in sin, the reader is subtly reminded of those words of John and that Jesus came to take away sins. The blasphemous behavior of the opponents is addressed by a new dedication. The Temple of "his

---

[277] "The more fully Jesus reveals himself, the more hostile opponents become." Caneday, "Revealing and Concealing," 763.

body" is sanctified and becomes the place of the Father. The reader will now see the metaphor of the shepherd as it plays out in the rising of Lazarus.

The Sleep of Lazarus

The purpose of this chapter is to exemplify the good shepherd discourse with a stage performance. In the last chapter, Jesus explains that he calls his own by name at the gate and the sheep come after him when they hear his voice. The shepherd offers eternal life to the sheep. In this chapter, Jesus calls Lazarus by name from the opening of the grave showing that those who hear his voice will go from death to life. The sheep needs a shepherd not only to provide life, but for protection from opponents who reject the word. Once again, a sign will force more Jews into a decision. Some will believe, while others will reject and become violent opponents to the Word. We will see how the chapter plays out the shepherd narrative.

The opening lines in chapter 11 devote more ink to Mary than Lazarus with a particular reference to the anointing of Jesus' feet, providing the reader with a peculiar perspective. Mary anoints Jesus to prepare for his death: "Leave her alone. She bought it so that she might keep it for the day of my burial" (12:7). This places the context of the entire scene in the light of Jesus' death. The listener has just heard how the good shepherd must lay down his life for the sheep. So there are numerous thematic links to the previous chapter. Thomas is somewhat aware of the serious implications of Jesus' return to Judea: "Let us go that we may die with him" (11:16). Although this statement appears crass, it allows the reader to note that if Lazarus is going to escape the tomb, there may be consequences. This is a job for the good shepherd. This is not the only time that Thomas appears emboldened. He is not present with the other disciples in the upper room on the evening of the Resurrection. The other disciples are locked in seclusion due to fear. Thomas, who is not with them, apparently has no cause for fear because he is moving about without the security of locked doors. One moment he is absent, another he is with them. He also challenges the claims of his associates: "I will not believe" (20:25). And Thomas is the only one who acknowledges Jesus as his Lord and God when He appears in His resurrected state, something the other apostles did not do. His bold character provides the author with characterization that challenges fear and intimidation, the obstacles that block one's belief in true testimony.

The story begins with a travel delay that allows time for the illness to spread, resulting in Lazarus's death and burial. Two dialogues take place when Jesus finally arrives at Bethany, one with each of the two sisters. Martha and Mary repeat the same line at each of their encounters with Jesus: "If you were here, my brother would not have died" (11:21, 32). They both believe, but Jesus needs to expand their expectations: "I am the resurrection and the life…do you believe this?" (11:26). Martha uses the title "Son of God" to respond to Jesus' words. Thomas also declares Jesus as God when he encounters the risen Lord (20:28). Death to life is recognized as a divine activity for both. Martha and Mary meet Jesus at different times. This allows the author to employ two conversation partners. The repetition in the dialogue provides the audience with proof. We have seen such replication with the consistent witness of the man born blind. When

Mary repeats the phrase, Jesus becomes upset with the mourning and weeping.

It is very likely that the evangelist here is presenting Jesus as one who is angry with the crowd. When Jesus first informed the disciples about Lazarus's death, he called it sleep: "Our friend Lazarus has fallen asleep." The disciples take this literally so Jesus has to qualify his words by telling them plainly "Lazarus is dead." Death is often described as sleep (cf., 1 Thes 4:13-16; 1 Cor 7:39;11:30' 15:6; 18, 51; Acts 7:60; 13:36; 2 Pet 3:4), yet death for Jesus, as the reader knows, is not permanent but temporary for the believer. For this reason, he describes death as something as transitory as sleep. After observing everyone's tears with deep emotion, "He said, 'Where have you laid him?' they said to him, 'Lord, come and see'" (11:34). There seems to be a role reversal from the dialogue that took place between Jesus' and John's two disciples: "They said to him, 'Where are you staying.' Jesus said to them 'come and see.'" Jesus is now asking the question "where" and the mourners respond using similar words that Jesus used when he responded to the two by saying "come and see." Jesus said, "'Where have you laid him?' they said to him, 'Lord, come and see'" (11:34). The irony is effective. When Jesus says "come and you will see," he brings others to the presence of God. When the Jews say "come and see," they bring him to a place of death, doom, and despair. Jesus offers life, the Jews death. The contrast is overwhelming and Jesus begins to weep.

The word that describes Jesus' "tears" (δακρύω) is different from the "crying" (κλαίω) of the Jews and Mary. Some interpret Jesus' tears as a shared sorrow with Mary, not a rebuke from a lack of faith.²⁷⁸ However, the sweep of emotion over Jesus is not the outcome of a loss of a friend as the Jews interpret it: "See how he loved him" (11:36).²⁷⁹ This has been an ongoing problem with the Jews. They never understand Jesus. Jesus' emotion is directed as a rebuke at the despair of the mourners who lost their friend.²⁸⁰ Jesus never lost his sleeping friend. The mourners, however, have lost their friend to the permanent state of death. Mary too has joined the Jews in their despair while they are standing beside the "resurrection and the life." The lack of faith is overwhelming and the disappointment

---

²⁷⁸ Schneiders, *John*, 181; Stephen S. Kim, "The Significance of Jesus' Raising Lazarus from the Dead in John 11," *Bibliotheca Sacra* 168 (2011): 59. Pino Di Luccio reads the cry of Jesus in the light of the Old Testament as an expression of indignation at the incompleteness of life and the yearning for full and fulfilled life in the presence of God. See his "La Risurrezione Di Lazzaro," *La Civilta Cattolica* 166 (2015): 22-23.

²⁷⁹ Joan S. Infante concludes from her investigation that the shedding of tears in John 11:35 is due to the frustration of Jesus at the lack of faith around Him. See "Jesus Shed Tears in Frustration: The Contribution of dakryō and klaiō to the Interpretation of John 11:35," *Pacifica* 27 (2014): 251-52. The article suggests that the lexical shift from κλαίω to δακρύω alerts the reader to differentiate the weeping of Jesus in 11:35 from the weeping of Mary and the Jews in Jn. 11:33.

²⁸⁰ Numerous scholars argue this including Barnabas Lindars who investigated the ambiguous verb ἐμβρῑμάομαι in 11:33 and concluded, "though the word often refers to anger or indignation, its primary application is to vehement expression of emotion, and can denote behaviour of this kind without necessarily revealing the inward state of the subject. Thus it is used in contexts where the action is a threat or verbal rebuke." "Rebuking the Spirit: A New Analysis of the Lazarus Story of John 11," *NTS* 38 (1992): 103. See also Francis Moloney, "The Faith of Martha and Mary: A Narrative Approach to John 11,17-40," *Bib* 75 (1994): 485.

and frustration affect Jesus in an emotional way. The crowd expresses doubt and even questions Jesus, as if death may be beyond his power: "Could not he who opened the eyes of the blind man have kept this man from dying?" (11:37). Again, death is not an end for the one who calls himself the resurrection and the life. Death is a door. The gatekeeper opens the door for the shepherd. The shepherd calls each by name and the sheep follow his voice. Jesus is connected to his sheep by his own voice.

The metaphor of the sheep is now about to be played out when Jesus asks that the stone be moved.[281] Even Martha fails to understand accepting only that her brother is decomposed beyond recognition: "Lord, already there is stench" (11:39). Both Mary and Martha claimed to believe, but they both fall short by believing in the permanence of death: one by weeping, the other by warning Jesus of rot and decay. Jesus offers a prayer of gratitude because this is the moment he will show the world God's greatness. The act of revelation produces glory. That is, the divine invisibility becomes visible by way of his action. He is the light of the world. Like the act of giving sight to the blind man from birth, no one has ever raised a dead man from the grave. Jesus shows them the Father: "Did I not tell you that if you believed, you will see the glory of God" (11:40). It is now clear that God sent the Word to create life, and he creates this everlasting life through the Word: "That they may believe that you sent me" (11:43). This passages explains the purpose of the sign that is about to unfold. Once again location is dominant. Jesus is from the

---

[281] For similar viewpoints, see also Kim, "Raising Lazarus," 59; Culpepper, *John*, 189.

Father. Here Jesus prays that the obstacle to faith be eliminated by providing knowledge of where Jesus is from. Once the crowd knows where Jesus is from, they will be able to believe and have access to everlasting life. They are about to see a preview of their own access to this life through the rising of Lazarus. Note the emphasis of the prayer is not Lazarus but, on the crowd, to believe.

The act, indeed, produced believers: "Many of the Jews therefore, who had come with Mary and had seen what Jesus did, believed in him" (11:45). It also generated resistance. Ironically, the price for one man to be freed from the grave is death. One corpse replaces another. The error on the part of the conspirators is that they believe that death will be permanent; however, for Jesus, it is passage to the Father. The conspirators have no control over Jesus' return to the Father. Jesus lays down his own life when the time is right, when the work is complete: "It is finished. Then he bowed his head and handed over his spirit" (19:30). God's glory (manifestation) and Jesus' death are understood in the light of the good shepherd narrative, where it was explained that the sheep lays down his life for the sheep. Lazarus regains his life, but the event immediately leads to a council of leaders where it is agreed that Jesus must die (11:47-53). In the Gospel, the hour (2:4; 7:7-8, 30; 8:20) has already been linked to Jesus when he is "lifted up" (3:14; 8:28).

We have seen numerous times that not knowing where Jesus is from is cause for disbelief. It is not that the non-believer lacks evidence. They are always given two witnesses: Himself and the Father. If they refuse to accept indisputable evidence, then their location is the "world" and their activity is violence. The world has two types of inhabitants: one is the person who has not been given revelation, the other is one who has been given revelation but refuses to accept the truth. Those who do not belong to the world are believers. Both believers and non-believers are empowered to act: one witnesses, the other destroys and kills. Yet even believers have two options, those who reveal the truth to others and those who fear. They fear violence from the non-believers. So, Jesus needs to provide a remedy for this new obstacle.

The Jews are afraid of the Romans: "Romans will come and destroy both our holy place and our nation" (11:48). This may be a fear to which the intended Christian audience in the first century could relate. There may have been fears that their confession of faith in Jesus would have them expelled from the synagogue, exposing them to the Roman authorities. To the Romans, Jesus was an executed enemy of the state and any group that circulated in his name would expose members as a possible rebellious threat against the Empire. It is very possible that the primitive church had to deal with fear among its members. There is no way to verify this from the text or other historical sources. Still, scholars believe that this may be behind some of the treatment of fear in the Gospel, such as the disciples hiding in the upper room before the resurrected Christ appeared and the reaction of the parents of the man born blind who feared expulsion from the synagogue. In any case, fear is an obstacle that prevents people from accepting Jesus and confessing his divine origin. Jesus' popularity after Lazarus' resuscitation presents new concerns among the leaders of the Jewish people.

Caiaphas offers a compelling reason to move forward with the plan to have Jesus killed. His sinister rejection of Jesus is benignly masked by expressing his love for the nation: "It is better for you to have one man die for the people than to have the whole nation destroyed" (11:50). Caiaphas and the other plotters never consider Jesus as a martyr for the nation, as if his death will bring about the unification of the dispersed children of God. Jesus always brought about division among the Jews, never union: "Again the Jews were divided because of these words" (10:19); "and they were divided" (9:16); "So there was a division in the crowd because of him" (7:43). Union is only possible among believers. "But also on behalf of those who will believe in me through their word, that they may all be one. As you, Father are in me and I am in you" (17:20-21). The comment that Caiaphas is a prophet is a statement that the author does not mean literally. The final line at 11:53 puts his prophetic posturing in proper context: "so from that day on they planned to put him to death." Plotting the destruction of a prophet is not the work of a prophet. Caiaphas and the conspirators stand in the same tradition as the prophet killers of the past. This time, however, they are scheming the execution of the Son of God. Note that the term "children of God" is used in the commentary to defend Caiaphas' prophetic words. It is the same expression that is used in the prologue. Caiaphas wants to destroy the "Word." On one hand, Caiaphas wants to sacrifice Jesus to save the Jewish nation; on the other hand, Jesus wants to sacrifice himself so God is known by all.[282] Yet, according to the prologue, without the Word, "children of God" have no access to eternal life. In 11:52, the phrase "children of God" refers to the chosen people, but it remains an empty title if deprived of the

---

[282] See Heil, "High Priest," 731, 34.

"Word." The ironic tongue-in-cheek commentary on Caiaphas's prophecy underscores the absurdity of placing the plot in a favorable light. As if one can destroy the "Word," and the children of God will remain united. Jesus came to create children of God by revealing truth. Those who believe in His revelation are transformed. It is not by rejecting Jesus but accepting him and believing in Him that the children of God are saved. Later the Jews will choose a rebel against the Romans, Barabbas, over Jesus, underscoring their lack of concern to save the "children of God" from a possible Roman threat. Rather, without the Word, there are no children of God, as the prologue guaranteed.

It is now the Passover when the Jews are gathered together in place. As Jesus distances himself, the chapter appropriately ends with the Jews collectively puzzling over "where" Jesus is.

Mary and Judas

As preparations of the Passover are underway and the plotters gather in Jerusalem, Jesus dines with Lazarus and his two sisters, Mary and Martha. There are numerous parallels between chapters 11 and 12. Both name Bethany, Lazarus, Mary and Martha 11:1; 12:1; both mention the anointing of Jesus by Mary (11:2; 12:3); both describe scent/odor with stench (11:30) and with fragrance of the ointment (12:3); both involve Pharisees (11:47-48; 12:19); both discuss belief in Jesus (11:48; 12:11); both highlight one character ("But one [εἷς] of them, Caiaphas," 11:49-50; "But Judas Iscariot, one [εἷς]

Part 2: The Books of Signs (Section II: Non-Believers) 217

of his disciples," 12:4-5); and both deliberate on a plot to put Jesus to death (11:53; 12:10).[283]

Earlier, Mary's weeping at her brother's tomb was emotionally offensive to Jesus; here, she rebounds with her generous anointing. One notes that she anoints the feet (not the head) depriving the deed of any messianic significance. The text explains the gesture as a burial ritual, not a confirmation about the kingship of Jesus. At Lazarus's tomb, Martha mentioned that there will be a stench if they remove the stone. Mary, in contrast, fills the room with perfume.[284] Dominika A. Kurek-Chomycz argues that John's unique focus on the aroma of the anointing as contrasted with the other Gospel traditions (i.e. Luke 7:36-50; Matthew 26:6-13; Mark 14:3-9), "is well integrated in his narrative and consistent with his interest in sense imagery."[285] The explicit olfactory reference to Jesus burial contrasts with Martha's statement about her brother's entombment. Mary is allowed to keep the ointment: "Leave her alone. She bought it so that she might keep it for the day of my burial" (12:7). According to Gerd Häfner Diana Pettinger and Stephan Witetschek, the meaning of the debated phrase: "let her keep it" refers not to the burial of Jesus but it is rather a reference to Mary who is the ideal disciple. That is why she is contrasted with Judas the anti-disciple, who wants to take

---

[283] For a detailed discussion on the parallels between chapter 11 and 12, see Lyle Eslinger, "Judas Game: The Biology of Combat in The Gospel of John," *JSNT* (2000): 45-73.

[284] John 12:3 is the only place in the New Testament where there is a reference to the scent (οσμή) of the oil outside of the Pauline corpus.

[285] See her, "The Fragrance of Her Perfume: The Significance of Sense Imagery in John's Account of the Anointing in Bethany, *Novum Testamentum* 52 (2010): 336.

away the valued ointment. She is instead allowed to keep the ointment.[286]

Both Mary and Jesus attend to feet in preparation for his death. He will wash the feet of the disciples, but he will upgrade by using water packed with all its theological significance for revelation.

However laudable Mary's actions, she is upstaged by Judas. The reader, who already knows that he will betray Jesus (παραδίδω, 6:60, 71), is now presented as another plotter deep inside the sheepfold. They are everywhere, even hidden among his own followers. One recall's again the prologue, "and his own people did not accept him" (1:11). The previous discussion about the good shepherd provides interpretive background here. Both this and the shepherd account include thieves and death. The reader is given information about Judas. "He is a thief" (12:6). From the passage of the good shepherd, one is aware of the activities of thieves: "They do not enter the sheepfold by the gate but climb in by another way…to steal and kill and destroy" (10:1, 10). The gate represents Jesus, who gives his life for the sheep: "I am the gate" (10:9). The thief, rather, kills the sheep. The only way to be saved and to have life is to have access to the gate: "Whoever enters by me will be saved…I came that they may have life" (10:9, 10). Thieves refuse to use the gate because they want to steal and kill the sheep. Judas is the thief who steals as well as kills and destroys. The evil he plots is masked with intentions of helping the poor. Caiaphas, like Judas, hides his evil plan with intentions of saving others. Both plotters of Jesus' death want to deprive others of

---

[286] See their "Die Salbung Jesu durch Maria (Joh 12,1-8). *Biblische Notizen* 122 (2004): 101.

access (gate) to eternal life. One is inside the sheepfold while the other is outside. They will form a team and execute the plan. Judas will personally deliver Jesus into their hands, and Jesus will die.

Once again, John is a master with irony. Once Jesus makes revelation available to all, he will return to the Father. This is the movement of the Word that is expressed in the prologue. The Word leaves God to create, and then returns. The irony is that the evil plotters think they are putting an end to Jesus and revelation, but they are really setting up the finish line that complete the success of the mission.

So their plan completely foils. They cannot destroy the sheep because Jesus is a gate that allows passage from death to life. Jesus' death is not an end. It is a passage because his tomb will be empty with an open door where people will "come in and go out" (10:9). Simon Peter went into the tomb (20:6) …the other disciple also went into the tomb (20:8) …then the disciples returned to their homes" (20:10). The beloved disciple went in and came out of the tomb yet during the passage he became a believer: "he saw and believed" (20:8). He then left the tomb to go home. Earlier the beloved disciple was instructed to take the mother of Jesus into his home in order that the two witnesses form a family: "And from that hour the disciple took her into his own home" (19:27). On the cross, Jesus is the shepherd who gives his life for the sheep. He leads them to pastures where they have access to true food and drink (revelation) that will give them eternal life. Jesus' side is pierced and immediately blood and water flow, the two fluids of which he spoke that offer eternal life. The two witnesses represent the sheepfold. The empty tomb recalls Mary's anointing: "that she might keep it for the day of my burial."[287] A tomb that has an open gate allowing passage from death to life. The plot to kill Jesus fails because of the gate, to which the robber has no access.

The Passover is six days away. The creation motif that first appeared in the prologue has returned. In Genesis, God worked six days and rested on the seventh. Jesus has six days to work. He will die on the final day of preparation for the Passover. The day after his death will be the seventh when he will be reunited with the Father. The reader knows that Jesus will return to the Father from the Final Discourse to his disciples: "where I am going you cannot come…I am going to the Father" (13:33; 14:12). The Genesis reference puts the reader back in contact with the prologue that first announced the creation of children of God. One can see how intratextuality can provide an interpretive lens for understanding the complexity of metaphors and imagery.

---

[287] It is questionable whether Mary was cognisant of the burial implications of her gesture, and that Jesus upgraded her gratitude with a deeper meaning. Kurek-Chomycz claims that Mary foreknew the impending events, yet there is no explicit reference to this pronastication. 341. I disagree with Moloney who states "For the first time in the narrative, Jesus' proximate death is recognized. Mary is the first to accept that the illness and death of Lazarus will be the means by which the Son of God will be glorified (11.4)." See his "Can Everyone Be Wrong? A Reading of John 11.1-12.8," *NTS* 49 (2003): 525. Thomas implicitly suggests that death would be an outcome of Jesus' trip to Lazarus in 11:16.

The Welcome in Jerusalem

The next day Jesus enters Jerusalem. The day is full of activity. People are busy with Passover preparations and plots to destroy Jesus. He enters Jerusalem and meets the crowd, the same crowd that wanted to make Jesus a king after he gave them bread before the Passover. Now in preparation for the Passover, they call him king: "Blessed is the one who comes in the name of the Lord—the King of Israel" (12:13). The author quotes "'Do not be afraid, daughter of Zion'" (12:15). Two themes (king and fear) are joined together here: (1) fear which prevents belief, and (2) king, a role that will play an important part of the trial of Pilate as the author will use it to show where Jesus is from. His kingdom and power are not from this world but from above. The author of the Gospel once again underscores the conditions for unbelief. Both fear and not knowing Jesus' origin are the two obstacles that prevent one from accepting divine truth/revelation. Pilate will accept the fact that Jesus is a king but rejects him on account of his fear of the Jews. This passage prepares the reader for Jesus' trial.

News of Jesus' reputation is vastly spreading throughout the crowds that gather for the Passover because of the testimony of those who were present when Lazarus walked out of the tomb. Those who were hearing the testimony wanted to meet Jesus, including some Greeks.

Part 3

Book of Glory

(World Access to Revelation)

The Greeks Want to "See"

The purpose of this passage is to underscore the reason for Jesus' coming to Jerusalem to suffer and die. He will reveal God by offering eternal life for those who believe. In the hour of glory, Jesus will make revelation available to all, even to foreigners such as the Greeks who seek to see Jesus. Remember, Jesus revealed God by raising Lazarus, but there was a price: "So from that day on they planned to put him to death" (11:53). He revealed God, providing a reason for rejecters to have him killed. Once again the author demonstrates his skills with irony. The leaders want to kill Jesus precisely because he gave life. Ironically, on the cross he will die and offer life to all who believe: When I am lifted up, I will draw all to myself." In this passage the author connects the narrative of Lazarus' death to life with Jesus' death which gives Him passage back to the Father. Both serve to glorify the Father.

Greek worshipers wanted to see Jesus.[288] They approach Philip, who has a Greek name. Ironically, Philip is the disciple who is consistently ignorant of any matters that have to do with location: "where" issues. He thinks Jesus is from Nazareth, cannot identify where to get bread, and later he will not know the way to the Father. So, he teams up with Andrew, the one who asked Jesus "where" he stays. They both go to Jesus with the request from the Greeks. At

---

[288] The sequence of ideas in this section is very much disputed. For discussions on this topic see Johannes Beutler, "Greeks Come to See Jesus (John 12,20f)," *Bib* 71 (1990): 333-347. R. Bultmann, *Das Evangelium des Johannes* (KeK; Göttingen 1941), 321.

first, it seems that Jesus ignores their inquiry, but the author provides clues in Jesus' rejoinder that relates directly to the request. One has to make a few intratextual connections to understand the link.

Instead of affirming or denying the request, Jesus raises the issue of his glorification. Glory is making divine invisibility visible. One needs to keep in mind that the Greeks want to "see." In actuality, the glorification of Jesus will fulfill the request, exceeding their expectations.[289] The Greek verb "to see" (eidon) is often associated with the acceptance or rejection of Jesus (cf. 1;18, 33, 34, 39, 50, 51; 3:3, 11, 32, 36; 4:45; 5:37; 6:2, 36, 46; 8:38, 57; 9:37; 11:32, 40). Apparently, they will have their request honored because "The hour has come for the Son of Man to be glorified" (12:23). The text never clarifies whether the Greeks are Jews living in the diaspora or foreigners who come to the feast to worship. Whatever the case, Jesus' governing role as a shepherd is inclusive to a larger contingent. One recalls the good shepherd discourse: "I have other sheep that do not belong to this fold. I must bring them also, and they will listen to my voice. So there will be one flock, one shepherd" (10:16). The theme of death is once again raised, connecting the audience back to the previous passages that treat Jesus' death.

Jesus uses the grain analogy to illustrate how God becomes visible by bearing much fruit (12:24): "unless a grain of wheat falls into the earth and dies, it remains just a single grain; but if it dies, it bears much fruit" (12:24) The dying grain of wheat refers to Christ. When he is lifted up he will draw all people to himself (12:32). This includes

---

[289] See Johannes Beutler, "Greeks Come to See Jesus (John 12:20f)," *Bib* 71 (1990): 334.

the Greek visitors who have just enquired about seeing Jesus. One death produces life for all people (Greeks included), just as one seed dies and produces much fruit. God becomes visible (glorified) when the Word reveals and produces much fruit, a reference to believers who have access to eternal life. That is, Jesus' divinity is most visible when he realizes his full potential on the cross. There, his life will be transformed into a family of believers who will share eternal life with him. The text interprets Jesus' death as a source of life for many. When Jesus reveals, he offers the gift of truth that provides life. However, he also exposes himself to those who choose to reject this truth. Jesus now addresses this dilemma. Does he save his life or does he continue his work of revelation by his words and deeds? (12:27). The text presents a choice to either love one's own life or to hate one's own life. The logic is meaningful. Those who believe that death is permanent must defend their lives at all costs, while those who believe also know that they can sacrifice their life for the benefit of others because death is temporary: "Whoever hates his life will keep it for eternal life" (12:25). Those who "hate" their lives can testify to the truth without any fear of loss. Like Christ, they will bear much fruit and gain eternal life for many others who will become believers through their witness. Witnessing is a profitable venture with nothing to lose and everything to gain. Those who confess Christ expose themselves to opponents who have rejected the truth. Yet, Jesus uses his own glorification to embolden his followers to service. "Whoever serves me must follow me, and where I am, there will my servant be also. Whoever serves me, the Father will honor" (12:26).

Jesus' perception of death as a gate to life provides incentive for the believer. He has no intention of saving his own life: "what should

I say—'Father, save me from this hour?'" (12:27). The "hour" is significant. In 7:30 and 8:20, the term "hour" refers to Jesus' suffering and death. But beginning here in 12:23 the term refers to glory: "The hour has come when the Son of man must be glorified." So the kind of suffering and death Jesus will experience reveals (glorifies) God. This Passover preparation formally initiates the hour that the author has been anticipating throughout the text: his "hour" had not yet come (cf. 2:4; 7:6, 8, 30; 8:20). The "hour" means that divinity will be made visible—in other words, glorified. The prologue stated that no one had ever seen God (1:18). The world is about to see God through Jesus' (temporary) death. Jesus once again turns to the Father at this critical moment and prays that God will be glorified. A voice from heaven responds to the prayer: "I have glorified it, and I will glorify it again" (12:28). This is the first time in the Gospel that the Father and Son share the same vocal stage. The crowds can no longer say that Jesus speaks on his own for his own glory. He and the Father are audibly connected. The heavenly message authenticates Jesus' voice and the crowds can no longer dispute where Jesus is from: "This voice has come for your sake, not for mine." It is for their sake because they have proof that the divine revelation Jesus offers is authentic and therefore believable.

It is appropriate, in the hour of glory, to talk once again about the light coming into the world: "Walk while you have the light. If you walk in the darkness, you do not know where you are going" (12:35). Once again refusing to accept the word as light is synonymous with not knowing "where": "you do not know where you are going" (12:35). More indisputable proof of Jesus' origin. Truth (represented by light) is exposed. Jesus brings up the issue of light once again. Those who are exposed to the truth are to walk in the light so that they may become "children of the light."[290] The prologue suggests that becoming a child of God is not an act of God alone. It can only come about when one believes. Revelation is a gift, but one must accept the creative Word to become a child: "But to all who received him, who believed in his name, he gave power to become children of God: (1:12). Isaiah is now cited to confirm this passage of the prologue "Lord who has believed our message, and to whom has the arm of the Lord been revealed" (12:37). There are two references to Isaiah. The first (Isa 51:3) is a close citation of the Septuagint while the second (6:1-5) appears to be a loose translation of the Hebrew text. Both texts contrast two realities that come from divine glorification: the power of God will benefit the believers while those who refuse will be unable to see making them powerless. They will not be able to walk in the dark (12:35).

The Greeks went to Philip and requested to "see" Jesus. The request gives Jesus the opportunity to define the terms as to what "seeing" really means. That is, Jesus will reveal the truth so one will have

---

[290] The phrase "children of the light" is an expression that is used in both Jewish and classical literature. This phrase is shared by many sources. In columns 3 and 4 of the *Community Rule,* reference is made to a cosmic dualism between two powerful forces (angels) expressed in terms of a light/darkness paradigm. At the center of the struggle, humans are divided into "Sons of Light" and "Sons of Darkness." According to the rule, the master instructs and teaches all the "Sons of Light" (1QS 3:13). It is hard to know if the author has a specific source in mind such as the *Community Rule* or if it is drawn from a common pool of terminology that was popular in the first century.

access to God. In other words, Jesus makes God visible. Jesus declares once again that he is the light of the world: "I have come as light into the world." (12:46). And whoever sees Jesus will see the Father (12:44). Light is revelation that transforms believers into eternal life. He was sent into the world with a command: "I know that his commandment is eternal life" (12:50). The Greeks request is accepted and answered beyond their expectations. They will see God as the Son reveals him by dying on the cross.

Through death, Jesus completes his work: "It is finished" (19:30). The divine becomes visible as if light has overcome the darkness, recalling the beginning of creation. Children of God are produced. A family of believers, like Christ, will witness to the truth. Their lives may also be at risk and taken away, but they know that, by dying, they gain eternal life and offer that life to others. In this way, they produce much fruit. They become collaborators with the Word: "Where I am, there will my servant be also" (12:26). In the book of signs, chapters 1-12, the author of John carefully identified two groups: believers and non-believers. In the hour of glory, focus specifically on this new third group: believers who will not testify to the truth due to fear. Peter and Pilate will represent this class of people. We are introduced to this class of characters just before the treatment of the washing of the feet: "But because of the Pharisees they did not confess it, for fear they would be put out of the synagogue" (12:42). The Gospel needs to address this fear because it prevents believers from witnessing to others. The antidote to fear is love. It will be a central theme when Jesus gathers with his disciples before he dies.

Part 3: Book of Glory (World Access to Revelation) 231

Washing Feet (13:1-38)

Intratextuality can clarify difficult passages that have generated multiple interpretations such as the narrative of the washing of the feet. Scholars differ in their opinion of the significance of this passage.[291] Some argue the narrative is analogous to the Eucharistic institutions in the Synoptic Gospels.[292] Others see the gesture of a humble servant fulfilling a hospitality need.[293] Thus, Jesus' example should likewise inspire others to serve others. Still, others connect the action as a symbol of Jesus' love that will be fully expressed on

---

[291] On John 13, see F. F. Segovia, "John 13:1-20: The Footwashing in the Johannine Tradition," *ZNW* 13 (1982): 31-51; Francis J. Moloney, "The Structure and Message of John 13:1-38," *AusBR* 34 (1986): 1-16; J. A. du Rand, "Narcological Perspectives on John 13:1- 38," *Hervormde Teologiese Studies* 46 (1990): 367-89; John C. Thomas, *Footwashing in John 13 and the Johannine Community* (JSNTSup 61; Sheffield: JSOT, 1991), 16-17.

[292] Schneiders, *You May Believe*, 189; Brown, *John*, 558-59; Craig R. Koester, *Symbolism in the Fourth Gospel: Meaning, Mystery Community* (Minneapolis: Fortress, 1995), 115-18. See Dunn who counters this viewpoint: "It seems then that sacraments and ritual washings are far from John's mind in this passage." James D. G. Dunn, "The Washing of the Disciples' Feet in John 13: 1-20," *Zeitschrift für die neutestamentliche Wissenschaft und die Kunde der älteren Kirche* 61 (1970): 247-252.

[293] See Barrett, *John*, 363. James D. B. Dunn claims "In John 13:1-20 the theme is of humble loving service as exemplified supremely in Jesus' voluntary death on behalf of his own." He cites other NT examples of humble service (Phil 2:5; 1 Pet 2:21ff). See his "The Washing of the Disciples' Feet in John 13:1-20," *ZNW* 61 (1970): 249. There is no evidence in the Gospel that reflects a doctrine that advocates humble service.

the cross.²⁹⁴ Michaels suggests that it signifies the forgiveness of sin.²⁹⁵ Some see the gesture as a sacramental sign of baptism.²⁹⁶ Yet,

---

²⁹⁴A partial list would include C. K. Barrett, "A symbolic narrative ... which prefigures the crucifixion itself," *John,* 363; Georg Richter, "The evangelist argues that the death of the cross is integral to Jesus' role as Messiah, "Die Fusswaschung Joh 13, 1-20," *Münchener Theologische Zeitschrift* 16 (1965): 13. Brown states that "all this serves to relate the foot washing to the death of the Lord." See his *John,* 551. See also James D. G. Dunn who states that the washing, "depicts not only Christ's death but also the benefits which flow from his passion," "The Washing of the Disciples' Feet in John 13 1-20," *ZNW* 61 (1970), 249. By contrast compare C. H. Dodd, who relates the foot-washing scene to Phil, 2:6-11, and sees in it a "sign" of the incarnation—a κατάβασης. *The Interpretation of the Fourth Gospel* (Cambridge, 1953,) 401-02.

²⁹⁵ J. Ramsey Michaels, "By Water and Blood: Sin and Purification in John and First John," in *Dimensions of Baptism: Biblical and Theological Studies* (eds. S. E. Porter and A. R. Cross; JSNTSup 234; Sheffield: Sheffield Academic, 2002), 153 n. 22.

²⁹⁶ John does not give a satisfying explanation as to the "deeper" meaning behind the washing of the feet other than a few clues. The event is meant to be clouded in mystery: "You do not know now what I am doing" (13:7). It is obvious that John intended the foot washing to be a symbolic act which forces the reader to seek the deeper meaning. Arland J. Hultgren suggests that the foot washing is a symbolic act of eschatological hospitality. See "The Johannine Foot-Washing," *New Testament Studies* 28 (1982): 542. Others see the foot washing as distinctively a sacramental cleansing. See Martin Dibelius and Hans Conzelmann, *The Pastoral Epistles* (Hermeneia; Philadelphia: Fortress, 1972), 75. However, the symbolic action is intended to be a physical washing because Jesus tells Peter that he is already clean. There are no references in the Gospel to a baptism of repentance or a baptism of reconciliation that suggest a purity ritual. The role of John's baptism is revelatory: "I came baptizing with water for this reason, that he might be revealed to Israel" (1:31).

these interpretations do not have much text support outside of this passage. This is the first time in the Gospel where Jesus takes the role of a humble servant, and there is no systematic teaching of baptism aside from a few mentions about people who baptize. I seek to offer an interpretation that is more consistent with the Gospel theme.

I will argue that the passage reflects how Jesus, the divine Word, cleans the disciples with revelation/truth, enabling them to bear much fruit when they also share divine revelation with others. The gesture itself has something to do with Jesus' love for his disciples and death: "He loved them to the end" (13:1). Brown and others are correct for connecting the death of Jesus to the foot washing.[297] However, they do not go far enough as to why Jesus dies. Brown uses the synoptic Gospels as background, calling to mind the instruction to serve rather than rule and lord it over others. Jesus came to serve and give up His life as a ransom for many (Mark 10:42-45; Matt 20:26-28; Luke 22:24-26).[298] Yet, nowhere in the Gospel does Jesus appear as a suffering servant. I will argue that Jesus dies because He offered others eternal life through revelation. He dies because those who rejected the truth seek to end His life. That is, Jesus gives up his life because he testifies to the truth so that those who believe will have eternal life. The washing of the feet, I will argue, symbolizes the divine gift of revelation/truth even if it costs the testifier to die.

---

[297] Brown, *John*, 568-72; Mary L. Coloe, "Welcome into the Household of God: The Foot Washing in John 13," CBQ 66 (2004): 412.

[298] John does not present Jesus as a servant of God, nor is there any reference to humble service. Coloe, "Foot Washing," 415.

At this stage of the Gospel, the reader is well aware of the central role of revelation/truth. Prior to this passage, water always represents revelation. One recalls manifold texts which include water containers (the Jordan River, six purification water jars, Jacob's well, the Sheep pool, the pool of Siloam, the basin of water at the Last Supper, the Messianic heart, and the Sea of Galilee), all of which discuss people who testify to the truth. If water represents revelation, then the water that washes the feet of the disciples likewise has a connection with revelation. The water that washes their feet symbolizes the revealed word of Christ: "You have already been cleansed by the word that I have spoken to you" (15:3). I will argue that the meaning of the washing of the feet is related to revelation.

There are important terms in the first few versus of chapter 13—"hour," "Passover," "Judas," "love"–that provide the background for understanding the symbolism of the foot washing. First, the reader is reminded that it is still the preparation of the Passover (13:1). The last time the Passover was near, Jesus multiplied the loaves and the fish. This time, Jesus gathers with his disciples for another meal (13:2). At the last Passover mentioned in John 6, He showed them a sign as the bread that came down from heaven. Bread symbolizes the divine word which offers eternal life to those who receive it. This time Jesus gives them the Word symbolized as not bread, but as water. Next, Jesus' hour is described as the moment he returns to the Father: "Jesus, knew that his hour had come to depart from this world and go to the Father" (13:1). Jesus will already be dead when the Passover begins. At the time of the Passover, Jesus will be with the Father as predicted: "I am going to the Father" (16:17). Presumably, he will occupy the same place before he was sent: "who is at the bosom of the Father" (1:18). In the last Passover Jesus is sent as the bread (revelation) from the Father to give eternal life. In this Passover, Jesus returns to the Father just as he fulfills his work, which is to bring light (revelation) into the darkness—thus the hour of Glory. The reader is then informed that Judas had internal contact with a demon, leaving him compromised. There is only one report of a possession in John's Gospel which seems to underscore the severity of Judas' role (13.2, 27). He will turn against Jesus and betray him. The verb that is used in Greek to describe the betrayal is παραδίδω which means "to hand over" (13:2). It best expresses the rejection of Jesus and will be used often during the trial of Jesus. The last time Judas appeared Mary bathed the feet of Jesus with expensive oil. Jesus is now going to bath his disciples' feet with water. The link between the two texts is meaningful. Mary prepares Jesus for his burial, and Jesus loves them to the end (13:1). In contrast to Judas's heart, which is filled with rejection (παραδίδωμι), Jesus' heart has love. The verb "love" (ἀγαπάω) will be used to describe Him twelve times (13:1 [twice], 23, 34; 14: 15, 21, 31; 15:9, 12; 17:23; 19:26; 21:7) during the period of his trial, death, and resurrection. Prior to this, it is only used one time to describe Jesus: "Though Jesus loved Martha and her sister and Lazarus" (11:5). There is a noticeable shift in focus as the narrative gravitates to expressions of love. The term is also used when Jesus exhorts his disciple to love (9 times) in the same way he loves (13:34 [twice] 14:21 [twice], 23, 28; 15:9, 12, 17) and when he describes the Father 6 times (14:21, 23; 15:9; 17: 23, 24, 26).

    There are a number of parallels between this narrative and the prologue. Jesus' origin is stated (1:1; 13:1, 3), there is mention of his "own" (1:11; 13:1 ἴδιος), the term "world" is used (9, 10; 13:1), and a contrast is presented between light and darkness (1:5) and Jesus and the devil (13:1-2).[299]

Jesus is leaving for the Father which indicates a transition. The revealer of divine truth will pass his work over to the disciples: "The one who believes in me will also do the works that I do and, in fact, will do greater works than these, because I am going to the Father" (14:12). The washing of the feet represents a transition because he is "going to the Father": "So if I, your Lord and teacher, have washed your feet, you also ought to wash one another's feet" (13:14). What then is meant by washing feet?

After taking off his outer garment, He pours water into a basin. This is one of many water containers in the Gospel. So far, the reader has seen the Jordan River, six purification water jars, Jacob's well, the Sheep pool, and the pool of Siloam.

First century hearers of the Gospel may have been familiar with references to water containers from Jewish literature. Each Jewish citation that refers to "living water," makes reference to a water container. See the following texts:

> Thus says the LORD, for my people have committed two evils: they have forsaken me, the fountain of living water, and dug out cisterns for themselves, cracked cisterns that can hold no water (Jer:2:13).

---

[299] Jesus and the devil stand in sharp contrast. Jesus offers truth and light while the devil offers lies and death.

O hope of Israel! O LORD! All who forsake you shall be put to shame; those who turn away from you shall be recorded in the underworld, for they have forsaken the fountain of living water, the LORD. (Jer 17:13).

On that day living waters shall flow out from Jerusalem, half of them to the eastern sea and half of them to the western sea; it shall continue in summer as in winter. (Zech 13:3).

Wherever the river goes, every living creature that swarms will live, and there will be very many fish, once these waters reach there. It will become fresh; and everything will live where the river goes. (Ezek 47:9).

"So are all the men who entered into the New Covenant in the land of Damascus and yet turned backward and acted treacherously and departed from the spring of living waters" (CDC 9:28).

The well is the Law, and they who dug it are the penitents of Israel who went forth out of the land of Judah and sojourned in the Land of Damascus (CDC 8:6). With joy you will draw water from the wells (belly[300]) of salvation.

---

[300] Some versions of the LXX read "belly" instead of "fountain." See Marcus, "Rivers of Living Water," 328-30.

There are numerous references that link living water to water containers such as a cistern (Jer 2:13), a fountain (Jer 17:13; 14:27; 16:22, Psa 36:9), a river (Ezek 47:9), a well (CD 3:16; CDC 9b:28; 8:6), and a belly (Isaiah 12:3 LXX). Pooled together, these texts yield a list of water containers that is strikingly close to the list of water vessels in John's Gospel: a river (1:28), jars (2:6), a well (4:6), a pool (9;7), basin (13:5), and the Messianic side (19:34). Likewise, John links water containers with his two references to "living water": "Sir, you have no bucket, and the well is deep. Where do you get that living water?" (4:11), and "Out of the belly shall flow rivers of living water" (7:38). If John is tapping into ancient Jewish tradition here and associating water contains with living water, then what is the role of living water?

If we turn first to Jewish writings we find numerous citations that confirm the role of "moving water" as an action that purifies. According to Jewish texts, the most basic and fundamental role of water was for ablution.[301] Here are a few examples:

> I will sprinkle clean water upon you, and you shall be clean from all your uncleanness, and from all your idols I will cleanse you (Ezek 36:25-26).

---

[301] Scholars show that there was an interest in washing practices during the first temple period (2 Sam. 11:2; 2 Kgs 5:10). There are also texts that refer to water initiations in the Priestly and Levitical circles (Lev. 8:6; Num. 8:7). In light of the entire Pentateuch, water washing seems to be an exclusive interest for the Priestly source in Leviticus.

> On that day a fountain shall be opened for the house of David and the inhabitants of Jerusalem, to cleanse them from sin and impurity (Zech 13:1).

> And thus you shall do to them, to cleanse them: sprinkle the water of expiation upon them, and let them go with a razor over all their body, and wash their clothes and cleanse themselves (Num 8:7).

Turning back to John's Gospel, one sees that the containers themselves represent purification. In John 3, John's baptism at the Jordan was the occasion of a clarification requested by his disciples concerning purification: "Now a discussion about purification (περὶ καθαρισμοῦ) arose between John's disciples and a Jew" (3:25). The six water jars at the wedding at Cana are described as καθαρισμός (purification, 2:6).[302] The waters of the pool of Siloam are used to wash (νίπτω) the eyes of the man born blind. Jacob's well is a source of water for domestic use. Both Jews and Samaritans considered living water as a means of purification.[303] The basin at the Last Supper washes the feet of the disciples, assuring Peter that they are clean (καθαρός, 13:10-11). However, in this Gospel, it appears that the water is not the purifying agent itself but a symbol: "You are clean, but not all" (13:11). It is the acceptance of Jesus' words that make His disciples pure: "You have already been cleansed (καθαρός) by the

---

[302] Hannah K. Harrington, "Washing in Water: Trajectories of Ritual Bathing in the Hebrew Bible and Second Temple Literature," *JSS* 54 (2009): 118.

[303] Koester, *Symbolism,* 168.

word that I have spoken to you" (15:3). Jesus clarifies further the purifying role of his words by then speaking of them as commandments: "If you keep my commandments, just as I have kept my Father's commandments… I am giving you these commands" (15:10, 17).

I mentioned in the introduction that outside sources can import meaning that was not intended by the author. Here is an example of this. Water plays a unique role with John. The process of purification has shifted from washing with water to accepting revelation.

All the witnesses to Christ in the Gospel, starting with John, have one essential connection with one another: water. Water is one of a number of symbols that represents revelation (i.e., spirit, bread from heaven, blood, etc.). The reader is already well informed that water has this meaning from the encounter with the Samaritan woman and the feast of Tabernacles. Revelation is the linchpin because it produces eternal life. Once again the prologue confirms this. As stated before, Jesus is at the bosom of the Father. He hears everything the Father says. The Father sends the Son who has knowledge of what the Father tells him in order to reveal the word of the Father to others. Likewise in the Gospel, the reader has seen how Jesus shares his knowledge of the Father, and how the believer now has access to eternal life. The believer knows what the Son says is truth because s/he knows that the Son is from God. Knowing "where" provides the believer with proof of the authenticity of His message. In essence, the truth is a gift from God that empowers the believer to become a child of God according to the prologue. The creative Word produces children by revelation. In the Gospel, water symbolizes the transformative power of revelation/truth. Truth transforms the believer just as the gift of living water gives eternal life. For one to receive this transformative gift, one has to receive the revelation of truth by a witness. I suggest that Jesus offers this transformative revelation as a witness to the truth symbolized by the bathing of the disciples' feet with water. Jesus loves them to the end; this means that the act of witnessing will cost him his life. The disciples are asked to do the same as Christ, which is to offer the truth to others as witnesses. They too may risk their lives for their testimony, but they will be giving the divine gift of eternal life to others.[304] In other words, the washing of the feet is a ceremony that produces future witnesses to the truth after the Son has returned to the Father. Offering divine truth to others is the ultimate act of love, sacrificing oneself so that others may have eternal life. This is what Jesus does when he dies on the cross. He offers his life to reveal the Father: "That you also may believe" (19:35).

Water is intricately connected to the empowerment to witness about Jesus. That is because the witness always seems to have access to water. John the Baptist, who was sent to "baptize with water"—three times the phrase is used (1:26, 31, 33)—is a witness because he saw the Holy Spirit descend upon the Son of God at Jesus' baptism (1:31-34). John subordinates his baptizing work to his mission of witnessing to Israel: "but I came baptizing with water for this reason, that he might be revealed to Israel" (1:31). Likewise, the Samaritan

---

[304] "The Gospel bears witness to a life-giving, life-changing Savior who invites others both to receive that life and to pass it on." Gorman, "Missional Gospel," 150.

woman at Jacob's Well testifies to the entire village (4:39). The paralytic at the Sheep Pool "proclaims" (ἀναγγέλλω, 5:15) the identity of his healer to the Pharisees. The blind man washes his eyes in the pool of Siloam, and he witnesses to diverse unbelieving groups (9:9-12; 15-17; 25-32). The beloved disciple will later witness that he saw water flowing from the side of Jesus (19:34-35). During the festival of Booths, Jesus speaks about the believer having access to water: "Let the one who believes in me drink, as the scripture has said,' Out of the believer's heart shall flow rivers of living water'" (7:38). Every witness, beginning with John, has some connection with water. This vital connection has symbolic significance that will give meaning to the washing of the feet narrative that begins the anticipated "hour" of Jesus. However, there are more factors that connect those who witness to the truth in addition to water: obedience, humility, and the knowledge of "where" Jesus is from. All the witnesses in the Gospel have in common a pattern of behaviors that are also reflected in the narrative of the washing of the feet. It is important to see these multiple similarities that indicate that the foot washing narrative reflects a commissioning of new witnesses in the absence of Jesus who returns to the Father. I will now examine these common factors: obedience, humility and knowledge of Jesus' origin, respectively.

Obedience

There is a striking consistency that weaves throughout this Gospel. Witnesses who have access to the water containers obey Jesus' words. For example, John the Baptist describes his relationship with the bridegroom as that of a "friend" (φίλος, 3:29), calling to mind

Jesus' definition of friendship: "You are my friends (φίλοι) if you do what I command you" (15:14).[305] John accomplished the work that he was sent/commanded to do. John, who described himself as a friend, fulfills the requirement of friendship by accomplishing the will of God. Also, according to Josephus, John's baptism presupposed a life of obedience to the law:

> In his (John the Baptizer) view this (leading righteous lives) was a necessary preliminary if baptism was to be acceptable to God. They must not employ it to gain pardon for whatever sins they committed, but as a consecration of the body implying that the soul was already thoroughly cleansed by right behavior (*Antiquities* 18:117).[306]

"Do what I command you" is a phrase that also successfully describes the servants at the wedding: "Do whatever he tells you" (2:5). Water management for the servants will come at a cost and will test their obedience to "do whatever he says." Considering the scarcity

---

[305] Jesus' discourse with his disciples on friendship in John 15 includes joy. Joy and friendship with Jesus go together: "I have said these things to you so that my joy (χαρά) may be in you, and that your joy (χαρά) may be complete" (15:11). That is why John describes his friendship with the bridegroom in terms of joy: "rejoices (χαρά) greatly at the bridegroom's voice" (4:29).

[306] James H Charlesworth, "John the Baptizer and Qumran Barriers in Light of the Rule of the Community," in *The Provo International Conference on the Dead Sea Scrolls: Technological Innovations, New Texts, and Reformulated Issues*. (ed. Donald W. Parry and Eugene Ulrich; Boston: Brill, 1999), 357-58.

of water sources in Palestine, the limited rain supply required the digging of wells and the construction of cisterns and pools to collect the runoff water during the rainy season.[307] Filling stone water jars in Palestine was no small task. Two and three measures each, at nine gallons a measure, averages to about eighteen to twenty-seven gallons per jar.[308] The weight of each jar could be as much as 200 pounds. Then, add another 1,500 pounds of water to fill the six jars with water to the brim.[309] Such a labor intensive job, while serving guests at a wedding, was quite a demand—not the most welcome chore if one was busy with the burden of table service. Then there was the risk of approaching the headwaiter with a sample of the water, especially if the servants did not know it had been changed to wine. It certainly would not be the first prank devised by a mother and son team. One can recall Rebecca tricking Isaac so that Esau's blessing would fall on the younger son Jacob (Gen 27). The request for the servants, "Do whatever he says," is not going to be so easy. Yet, their obedience to Jesus' word resulted in much gain: "and his disciples believed in him" (2:11). Like the servants of Cana, the Samaritan woman also encounters the threat of difficulty in her encounter with a Jewish man. Yet, despite the years of bad blood between Jews and Samaritans, she obeys the Jewish man's words: "Go, call ... and come back" (4:16).

---

[307] Gerald Klingbeil, "Water," in *The New Interpreters Dictionary of the Bible* (ed. Katharine Sakenfeld; Nashville: Abingdon, 2009), 5:819.

[308] Ernst Haenchen, *A Commentary on the Gospel of John: Chapters 1-6* (trans. Robert W. Funk; Philadelphia: Fortress, 1980), 173.

[309] Ibid.

The man born blind likewise obeys Jesus.[310] Obedience becomes part of the blind man's testimony: "He told me to wash; I washed at the pool of Siloam" (9:11).[311] The blind man accepted the water and earth mixture on his eyes. The washing of the feet is another occasion for obedience for Peter. Finally, Jesus obeys the Father. Jesus reveals that the Father gives him the words which he obediently speaks: "The Father who sent me has himself given me a commandment about what to say and what to speak. And I know that his commandment is eternal life. What I speak, therefore, I speak just as the Father has told me" (12:49-50). Obedience is a requirement for those who will become witnesses to the truth.

Humility

Those mentioned above all share the quality of humility. John the Baptist describes his relationship with the "Word" as a servant: "I am not worthy to untie the thong of his sandal."[312] The job of untying sandal straps was delegated to the lowest among the class of

---

[310] The term water is not used in the narrative of the Man Born Blind (John 9). However, it has an important role in the event. Ng, *Water*, 64.

[311] The church fathers almost unanimously interpret the washing in the pool as a Christian baptism. L. Sciberras, *Water in the Gospel of St. John According to the Greek Fathers and Writers of the Church*, (Thesis for the licentiate, Studium Biblicum Fanciscanum, Jerusalem, 1975), 80-88.

[312] The passage is cited in all four gospels and Acts (Mark 1:8; Luke 3:16; Matt 3:11; John 1:27; and Acts 8:25). There are a few word variations between the Evangelists. John and Acts use the term ἄξιος, and John's sandal is singular.

servants and slaves.[313] In the Babylonian Talmud, Rabbi Joshua ben Levi writes: "All services which a slave does for his master a pupil should do for his teacher, with the exception of undoing his shoes" (b. *Ketub.* 96a).[314] Hebrew slaves were even exempt. John would have to lower himself below the status of a slave.[315] The servants at a wedding, the Samaritan woman ("for Jews have no dealings with Samaritans," 4:9), the man born blind ("Rabbi, who sinned, this man or his parents, that he was born blind?" 9:2), are considered to be the marginalized and from the lower levels of society. Finally, Jesus takes the role of a humble person when He washes the feet of the disciples.

Knowing Jesus Origin

"The word 'where' is a *leitmotif.*"[316] Knowing "where" (πόθεν, 2:9; 3:8; 7:27; 9:29, 30; 19:9) indicates origin, which is essential for validating revelation. The reader has already seen a number of references throughout the Gospel emphasizing this point: "Where does this man intend to go that we will not find him?" (7:35); "Where do you stay?" (1:38); "Where is he?" (7:10); "Where did you get to know me?" (1:48); "Where are you from?" (19:9); "Where are you going?" (13:36); "Where do I get this water?" (4:11). Every witness is able to answer the question "Where?" John the Baptist claims that he has a

---

[313] Moloney, *John,* 57.

[314] Quoted from Francis Moloney, *The Gospel of Mark: A Commentary* (Peabody, MA: Hendrickson, 2002), 35.

[315] Robert A. Guelich, *Mark 1-8:26* (WBC 34A; Dallas: Word, 1989), 24.

[316] Schneiders states: "To know where Jesus comes from is to know *who* he is." See her "You May Believe," 161.

special kind of knowledge: "The one who sent me to baptize with water said to me, 'He on whom you see the Spirit descend and remain is the one who baptizes with the Holy Spirit.' And I myself have seen and have testified that this is the Son of God" (1:33-34). Twice, John indicated that he "did not know him" (1:31, 33),[317] supporting the claim that his knowledge was received from above. Information from above is given to John. The emphasis is not on the communication itself but on from where the report came. After all, he was sent from above: "He whom God has sent speaks the words of God" (3:34). Even John's disciples know what question is most important to ask: "Where do you stay?" (1:38). John knows the answer to the question "where" because he previously stated "I myself have seen and have testified." J. A. Kowalski links all the water narratives with the revelation of the word of God. That is why the purpose of water baptism is "to reveal Jesus by John's witness."[318]

The mother of Jesus knows "where" to get the "good" wine. When the bridegroom tasted the water made wine the text states that "they did not know where (πόθεν) it came from" (2:9). The servants know from where the wine came. The Samaritan woman first asks Jesus: "Where do you get that living water?" (9:11). Later, she indi-

---

[317] There are a number of repetitions in the John the Baptist narrative. There are two sets of sent representatives (1:19, 24,) as well as a number of phrase doublets: "They questioned him further" (1:21, 25), "Look, the Lamb of God" (1:29, 36) "I myself did not recognize him" (1:32, 33). John 1:15 and 1:30 are the same. Boismard puts out the theory that there were two introductions to Jesus and a final redactor included both. Boismard, "Bapteme a Cana," 39-44.

[318] Kowalski, *Water and Spirit*, 72.

cates that she knows the answered by leaving her water jar with Jesus. The blind man likewise knows "where" Jesus is from. In this narrative, the neighbors ask the "where" question (9:12). The blind man initially does not know. Yet at the end, he schools the Pharisees: "Here is an astonishing thing. You do not know where he comes from, and yet he opened my eyes...If this man were not from God, he could do nothing" At the scene of the dinner with his disciples, Jesus knows where his place is with the Father: "Jesus knew that his hour had come to depart from this world and go to the Father" (13:1).

Christ at the foot washing shares striking similarities with the Baptist and the other witnesses in the Gospel. The newly commissioned witnesses, the disciples, will also be required to be humble, obey, and know "where." The initiation rite with the water basin transforms the disciples into those who are humble: "So if I, your Lord and Teacher, have washed your feet, you also ought to wash one another's feet" (13:14). Obedience is also required of the disciples. They are to provide revelation/word to others. The washing of others feet is symbolic of offering others transforming "water" (witness) that will provide them with eternal life. The new witnesses are also required to know where.

Peter inquires: "Lord, where (ποῦ) are you going?" (13:36). It is a question that will always be answered for the witness: "Where I am going, you cannot follow me now; but you will follow afterward" (13:36). Thomas asks: "Lord, we do not know where you are going. How can we know the way?" (14:5). Again, Jesus provides the answer for his witness: "I am the way, and the truth, and the life" (14:6). The need to know "where" is a vocational requirement. "Where" is a location that is known by the true witness. There is a consistent pattern that connects the witnesses with water containers. The story of the washing of the feet fits nicely into this pattern.

Once the consistent pattern that weaves throughout the Gospel is acknowledge, one can look carefully at the details of the washing of the feet narrative.

The Details

Jesus begins by shedding his outer garment (τα ιμάτια), the one that will be divided by the soldiers: "He got up from the table, took off his outer robe" (τα ιμάτια, 13:4). Immediately we have a verbal link to Jesus' death on the cross, as well as with the good shepherd narrative. The two terms τίθημι ("put" or "place") and λαμβάνω ("take up") that are paired in the phrase "the good shepherd lays down (τίθημι) his life in order to take it back up again (λαμβάνω)" in 10:17-18 are found together in 13:4 when Jesus removes (τίθημι) his outer garment and takes (λαμβάνω) a towel and wraps it around his waist.[319]

We recall earlier how Jesus "loved them to the end" (13:1).[320] There is no explanation, no instructions, and no dialogue as Jesus

---

[319] See Skinner, "Good Shepherd," 110, n. 41.

[320] Heil sees a verbal connection with the passion narrative as well. "Jesus himself takes off his clothes (τα ιμάτια, 13:4) when he washes his disciples' feet in order for them to have a share (μέρος) with him (13:8)." By taking his clothes (τα ιμάτια) and making four shares (μέρη), one for each soldier (19:23), the Roman soldiers ironically anticipate Jesus' death offering a "share" in eternal life to individual persons—even those who are Gentiles. See his "High Priest," 741.

washes, until he comes to Peter. This is the opportunity for the evangelist to give the reader a few clues about the purpose of this unusual interruption at dinner. After Peter questions Jesus about the foot washings, Jesus tells Peter that he will not understand what is being done to him until later. Peter, however, goes on to assume that he understands what Jesus is doing by telling him not to wash his feet. Peter must think that Jesus' purpose is to provide his guests with clean feet. Thoughtful hosts would offer a basin of water for the guests to wash their feet before they entered the household.[321] Slaves would often times assist the guests with this task. This ancient practice of providing water for guests to wash their feet is well attested (Gen 18:4; 19:2; 24:32; 43:24; Judg 10:21; 1 Sam 25:41; 2 Sam 11:8).[322] Ancient hospitality is simple but tangibly practical. When Jesus saw that no one provided hospitality to the others, no water basin, no towel, no assistance, he assumed that role. At least, this is what Peter thinks is behind the washing.

It is possible that Peter finds scandal in the procedure because it does not follow Jewish protocol. The *Midrash Mekhilta* on Exod 21:2 explains that the master could not allow the slave to wash his feet.[323]

---

[321] There was a custom among hosts to provide water so quests could wash their feet before reclining at table. See Brown, *John*, 564.

[322] Usually the host provides the water in a basin and the guest washes his own feet. There is an exception. In 1 Sam 25:41, Abigail washes the feet of David's servant as a gesture of service. Jesus tells Simon the Pharisee that he did not offer him water to wash his feet (Luke 7:44). In 1 Tim 5:10, washing the feet of the saints is an act by widows as a sign of humility and hospitality.

[323] Barrett, *John*, 440.

Peter's refusal would have been an appropriate Jewish reaction. Apparently, he misunderstands Jesus' gesture as inappropriate behavior for a teacher.[324] Jesus' commissioning of his disciples as witnesses has precedence over simply crossing class lines or correcting a hospitable misstep. Peter doesn't realize the seriousness of his rejection. It makes sense why Jesus is so stern with a rebellious Peter who is about to refuse water (revelation). He warns Peter what will happen if one does not receive the Word that is symbolized by the water, "If I do not wash your feet you can have no part of me." In fact, Peter's three denials, predicted by Jesus (13:38), do not carry the same consequences as a refusal of allowing his feet to be washed: "You will have no part of me" (13:8). Jesus is giving Peter the revelatory word that cleanses, which will allow him to bear much fruit as later explained in the analogy of the vine and the branches: "Every branch that bears fruit he prunes to make it bear more fruit. You already have been cleansed by the word that I have spoken to you" (15:2-3). This passage verifies the role of the Word as a pruning agent that allows the branch to bear much fruit. Apart from the word, Peter is a branch without the vine, "You can have no part of Me." Refusing water from Jesus would be the same as rejecting the truth, since water symbolizes transformative revelation. Both water and the words of Jesus make a person clean. Thus, it makes sense that the washing of the disciples' feet represents the cleaning action of the divine word which empowers the disciples to produce believers.

---

[324] Carson, *John*, 1991; Andreas Kostenberger. *A Theology of John's Gospel and Letters* (BTNT; Grand Rapids: Zondervan, 2009).

Again, one can turn to first century Jewish thought from the Community Rule from the Essenes:[325] "He will cleanse him of all wicked deeds with the spirit of holiness; like purifying waters. He will shed upon him the spirit of truth (to cleanse him)…he shall plunge into the spirit of purification" (1QS 4:21). Spirit is identified with purity.[326] "Purify in his truth all the works of man, rooting out iniquity and purifying man's flesh of all impurity by a holy spirit" (1QS4:21-24).[327] Spirit is especially used as the symbolic link between purity and special knowledge. According to the Community Rule, the purification of the spirit gives access to special knowledge: "he shall plunge into the spirit of purification, that he may instruct the upright in the knowledge of the Most High" (1QS 4:22).[328] Purification from water anticipates revelation because purity and knowledge are related to the spirit: "A spirit of humility, patience, abundant charity, unending goodness, understanding, and intelligence; a spirit of might wisdom" (1QS 4:4). Purity is attributed to truth: "God will then purify every deed of man with his truth" (1QS

---

[325] The Essenes were a separatist Jewish sect, who were responsible for the Dead Sea Scrolls. The Community Rule provides the rules and regulations of this community and offers a glimpse into the diversity of Judaism at the time of Jesus.

[326] Rabbinic literature links obedience to God's laws to the Spirit: "He who undertakes a command in faith is worthy that the Holy Spirit rest on him" (Rabbi Acha, Lev.R 35:7). See Sjober, "πνεῦμα" *TDNT* 6:383.

[327] Cf. 1QS 3:6-8; 11:10-14; 7:6; 9:32, 12:12; 16:12; 17:20 all refer to purification rites which were signs of inward purity and renewal.

[328] Purification in water anticipated the work of the Spirit which brought about divine revelation and ushered in the eschatological expectations. Harrington, "Purification," 119.

4:19). In all of these texts, "spirit" is associated with divine knowledge. Here is another compelling text from the Damascus Rule:[329] "And through his Messiah, He shall make them know his holy spirit, and he is truth" (CDC 2:10).[330] Finally, the purified one has access to this special divine knowledge in order to instruct others: "he shall plunge into the spirit of purification, that he may instruct the upright in the knowledge of the Most High" (1QS 4:22).

There are other clues that suggest that the water used to wash the feet symbolize witnessing. One should note that Jesus washes the feet, not as a slave, but as a teacher, Lord, and master. In fact he notes his status twice: "You call me Teacher and lord…So if I, your Lord and Teacher, have washed your feet, you also ought to wash one another's feet" (13:13, 14).[331] Witnesses are teachers of the truth. The reference to sending also hints that the passage refers to witnessing:

---

[329] The Damascus Rule or the Book of the Covenant of Damascus(CD) was recovered from three of the Qumran caves which discusses Admonition (moral instruction, exhortation, and warning addressed to members of the sect) and Laws of the new covenant expressed through the Teacher of Righteousness

[330] Raymond Edward Brown, *The Dead Sea Scrolls and the New Testament* (London: Geoffrey Chapman Pub, 1972), 559.

[331] There are numerous examples of the conditional clause formula (εἰ + the indicative in the protasis). See 1:25; 3:12; 5:47; 7:4; 7:23; 9:33; 10:35; 10:37; 12:26; 13:14; 13:32; 14:7; 15:24; 18:8; 18:23b; 19:11; 14:11; 15:22; 8:39, 46; 9:25; 10:24; 11:12; 15:18; 15:20a and b; 18:23a; 20:15. According to Michael J. Thate, "any classification of the conditional construction must remain wide and flexible and allow for context to determine the precise relation of the protasis with the apodosis. See his "Conditionality in John's Gospel," 572.

whoever receives one whom I send receives me; and whoever receives me receives him who sent me" (13:20). Recall how John the Baptist and the Samaritan woman were sent to witness after receiving Jesus' testimony. Finally, Peter invites Jesus to wash his head and hands. Peter misunderstands again. The foot washing is symbolic; it is not about bathing: "One who has bathed does not need to wash" (13:10). Judas, who also had his feet washed, did not become clean: "Not all are clean" (13:11). The reason for his impurity is because of his rejection (παραδίδωμι) of Christ, who reveals the Father by word and deed. This is the second time Judas is described with this term (cf. 13:2).

Then, Jesus tells his disciples to wash each other's feet. If water represents revelation, then they too will make truth (water) available by becoming witnesses to the divine word whereby others may believe and have eternal life. Jesus then tells them to follow his example: "For I have set you an example, that you also should do as I have done to you." He models for them by testifying to the truth so that his disciples may believe.

Of course, His testimony generates resistance that will cost him his life on the cross: "he loved them to the end" (13:1). Death is the price for testifying, and his death on a cross is a result of a rejection of the truth which he made available to others so that they may have access to eternal life.[332] The disciples who are cleaned (pruned) by

---

[332] Herald Weiss states that "We must interpret the scene of the washing of the disciples' feet in the context of a community facing persecution and martyrdom." See his "Footwashing in the Johannine Community," *Novum Testamentum,* 21 (1979): 310. Ron Belsterling states: "As one reads

the word are now able to bear much fruit by offering eternal life to the others and witnessing to the truth. Bultmann uses 15:3 to interpret the foot washing as a symbol of the cleansing power of the word. He also indicates that the believer is cleaned by the revealer's word alone, not by sacramental means.[333] This interpretation of the washing of the feet is consistent with the Gospel narrative that has prepared the reader to recognize the symbolism of water as revelation/truth. All this complies with the prologue. The Word was sent to reveal. In the prologue, the Word was rejected by his own as it is exactly played out in Jesus' passion. Those who believe will become children of God. The washing of the feet expounds on this theme by using water as a symbol of revelation. Once again, coherence, as I suggest, allows the reader to tap into the basic theme of the Gospel as outlined in the prologue.

Why feet? Recall that Jesus' feet were anointed with a costly perfume, and Jesus interpreted the gesture as a preparation for His death. Now Jesus washes the feet of the disciples, preparing them to make the ultimate sacrifice when they offer revelation to others as Jesus does for them: "For I have set you an example, that you also should do as I have done to you" (13:15). The washing of the feet is a symbolic gesture of the words of revelation that empower the disciples to witnesses to others. With water as a symbol of revelation, the disciples have access to the truth that gives them eternal life.

---

the rest of John 13–18, it becomes obvious that Peter also did not immediately realize that following Jesus' example might cost him his life. See his "The Mentoring Approach of Jesus as Demonstrated in John 13," *Journal of Youth Ministry* 5 (2006): 85.

[333] See Brown's treatment of Bultmann in *John*, 677.

They also have the resource to offer this gift to others. The reader has absorbed enough information about water and witnesses to be able to understand the precise meaning of the washing of the feet. This interpretation is consistent with the message and purpose of the Gospel according to the prologue. The "hour" (ἦλθεν αὐτοῦ ἡ ὥρα, 13:1)[334] begins with pouring water into the basin that washes. The hour will end with flowing water from Jesus' pierced side. Water represents the Word which generates eternal life. The word washes the disciples clean so that they can produce much fruit—that is, believers—and the water that comes from the Messianic side makes available the living water which produces eternal life. All they need to do is do likewise, and reveal to others as Jesus revealed the truth to them.

Judas, the Beloved Disciple, and Peter

The audience is first introduced to the beloved disciple in chapter 13 at the news of a betrayer at the table. He provides contrast with Judas: two believers, one who rejects Jesus, the other witnesses about Jesus: "He has testified so that you also may believe" (19:35). Special attention is given to the precise location of the beloved disciple at table, and to him only. He reclines at the bosom (κόλπος) of Jesus, the same word that described Jesus' place with the Father in 1:18. Jesus has the truth because of his location next to the Father; he can hear everything the Father says from His bosom. The beloved disciple, likewise, has the truth because of his location. He is a receptor

---

[334] The hour had come (11:55-57; 12:20-24, 27-33). The hour had not yet come (2:4; 7:30; 8:20).

of the word. Judas, on the other hand, receives Satan: "Satan entered into him" (13:27). Satan represents the opposite of divine revelation: lies. This fulfills Jesus' prophecy "Did I not choose you, the twelve, yet one of you is a devil" (6:70). Judas has a devil because he rejects the truth and will be a part of the destruction of Jesus. Jesus does not cast the demon out—as he normally does in the Synoptics—but rather dismisses Judas so he can carry out the plan with the other plotters.[335] The disciple who could have received food (truth) that would give him eternal life is handed a "morsel" (13:26, 30) of perishable food.[336]

The beloved disciple and Judas are well contrasted: one symbolizes the believer who receives the truth and will testify. The other rejects Jesus, distancing himself from the "light (truth) of the world" and casting himself into the night: "he immediately went out. And it was night" (13:30). So there are two realities when the word is offered: One rejects, the other believes and testifies. Still, there is a third option, one who believes but does not testify due to fear. Peter who just insisted that he would not have his feet washed ("you will not wash my feet"), now wants to make the journey with Jesus, even if it means death. However, the reader is informed that Peter instead will deny Jesus three times. Peter represents the believer who fears.

---

[335] According to Andre van Oudtshoom, Jesus' death on the cross is portrayed as the exorcism of the devil from the whole world. See his "Where Have All the Demons Gone?: The Role and Place of the Devil in the Gospel of John," *Neot* 51 (2017): 80.

[336] Moloney maintains that "Jesus' meal with his fragile disciples and his gift of the morsel still has hints of the Johannine Community's Eucharistic theology and cult." See "A Sacramental Reading of John 13:1-38," *CBQ* 53 (1991): 256.

When he has the opportunity to testify about Jesus, he will fail. Fear is the obstacle that prevents one from witnessing. The author presents three characters that represent three modes of reception of the word: one rejects the word, one believes the word but will not witness because of fear, and one believes and witnesses. The reader has already seen these three representations in the story of the man born blind. They will be exemplified again during the trial of Jesus by Jesus (the one who testifies), Pilate (the fearer), and the crowd (rejecters).

The Final Discourse (13:31–17:26)

The final discourse is greatly disputed among scholars as to how to explain the numerous repetitions, seeming contradictions, and unusual breaks in the narrative. For example, Jesus appears to depart in 14:30-31, yet continues to teach for three more chapters. In 13:36 Peter asks Jesus where he is going and in 16:5 he states: "Not one of you asks me, "Where are you going?" There appears to be no connection between the discussion of Jesus' departure and the allegory of the vine and the branches that follows. Jesus repeats several things throughout the discourse: he is going away (14:28; 16:4-33), the disciple should avoid being troubled (14:1; 16:6), the Paraclete is a gift from God (14:15-17; 16:7-11), he himself will no longer able to speak (14:30; 16:12), he will return to the disciples (14:18; 16:22), the son is glorified (13:31-32; 17;1-5), his disciples should love one another (13:34-35; 15:12-13, 17), and one should have courage (14:27; 16:33). He also repeats the following phrases: "On that day" (14:20; 16:23), "I have said this to you" (14:25; 1625), "I am going to the Father"

(14:12; 16:28). Many have agreed that the unit is a varied collection of texts, but there is no consensus as to where they came from or how they were compiled together.[337] I leave this analysis with other commentators. What is clearly evident is that someone brought them together in the order and manner they are found today. I will read the discourse as a singular unit. The repetitions are used by the final editor to tie sections of the discourse together. The speech, I will argue, is intended to make a transition from Jesus, who reveals God to others, to believers, who will be the next source of revelation in Jesus' absence.

To be witnesses like Jesus, the disciples will need to receive the truth from God as He did, and verify how their origin in God for the purpose of authenticating Divine revelation. In the discourse, the disciples are instructed by Christ to abide in God, receive the Spirit of Truth to guide them to all truth, to do what Jesus did, and produce much fruit because of the Word that is in them. They are also warned of rejecters who will resist the truth by resorting to violence, as they do with Christ. They do not speak the truth on their own because they have the Spirit, giving authenticity to their witness. They also have origin because they are sent by God, with whom they now abide by accepting Jesus' word with their obedience. All the factors that made Christ a true witness (origin, truth) are passed on to the disciples who will now witness in his absence. This describes the purpose of the final discourse. To argue this, I will first look at how these themes are repeated throughout the discourse.

---

[337] See Brown, *John*, 582-603 for a report on the various theories about the composition of the discourse.

There is a particular interest in Jesus' origin in the final discourse:

> "Simon Peter said to him, 'Lord, where are you going'" (13:36), "And you know the way to the place where I am going" (14:4), "Thomas said to him, 'Lord, we do not know where you are going. How can we know the way?'" and "show us the Father" (14:5), "I am going to the Father" (14:12), "On that day you will know that I am in my Father and you in me, and I in you" (14:20), "The word you hear is not mine, but is from the Father who sent me" (14:24), "Because you have loved me and have believed that I came from God" (16:27), "I am going to the Father" (13:33), "You have heard me say to you, I am going away, and I am coming to you" (14:28), "I am going to the Father and you will see me no longer" (16:10), "A little while longer, and you will no longer see me" (16:17), "Because I am going to the Father" (16:17), "I came from you; and they have believed that you sent me" (17:8), "that the world may believe that you sent me" (17:21), "that the world may know that you that you have sent me and have loved them even as you have loved me" (17:23) "Father, the world does not know you, but I know you; and these know that you have sent me" (17:25).

The discourse places the believers with God as their new place of origin:

"So that where I am you also may be" (14:3), "You know him because he abides with you and he will be in you" (14:17), "Those who love me will keep me word, and my Father will love them, and we will come to them and make our home with them" (14:23), "Abide in me as I abide in you" (15:4-5), "You do not belong to the world" (15;19), "Father, I desire that those also, whom you have given me, may be with me where I am, to see my glory, which you have given me because you loved me before the foundation of the world" (17:24), "They do not belong to the world (17:16), "You also are to testify because you have been with me from the beginning" (15:26-27).

The discourse discusses the separation between Jesus and the disciples:

"Where I am going, you cannot come" (13:33), "Where I am going, you cannot follow me now" (13:37), "the one who believes in me will do my works" (14:12), "I will not leave you orphans" (14:18), "it is to your advantage that I go away, for if I do not go away, the Advocate will not come to you; but if I go, I will send him to you" (16:7).

Believers are expected to obey with particular attention to the commandment of love:

"If you love me you will keep my commandments" (14:15), "They who have my commandments and keep them are those who love me; and those who love me will be loved by my Father and I will love them and reveal myself to them" (14:21), "Those who love me will keep my word" (14:23), "If you keep my commandments, you will abide in my love, just as I have kept my father's commandments and abide in his love" (15:10), "This is my commandment, that you love one another as I have loved you" (15:12), "I am giving you those commands so that you may love one another" (14:17).[338]

As Jesus obeys the Father ("The Father has commanded me, so that the world may know that I love the Father," 14:31). believers will receive the Advocate, the Spirit of Truth in the absence of Christ when He is reunited to the Father:

> "I will ask the Father, and he will give you another Advocate" (14:16), "The Advocate, the Holy Spirit, whom the Father will send in my name, will teach you everything and

---

[338] There has been a broadly accepted consensus that the Fourth Gospel contains no ethics, apart from brotherly love. "…for the "only rule [of the Johannine Jesus] is 'love one another,' and that rule is both vague in its application and narrowly circumscribed, being limited solely to those who are firmly within the Johannine circle. See Wayne A. Meeks, "The Ethics of the Fourth Evangelist," in *Exploring the Gospel of John. Essays in Honour of Dwight Moody Smith*. (eds. R. Alan Culpepper and C. Clifton Black; Louisville, Ky.: Westminster John Knox, 1996), 318-319. A counter position is offered by Richard Hays in *The Moral Vision of the New Testament: A Contemporary Introduction to New Testament Ethics* (San Francisco: Harper San Francisco, 1996). For further review of the question of ethics in John see Zimmermann, "Abundant and Abandoning," 31-53.

remind you of all that I have said to you" (14:26), "When the Advocate comes, whom I will send to you from the Father, the Spirit of truth who comes from the Father, he will testify on my behalf. You also are to testify because you have been with me from the beginning" (15:26-27). When the Spirit of Truth comes, he will guide you into all the truth; for he will not speak on his own, but will speak whatever he hears, and he will declare to you the things that are to come" (16:13).

They will suffer like Christ:

"If they persecuted me, they will persecute you; if they kept my word, they will keep yours also 15:20, In the world you face persecution. But take courage; I have conquered the world" (16:33), "They will put you out of the synagogues" (16:1).

There is also a reference to each of the ways people respond to revelation. They either reject the truth (sin), accept it and testify (joy), or accept the truth, but refuse to testify to it (fear):

Sin

"If I had not come and spoken to them, they would not have sin; but now they have no excuse for their sin" (15:22), "Whoever hates me hates my Father also" (15:23), "About sin, they do not believe in me" (16:9).

Fear

> "You will deny me" (13:38), "Do not be troubled" (14:1), "Do not let your hearts be troubled, and do not let them be afraid" (14:27).

And Joy:

> "I said these things to you so that my joy may be in you, and that your joy may be complete, (15:11), "But your pain will turn into joy" (16:20), "In the world so that they may have my joy made complete in themselves) (17:13).[339]

Next, I will show how these themes tie together in a cohesive theological message that reflects the prologue mission and the Gospel's agenda. When Judas leaves, Jesus begins to teach: "Now the son of Man has been glorified, and God has been glorified in him" (13:31). This is a reference to revelation. God was once invisible according to the prologue (1:18), and now God is visible: "Whoever sees me, sees the Father" (14:9). From this the "where" issue resurfaces: "Where I am going; you cannot come" (13:33). This statement refers to both his death and origin. First, the reader knows he is making an allusion to his death. Death for Jesus is passage to the Father. Jesus dies because he testifies to the truth, and His testimony will produce believers. So if death is not an end but a reunion with the

---

[339] Belief in Jesus leads to joy, but this joy is unique in that it is Jesus' own joy, given to those who believe in him.

Father, then Jesus loses nothing by dying; instead, He gains a family of believers: "behold your mother" (19:27). After telling the disciples that they cannot come where he is going, Jesus seems to change the subject by giving them a new commandant: "I give you a new commandment, that you love one another. Just as I have loved you, you also should love one another" (13:34). Death and love are both interrelated, so there has not been a shift of focus. Peter may have a sense that Jesus is going to die. He even makes reference to death: "I will lay down (τίθημι) my life for you" (13:37). This is not the first time the terms lay down (τίθημι) and life (ψυχή) are strung together to refer to death: "No one has greater love than this, to lay down (τίθημι) one's life (ψυχή) for one's friends" (15:13). In essence, Jesus questions Peter's ability to obey this new commandment: "Will you lay down (τίθημι) your life (ψυχή) for me?" (13:38). He then presses the issue forward by predicting that Peter will deny him three times (13:38).

If denial means refraining from witnessing to the truth, then laying down one's life by testifying to the truth is the concrete expression of love. Jesus will soon be absent and so he now commands the disciples to love as he loves. Jesus will need to replace Peter's fear with love, and He will do this in the last chapter when He asks Peter three times if he loves. This means that Peter will have to bring divine truth to others in Jesus' absence. One recalls the meaning of the water in the foot washing and the command to do for one another what Jesus did for the disciples. Everyone will know they are connected to Him when they love in the manner Jesus loves: "By this everyone will know that you are my disciples, if you have love for one another" (13:35).[340] The new commandment is revealed at the announcement of Jesus' departure to highlight Jesus' death as a consequence for revealing the Father. Love is not only related to death, but it is also tied to having one's origin in God, the necessary prerequisite if one offers authentic divine truth to others.

The statement "Where I am going; you cannot come" (13:33) also raises the issue of Jesus' origin. The reference to his going to the Father clarifies "where" Jesus is from. Note the frequency of this topic so early in the discourse:

> "Where I am going you cannot come" (13:33). "Simon Peter said to him, 'Lord, where are you going'" (13:36), "And you know the way to the place where I am going" (14:4), "Thomas said to him, '"Lord, we do not know where you are going. How can we know the way?"' and "show us the Father" (14:5), "I am going to the Father" (14:12), "On that day you will know that I am in my Father and you in me, and I in you" (14:20), "The word you hear is not mine, but is from the Father who sent me" (14:24).

Jesus now reveals that he must return to his origin, the Father.[341] It is appropriate that Jesus paints a picture of a home with many

---

[340] Jesus uses nineteen conditional expressions in his farewell discourse, most of which function rhetorically to structure his discourse. Brown, *John*, 693.

[341] Sending and returning are part of the creative action. So too, Jesus returns to the Father (13:1,3; 14:2-3, 12, 27-28; 16:28; 17:11) as the word

rooms. He must first go to his Father's house to prepare these rooms and return to them.³⁴² However, the disciples' image of a home in a far distant location raises another set of questions that are related to "where" Jesus is going: "How do we know the way…show us the Father" (14:5, 8). They did not remember what Jesus said after the wedding in Cana, that the Father's home is the body of Christ: "He was speaking of the temple of his body" (2:21). Of course they forgot; the disciples will not recall the reference until after the resurrection: "After he was raised from the dead, his disciples remembered that he had said this" (2:22). That is why Jesus tells them, "the Father who dwells in me…."

Jesus responds to Thomas's "where" question ("How can we know where," 14:5) by forging together three terms that refer to revelation: "way," "truth," and "life": "I am the way, the truth and the life" (14:6). The reader knows that divine truth leads to eternal life for those who believe. Jesus as the way refers to the fact that revelation is an invitation: "come and see" (1:39). That means it is a gift: "You did not choose me, but I chose you" (15:16). The "way," that is Jesus, represents the only access to the Father: "No one comes to the

---

returns to God as a part of the creative mission. According to the prologue dynamic, the return of the Word to its origin is equally important as the sending. In many places the Fourth Gospel depicts Jesus' death as a return to his Father. The death of Jesus has meaning as his return to his Father, signifying the completion of the divine mission.

³⁴² Jesus' return to the disciples is understood by Brown to be the parousia, he cites Matt 26:29, and claims that John himself alludes to it in 21:22 with the same verb "to come." See his *John*, 626. However, Jesus speaks about the gift of the Spirit that will unite them to God, the same way Jesus is united to the Father.

Father except through me" (14:6). Jesus provides access to the truth that provides believers with life. The house imagery is now understood as a place "where" Jesus is united with the Father. The extra rooms suggest that the disciples will also enjoy a union with the Father and the Son, indicating that they now have a place with God. In 14:23 Jesus reassures them again of their place with God: "the father will love them, and we will come to them and make our home with them" (14:23). In light of Jesus' comment about slaves who do not have a permanent place, the image of the rooms also implies that the disciples are there permanently by reason of their adoption into the household: "The slave does not have a permanent place in the household; the son has a place there forever" (8:35). Now that the believer has a place with God, s/he can offer authentic testimony as Christ did when the Jews questioned Jesus' legitimacy. Like Christ and John the Baptist, the believer can claim that they are from God. When they become witnesses like Jesus, they will have their origin in God, which will authenticate their revelation. From the prologue and down through the Gospel narrative, the issue of Christ's origin is vital to His testimony. Now that Jesus is returning to the Father, the issue of origin is addressed to the future witnesses. The prologue sheds light on how those who believe in the truth are empowered to become children of God. From this perspective, one can see why the author placed the Temple scene immediately after the wedding. Children of God are located with God in the home of Jesus' body. Jesus, however, questions the belief of the disciples: "Do you not believe that I am in the Father and the Father is in me" (14:10). He offers proof of his claim by reminding them that his words belong to the Father. The author continues to emphasis the need for forensic evidence. Legal testimony requires two witnesses. Otherwise it is one person's word against another: "The words that I say to you I do not speak on my own; but the Father who dwells in me does his works" (14:10).

The origin with God is further developed and emphasized when Jesus discusses the Spirit. The role of the Spirit fills a gap.[343] When Jesus leaves the disciples to return to the Father, the future witnesses will have a problem. If the disciples are sent into the world for the same reason Jesus was sent into the world, how will they legitimate their testimony?[344] Without Christ—the true Word in the world—how are the disciples going to witness without forensic proof? Jesus had the Father to legitimate his testimony. The disciples, in contrast, have no divine link to legitimate their claims without Jesus. Jesus' departure creates a void in the legal system. To remedy this, the Father, at the Son's request, will send an advocate whom Jesus calls "the Spirit of Truth" (14:17): "He will not speak on his own, but will speak only what he hears…because it is from me that he will receive what he will declare to you" (16:13-14). The role of the Spirit is forensic.[345] The word "Advocate" is a legal term. The Gospel never suggests that the role of the Holy Spirit is that of a defense attorney who protects the disciples from danger. The Spirit provides proof

---

[343] "The Spirit will continue Jesus' revelatory work in the world through the disciples." Culpepper, "Theology." 429.
[344] Brown, *John*, 746.
[345] Ibid., 698.

for the disciples when they testify.[346] The disciples will not be orphans who are left without legal support: "I will not leave you orphaned" (14:18).[347] They will have the Spirit of Truth to authenticate their testimony. The Advocate, the Spirit of Truth, fills the forensic vacuum in Jesus' absence.[348] John 16:8-11 introduces the Holy Spirit as a great advantage to the disciples, providing the forensic proof of the truth/revelation and exposing those who believe (righteous) and those who do not (sinners).[349]

During the feast of Tabernacle, the author of John explains that the believers will receive the Spirit: "Now he said this about the Spirit, which believers in him were to receive; for as yet there was no

---

[346] See Raymond E. Brown, "The Paraclete in the Fourth Gospel," *NTS* 13 (1967): 116.

[347] Bruce D. Woll describes the purpose of the discourse narrative as an aid to prepare the disciples with the absence of Jesus by filling in the void with a successor. In conclusion, 14:12-17 "are to be understood as setting forth a doctrine of succession based upon the departure of Christ. The investiture of the believer with authority to do the works of Jesus is promised, an authority defined in terms of intercessory powers and based upon the indwelling of the Paraclete, also conceived as a successor figure who takes the place of the departing 'first' Paraclete." See his "The Departure of 'The Way': The First Farewell Discourse in the Gospel of John," *JBL* 99 (1980): 232.

[348] The term paraclete is found in 14:16, 14:26, 15:26 and 16:7. The expression the Spirit of Truth is used in 14:17, 15:26 and 16:13.

[349] See John Aloisi, who concludes that "according to this passage, the Spirit convicts the world of sin because people do not believe in Christ." "The Paraclete's Ministry of Conviction: Another Look at John 16:8-11," *JET* 47 (2004): 68. For more analysis on this text see D. A. "Carson. "The Function of the Paraclete in John 16:7-11," *BL* 98 (1979): 547-566.

Part 3: Book of Glory (World Access to Revelation) 271

Spirit, because Jesus was not yet glorified" (7:39). The statement is a commentary on the passage of Scripture which revealed that living water (representing truth) will flow from the believer's heart. As discussed above, "water" represents revelation, which transforms its recipients into believers. According to Jesus, the believers have access to the truth (living water). In his discourse with the disciples, Jesus confirms the fulfillment of that Scripture passage: "This is the Spirit of Truth…You know him, because he abides with you, and he will be in you" (14:17). Now that the believer has the Spirit of Truth, it makes sense in retrospect how out of the "belly" of the believer, revelation (symbolized as living water) will flow. The reader already knows that children of God are born by water and spirit. One recalls Jesus' words to Nicodemus: "Very truly I tell you that no one can enter the kingdom of God without being born of water and Spirit" (3:5). Revelation/truth is inside of the believer because the Spirit of Truth and living water (truth/revelation) dwell within the believer. As the reader processes the information that was received from earlier texts, the words of Jesus at the final discourse are better understood. This interpretation also makes sense in light of the washing of the feet where Jesus cleans with water (revelation), so that they will clean (with revelation) one another. The cleaning metaphor means that the believers represent pruned branches that able to bear much fruit. If cleaning represents pruning a branch to bear fruit, then the application of the metaphor makes sense, as we will see in the next section of the discourse. Believers have access to the Word so that they can testify for others.

The True Vine (John 15)

The analogy of the vine and the branches further underscores the believers' origin in God.[350] If they are to testify to the truth in Jesus' absence, they will need to have their origin in God to authenticate their witness. Jesus just told the disciples that if they love him, the Father and Son will dwell in them (14:23). Many of the themes Jesus raised in the discourse are present in the metaphor of the vine and branches, such as love (13:34, 35; 15:10, 12), indwelling (14:17; 15:9-10), obedience (13:34; 14:15; 15:10), and Advocate (14:26; 15:26). The passage will once again confirm that the believer expresses love by fulfilling their obligation to offer the Word to others because they are required "to bear much fruit," symbolic language meaning that they will produce many believers.[351] If the believer does not "bear fruit" they are cut off from the life source of the Word. In other words, if believers refuse to testify, they no longer have connections to eternal life. One remembers Jesus' words to Peter when he refused to have his feet washed, "You will have no part of me" (13:8). Here at 15:3 the author clarifies the role of the Word: The Word cleans the branches, allowing them to produce fruit. Metaphorically speaking, this means that the divine word provides life for them and is a source of life for others.

---

[350] The vine is the Jewish symbol for God's people: "Thus says the Lord of hosts: Glean thoroughly as a vine the remnant of Israel; (Jer 6:9) they shall blossom like the vine, their fragrance shall be like the wine of Lebanon (Hos 14:7)."

[351] Outside of the discourse on the vine, the metaphorical expression "bear fruit" is only found in 4:36 and 12:24.

Believers are given everything they need to successfully bear much fruit. They are supplied with the word that Christ gives them ("I have made known to you everything that I have heard from my Father," 15:15), origin ("abide in me as I abide in you," 15:4), the Spirit which authenticates their witness ("I will send to you from the Father, the Spirit of Truth who comes from the father, he will testify on my behalf," 15:26), and a model to follow ("I have set you an example," 13:15).[352] They have all the necessary components to be able to witness when Christ returns to the Father "I appointed you to go and bear fruit" (15:16). Now that Christ has provided everything to

---

[352] John 15:15 states that Jesus revealed everything to the disciples, which conflicts with the later statement in 16:12 that they will be given more information: "I still have many things to say to you, but you cannot bear them now." Either they know everything or they do not. Some scholars see a contradiction in this. The reader knows that the believer has consistently been a work in progress. This is true with the woman at the well who promoted Jesus' status as the narrative pressed forward, calling him a "Jew," (4:9) "Sir," (11) "Prophet," (19) and "Messiah" (29). The same is true with the man born blind, who refers to Jesus as a "prophet" (9:17), then "from God" (33) and "Lord" (38). Nicodemus is also one who progresses slowly. He does not understand Jesus, yet he appears publicly to bury Jesus in the tomb. The disciples, like Nicodemus, meet Jesus at night and fail to comprehend while Jesus teaches. Signs of progress are made after the resurrection: Thomas exclaims "my Lord and my God." And the beloved disciple in Jesus' tomb sees and believes. "Seeing" is always in stages and the text once again reflects this progression. Jesus will remedy this by giving the Spirit of Truth: "When the Spirit of truth comes, he will guide you into all the truth; for he will not speak on his own, but will speak whatever he hears, and he will declare to you the things that are to come" (16:13).

them in order to testify, he can say that they have received everything the Father has given him: "go and bear fruit, fruit that will last, so that the Father will give you whatever you ask him in my name" (15:16). In return for all of the gifts that God gives them, they are instructed not to fear (14:27) and to love. I will treat each of these two requirements as they are treated in the discourse.

Joy (acceptance) versus Sin (rejection)

Just after the prediction that Peter will deny Jesus three times—a behavior pattern generated by fear—Jesus tells the disciples not to be troubled. Now that Judas is gone, Jesus is specifically addressing believers who have accepted the truth. After the believer chooses to accept truth/revelation, they still need to choose whether they will testify or not. This is a question of love or fear. The downfall for most believers is fear, not rejection. Fear stops believers from witnessing. Jesus will deal with rejecters after he is arrested and tried. For now, he addresses believers and their major shortcoming. After the commissioning of the disciples to be witnesses to the truth, symbolized by the foot washing, Jesus must now offer advice on how to overcome fear. The counterpart to fear is love. Love encourages witnessing, fear discourages it. In 14:27 Jesus again addresses fear: "Do not let your hearts be troubled, and do not let them be afraid" (14:27). Love testifies; one who fears does not. Peter will demonstrate fear by denying Jesus three times when the opportunity arose for him to bear witness to the truth. The other disciples will likewise choose fear because they will be scattered: "The hour is coming, indeed it has come, when you will be scattered, each one to his home, and you will leave me alone" (16:32). If the believer succumbs to fear and does not give witness, then no fruit is produced and the branch is cut away according to the vine analogy. The fear is real because the threats from those who reject the truth are real. Only Jesus can offer a remedy to cure fear. Later, the disciples will be gathered in the upper room in fear (20:19). Jesus reveals himself and fear turns into rejoicing: "Then the disciples rejoiced when they saw the Lord" (20:20). Joy is the welcome reception of revelation.

The verb "rejoice" (χαίρω) is employed 9 times throughout the gospel (3:29; 4:36; 8:56; 11:15; 14:28; 16:20, 22; 19:3; 20:20). The Baptist has joy in hearing the voice of Jesus (3:29), the sower and the reaper rejoice over the fruit that is gathered for eternal life, joy as a result of receiving the word (4:36). Abraham rejoiced at seeing Jesus' day (8:56), Jesus rejoices that disciples will believe after Lazarus is raised (9:15). Disciples should rejoice to have Jesus go to the Father because they now continue the mission of Jesus bearing fruit (offering eternal life to others through revelation, 14:28).[353] Jesus rejoices so that the disciples may believe; seeing Jesus after his death causes believers to rejoice (16:22; 20:20). Joy is associated with revelation. Since Judas's question on why Jesus reveals Himself to disciples and not to the world in 14:22, Jesus has been speaking without interruptions. All the voices of the disciples have been silenced, similar to the Nicodemus narrative when the dialogue turned into a monologue. It is here that Jesus shifts his focus to joy. Jesus uses the analogy of childbearing as an example: "When her child is born, she no longer

---

[353] Brown, *John*, 680.

remembers the anguish because of the joy of having brought a human being into the world" (16:21).[354] The image is curious because this is not the first time the reader has encountered the topic of giving birth. The prologue discussed producing children of God (1:12) and Jesus discusses birth from above to Nicodemus in 3:3-7. Joy is once again seen by the reader as an effect of revelation, which produces children of God according to the prologue.

The opposite of joy (reception of truth) is sin (rejection of truth). The word "sin" is used 17 times in the Gospel. Jesus defines sin as the rejection of revelation: "about sin, because they do not believe in me" (16:9, 9:41); those who reject the truth claim that others sin when they speak the truth (8:34; 9:34); sin follows revelation: "If I had not come and spoken to them, they would not have sin; but now they have no excuse for their sin" (15:22); Jesus takes away sin (1;29); death and sin are synonymous (8:21, 24); sin represents slavery (8:34); those who reject Jesus by handing Him over are sinners: "The one who handed me over to you is guilty of a greater sin" (19:11); Jesus will prove the world wrong about sin (16:8). Disciples, who are believers in divine revelation, have the power to forgive and retain

---

[354] Calum M. Carmichael describes joy as a reference to marriage and bearing children. "An analysis of the Baptist's reference to his joy now that the bridegroom is around bears out the underlying concern with birth as well as with marriage. In fact, the reference has not been properly assessed. It has to do not just with the general joy associated with a marriage, but with the particular joy of the married couple's prospect of giving birth. It is this prospect that prompts the Baptist to say that Jesus, the bridegroom, must increase." See Carmichael's "Marriage and the Samaritan Woman," *NTS* 26 (1980): 333.

sin (20:21). Sin is, therefore, the conscious rejection of divine revelation. Jesus' persecution and death result from plotters and rejecters who do not know the source of his testimony because they do not know "where" Jesus is from. Those who believe do: "The Father himself loves you, because you have loved me and have believed that I came from God" (16:27). However, there is no excuse for anyone to reject the truth because Jesus offers forensic evidence that he is from God, which authenticates his testimony. The reason the rejecters sin is by a willful rejection of proven testimony (9:34). The reader recalls the Pharisees' rejection of the man who was born blind and his authentic testimony. They cast a blind eye to the indisputable evidence and for that reason, they have sinned: "Your sin remains" (9:41). Sin is again defined as a rejection of revelation: "If I had not come and spoken to them, they would not have sin; but now they have no excuse for their sin" (15:22). It is logical to conclude that rejecting the messenger is a rejection of the sender: "Indeed, an hour is coming when those who kill you will think that by doing so they are offering worship to God" (16:2). If sin is the rejection of truth, then the new commandment aptly addresses sin with love.

If the disciple is called to love as Jesus loves, who laid down his life by testifying, then the commandment to love means to testify to the truth. Love is not a genetic term without a specific significance. The connection between love and testimony is suggested a number of times in the Gospel. God expresses his love for the world by sending his son, "so that anyone who believes in him may not perish but may have eternal life" (3:16). John the Baptist, who testified, described himself as a friend of the bridegroom (3:29). The believers' testimony may lead to death, but it will be the greatest expression of love because they will be offering eternal life to others, just as Jesus offers eternal life with his testimony, a witness that cost him his life. The reader knows from an earlier account that the grain of wheat must die to bear much fruit (12:24). The only cause of death and persecution in the Gospel is that which generates opposition to those testifying. Death is the result of testifying to the truth, the ultimate expression of love because it generates eternal life. The dangers are real, and Jesus is upfront about them with his disciples. They will be hated (15:18), thrown out of synagogues (16:2), and be killed (16:2). The warnings are accompanied by examples of Jesus who likewise is hated, rejected, and will die. So, the text offers the disciples a model. It also anticipates the trial and death of Jesus. Jews will cast the believer out of the synagogue and expose them to Rome as enemies of the state just as they will hand Jesus over to Roman authority to be executed. They also have an example of one who loves, obeys, and hence, produces much fruit. Love, therefore, remedies the believers' Achilles heel: fear. Thus, they are commanded to love. Jesus mentions keeping commandments five times. He keeps his Father's commandments, and the disciples must keep Christ's commandments. No specific list of norms is given, but they are required to love: "This is my commandment, that you love one another as I have loved you" (15:12). Love defines the activity of witnessing because it offers others eternal life. Jesus will say that there is no greater love than to lay down one's life for one's friends (15:13). The author confirms this when he comments: "He loved them to the end" (13:1). The washing of the feet, as I argued above, symbolizes how the divine truth prepares one to bear much fruit. When Jesus loves, he gives eternal life by revealing truth. So, love should be seen as the act of witnessing to the truth which often results in suffering and/or death. They have the Word within them. They love by obeying the Word. They fulfill their obedience by revealing the Word to others.

Like a steady drumbeat, the message resonates with consistency. Intratextuality underscores the coherence of the message throughout the Gospel. It is a method that does not allow the narrative to be cut off from the mission of the prologue or the author's theological goals. The overall task of the reader is to remain engaged by processing what has been previously said and applying the data to interpret the collection of metaphors and symbols.[355] After teaching about love, the author composes yet another metaphor.

Death Wish: Jesus' Prayer before the Arrest

The disciples once again are silenced during Jesus' prayer to the Father. The passion narrative, which is about to begin, will be the divine answer to the prayer the reader is about to hear. Earlier, Jesus prayed to the Father in front of Lazarus's tomb. Its purpose was for the sake of the crowd so that they may believe: "That they may know

---

[355] Some contend that the allegory of the vine and the branches come from the Gnostics. See Bultmann, *John,* 407 S. Schulz, *Komposition und herkunft der johanneischen reden* (Stuttgart: Kohlhammer, 1960), 114-18. Others maintain John relied on OT and Jewish writings (Isa 5:1-7; 26:2-6 11:10-11,) where the vineyard typically symbolizes Israel. Some see a NT influence from Mark 12:1-11 and par. The vine and branches, like the image of the good shepherd, is different from other writings by identifying the vineyard to Christ as a source of life, not Israel. Also, the vineyard is depicted as a source of life, unlike anything found in OT and NT imagery. See Brown, *John,* 671.

so they will have eternal life" (11:42). The prayer was answered because Jesus raised Lazarus and many believed: "Many of the Jews therefore, who had come with Mary and had seen what Jesus did, believed in him" (11:45). In chapter 17, Jesus likewise prays so that others will believe. He begins by praying for visibility—i.e., glory. "That they may know (γινώσκω) you, the only true God, and Jesus Christ whom you have sent" (17:3). The mission of the prologue was to make known the one who was invisible (1:18). The word "know" (γινώσκω) is used seven times throughout John 17. In verse 23, Jesus prays that the "world may know (γινώσκω) that you have sent me." One recognizes the seriousness of this request because no one can believe unless they know "where" Jesus is from. Jesus' prayer takes place just before his arrest, trial, and death. The prayer effectively introduces the passion narrative because Jesus' death reveals the relationship between the Father and the Son, and makes God visible. The prayer anticipates this revelation: "That they may know." Up until this passage, revelation has been restricted to a cluster of groups and well defined locations. Now revelation is offered to all. When Jesus is raised up, He will be visible to all.

The focus of the prayer shifts to the believer. Jesus acknowledges the believers who will testify: "I ask not only on behalf of these, but also on behalf of those who will believe in me through their word" (17:20). One will recall the prayer when the beloved disciple testifies after Jesus' side is pierced: "He who saw this has testified so that you also may believe. His testimony is true, and he knows that he tells the truth" (19:35). The prayer also asks that eternal life be given to those who "know": "You have given him authority over all people, to give eternal life to all whom you have given him" (17:2). Eternal life is given to those who "know": "And this is eternal life, that they may know you, the only true God, and Jesus Christ whom you have sent" (17:3). Indeed, the passion narrative ends when blood and water flow from Jesus' pierced side. These are the elements that represent eternal life. Jesus' prayer is answered at death. The prayer, therefore, is used as an introduction to the passion narrative.

The prayer discusses the unity between the Father and the Son in terms of giving. The Father hands everything over to the Son ("everything you have given me is from you" 17:7) and Jesus hands everything over the Father ("All mine are yours, and yours are mine 17:10). Truth is the divine gift. The Word receives the truth from the Father according to the prologue and likewise, Jesus gives truth to believers: "The words that you gave to me I have given to them" (17:8). The believer is invited to the same reciprocity. Just as Jesus gave the word to the believers, they are to give the word to others. One recalls the vine and the branches' discourse. Jesus tells the disciples "I have made know to you everything that I have heard from my Father" (15:15). Because they have received "everything," they are now directed to bear fruit by revealing the word that was made known to them (15:16). The whole prayer is centered on the importance of knowing God by the Word. The Father gives words to the Son, the Son shares those words with his disciples, who are to communicate them to others. The sharing of revelation is the expression of love and unity: "I made your name known to them, and I will make it known, so that the love with which you have loved me may be in them and I in them" (17:20). Father, Son, and believers love by revealing divine truth, bringing about their unity: "I ask not only on behalf of these, but also on behalf of those who will believe in me through their word, that they may all be one. As you, Father, are in me and I am in you" (17:20-21). Love is obedience to Christ, who sends out the disciples with the word so that others can believe and have eternal life. Thus the Final Discourse concludes by addressing fear in the face of persecution: "Take courage; I have conquered the world" (17:33).

The Arrest: Jesus, Judas, and Peter

The author uses the narrative of Jesus' arrest to present the three responses we have seen so far to the revealed word: one rejects, one fears, and one offers eternal life to others. Jesus continues to be a model of one who is rejected, exposed to the Romans, and crucified. Yet, he is also providing eternal life to others. In other words, when one offers divine truth to another, this action is identified in the Gospel as the definition of love. When someone has to make the ultimate sacrifice and suffer consequences for making divine truth available to another, then that person has loved to the end. Peter, who has accepted the truth ("to whom shall we go, you have the words of everlasting life" [6:68]), fears and denies that he knows Jesus. He squanders an opportunity to testify to others. Finally, Judas rejects the Word by his betrayal. The representation of these three models of behavior will later shift in the next chapter where Peter and Judas will be replaced. The crowd will take Judas's role as the rejecters, and Pilate after finding the truth about Jesus, succumbs to fear because of the crowd and hands Jesus over to be crucified.

In the opening scene, Judas arrives in the garden with soldiers and police who are armed for war against the provider of peace.

Later, one will hear Jesus' first words to the disciples after the resurrection: "Peace be with you" (20:19). The reader is told that the plotters, (chief priests and Pharisees) who are not present, are behind the whole affair: "Judas brought a detachment of soldiers together with police from the chief priests and the Pharisees" (18:3). Judas is entirely irrelevant because Jesus voluntarily stepped forward. There is no need for a kiss to identify Jesus as in the synoptic narratives. He presents himself because he is about to reveal the Father's love to the world: "God so loved the world that he gave his only Son" (3:16). Three times Jesus identifies himself as "I am" (18:5, 6, 8). We have seen the "I am" statement accompanied by various characterizations throughout John's gospel: "I am the bread of life" (6:48); "I am the good shepherd" (10:14); "I am the resurrection and the life" (11:25); "I am the vine" (1:5:1). Other times it is not qualified: "When you have lifted up the Son of man, then you will know that I am he" (8:28); "truly, truly, I say to you, before Abraham was, I am" (8:58); "I tell you this now, before it takes place, that when it does take place you man believe that I am" (13:19). The fact that there is such a heavy concentration of the "I am" formula in the space of a few verses underscores its significance. Meanwhile, Judas stands there and does nothing in this scene. Jesus, in contrast to Judas, is the one in command. He makes the first move, asks questions, and gives out orders. Judas fades out of the drama as an insignificant bystander with no role. Neither will he hold great status among the plotters. They did not even need him. Still, his rejection goes on record: "Judas, who betrayed him" (18:5). The Gospel describes Judas eight times with this term (i.e., 6:64, 71, 12:4, 13:2, 11, 21, 18:2, 5). The soldiers appear incompetent despite the fact that they are armed to the teeth. They cannot even stand before Jesus without falling backward (18:6). It is almost comical, as if the keystone cops and Fredo from the Godfather team up to take out Jack Reacher. The characterization of the scene is brilliant because it highlights the majestic role of the revealer.

Then Peter comes on the scene. There is absolutely no reason to attack a slave. Jesus is in command and he orders the soldiers to let his disciples go free. The soldiers cannot be taken seriously. There is no reason to take a defensive stand. Nevertheless, Peter draws a sword and almost misses the slave, grazing the side of his face and cutting his ear. Jesus has to tell Peter to stay out of this, demonstrating again that Jesus is in control: "Knowing all that was to happen to him" (18:4).[356] The deceptive plot of Judas and the sword of Peter have no control over Jesus.[357] His authority will continue throughout the trial until his death. Peter's violent action is disturbing. He is specifically named here. Note in other synoptic gospels, the identity of the violence is unknown. Why is Peter identified here? It shows that he is leaning toward behaviors that are characteristic of non-

---

[356] "Moreover, when Peter's desperate act is interpreted in light of Jesus' statement "If my kingdom were of this world, my subjects would fight" (18:36), it becomes clear that the author of the Fourth Gospel has leveled a devastating indictment at Peter." Arthur J. Droge, "The Status of Peter in the Fourth Gospel: A Note on John 18:10-11," *JBL* 109 (1990): 311.

[357] "The most notable feature about Jesus in the Fourth Gospel, however, is the control He displayed over all persons and situations. Neither the treachery or stubbornness of His own disciples, nor the ridicule or machinations of the 'the Jews,' could hinder him from moving toward His 'hour' on the cross." See Tom Thatcher, Jesus, Judas, and Peter: Character by Contrast in the Fourth Gospel," *BSac* 153 (1996): 448.

believers. Fear can lead to rejection and violence. We will see this more clearly with Pilate.

The soldiers bring Jesus before Annas. He is the father-in-law of Caiaphas, the high priest. There is no Jewish trial, and there is no mention that Jesus meets the high priest. Still, there will be two trials, like in the Synoptics. By eliminating the Jewish trial, the author can add a second trial which runs concurrently with Pilate's trial. Jesus rules over his own trial as the judge of the world who does not condemn the world. Both Pilate and Jesus will succeed at getting to the truth. Pilate puts Jesus on trial and finds him innocent as well as a king, while Jesus puts the rejecters on trial and finds them guilty of sin (rejection of revelation).

Just the mention of the high priest's name recalls that it was Caiaphas who counseled the Jews to have Jesus killed for the sake of the nation. The brains behind the plot remain absent when Jesus faces and testifies to lesser authority. Note here that both plot leaders, Judas and Caiaphas have no significance other than their names have been mentioned. These are the same two who masked their evil plan with good intent. Their insignificance highlights Jesus as the force and leader of the narrative, who will use this moment to reveal God to the world. Unbelievers who use violence to stop revelation will fail.

As Jesus is lead away, the narrative turns to Peter, who will face slaves and other underlings with no power of authority. There is restricted access around the high priest courtyard (αυλή, 18:15). One immediately recalls the sheepfold (αυλή) of the good shepherd (10:1,16). Another connection with the shepherd narrative is the word gate (θύρα). Jesus is the gate (θύρα). From the passage, one learns that the gatekeeper opens the gate for the shepherd who calls the sheep. They hear his voice and they follow the shepherd to feed in the pastures. In the final chapter, Jesus will tell Peter to feed the lambs, tend the sheep, and feed the sheep. So three times Jesus asks him to take care of the lambs and sheep in 21:17. As a shepherd, Peter will have the task to lead the sheep to feed. These terms connect the narrative of Peter's denial with the good shepherd discourse. One will need to keep this in mind while reading the events that take place in the high priest's courtyard.

The gate at the high priest's residence is well guarded. One of the disciples had connections with the high priest and was permitted inside while Peter waited: "Peter was standing outside at the gate. So the other disciple, who was known to the high priest, went out, spoke to the woman who guarded the gate (θύρα), and brought Peter in" (18:16). John Paul Heil describes the scene: "He remained standing before the gate (θύρα), a symbol of Jesus, who declared, "I am the gate (θύρα) of the sheep" (10:7). "I am the gate (θύρα); if anyone enters through me, he will be saved and will go in and come out and find pasture" (10:9).[358] After Jesus' arrest, however, Peter enters inside of the gate and does not lead the sheep to feed by offering the truth. In light of how Jesus was described as the gatekeeper in an earlier text, it is now ironic that the first denial comes after a woman

---

[358] Heil, "High Priest," 738. M. W. G. Stibbe also relates the sheepfold of the good shepherd to the courtyard of the high priest in *John as Storyteller: Narrative Criticism and the Fourth Gospel* (SNTSMS 73; Cambridge: Cambridge University Press, 1992) 102-4, 25. See also A. Bottino, "La metafora della porta (Gv 10,7.9)," *RivB* 39 (1991): 207-15.

is introduced as the gatekeeper. Instead of offering divine truth about Jesus, Peter fears and denies at the gate, a place where people are led to the truth. After the resurrection, Jesus will address his three-fold denial out of fear and remedy it by calling him to love three times: "do you love me" (21:15, 16, 17). He is to lead the sheep and feed them with food (divine truth) that will endure forever: "Feed my sheep" (21:17). The reader knows that true food offers eternal life and the way to give this gift is by witnessing to the truth. In this scene, Peter is about to deny rather than to witness.

After the first denial the scene shifts to Jesus, who stands before Annas. The text does not cite specific questions from Annas, but it does refer to broad categories: disciples and teachings. If Annas is looking for truth, he needs to have two witnesses. Truth needs to be authenticated. Jesus' suggestion to go to those who heard his teaching is proper procedure. The defendant is more astute on juridical matters than the former high priest. Jesus has used the legal standards to legitimate his claims by his association with the Father. Jesus' suggestion is rejected because the plotters already made up their minds and are not interested in gathering evidence. Jesus exposes them. The slap on the face by the police is a rejection of the truth: "If I have spoken rightly, why do you strike me" (18:23). The author places the blow at the center of the passage by using the chiastic form, a literary pattern which is used to highlight one particular feature:

A. Annas questions Jesus
    B. Jesus replies to Annas
        C. Reaction of the officer: the blow

B. Jesus replies to the officer

A. Annas sends Jesus to Caiaphas[359]

Again, Jesus is the one asking the questions (Why do you ask me...Why do you strike me), advancing juridical protocol, and exposing wrongdoing (rejecting truth). Jesus continues to conduct himself as he did in the garden before the soldiers, the police, and Judas. Annas has Jesus restrained and sent to Caiaphas (18:24).

There is no report of what happens between the time of Jesus' meeting with Annas and his first encounter with Pilate. The narrative returns instead to Peter. Inside the courtyard, a group asks Peter about his status with Jesus: is he a disciple? The drama intensifies from one person to now many people. He denies it with the same answer he gave the woman: "I am not" (18:25). The "I am not" contrasts with Jesus' testimony to the soldiers in the garden: "I am." The third inquiry offers the biggest challenge when a slave of the high priest and relative of the injured Malchus appears. He was also at the garden at the time of the arrest and he would have noticed Peter because he stood out among the other disciples with his sword-wielding attack and his reprimand from Jesus. The slave asks Peter if he was the one with Jesus. Peter had reason to fear him due to his connections with the chief priest and the injured slave.[360] The text reports that Peter denied it, without quoting his response. The cock crowed confirming Jesus' prediction: "before the cock crows, you

---

[359] De la Potterie, *Hour of Jesus*, 46.

[360] "Indeed, the Johannine Peter would have had special reason to fear, once inside the *aulē* of the high priest." See Brown, *Death of the Messiah*, 2.593.

will deny me three times" (13:38). Judas exemplifies the rejecter who hands Jesus over (παραδίδωμι) to the soldiers. Peter models the believer who refuses to witness to the truth, demonstrating the paralysis which comes from fear.[361] Jesus will now represent one who testifies to the truth so that many may believe. Unlike Peter who stood before a slave, Jesus is about to appear before the governor representing Rome.

The Trials: The Crowd, Pilate, and Jesus

This passage, like the last one, also represents three responses to truth/revelation. The crowd rejects the Word, Pilate believes Jesus but fears the people, and Jesus continues to witness to the truth. The synoptic Gospels report a Jewish trial, but this has been omitted in the fourth Gospel. Still, I will argue that there are actually two trials in this Gospel that run concurrently. Pilate puts Jesus on trial and he finds truth ("So you are a king"). Jesus puts the rejecters on trial and he finds truth ("those who handed me over have the greater sin").[362] The reader needs to remember Jesus' authoritative demeanor. In the

---

[361] Peter also contrast with the beloved disciple who will witness at the crucifixion: "He who saw this has testified so that you also may believe" (19:35). Maurits Sabbe describes the denial in this way. "Since the main purpose of his narrative was theological, in describing the relationship between Peter and the Beloved Disciple." See his "The Denial of Peter in the Gospel of John," *Louvain Studies* 20 (1995): 239.

[362] Jesus is true judge. See Carroll and Green, *Death of Jesus,* 82-109; Jerome H. Neyrey, *The Gospel of John* (Cambridge: Cambridge University Press, 2007), 313.

garden, He asks questions, controls the conversation, and makes demands. With Pilate, he likewise asks questions, controls the conversation, and makes demands. He talks when he wants, but he also remains silent. Those handing Jesus over, in comparison, appear weak, desperate, and outmatched. Their only response to him is violence.[363] The soldiers bound him in the garden, Annas binds him as well, Pilate has him scourged, the soldiers place on his head a crown of thorns, and the crowd demands crucifixion. They resort to savagery because no one can disprove his testimony. Those who oppose Jesus force him to trial as a foil to prove his guilt and demonstrate that he is not from God.[364] Ironically, Pilate investigates and proves that both Jesus is innocent and that he is from God by way of his power (kingship) from above.

It was daybreak when Jesus arrived before Pilate. The timing is symbolic: Jesus is the light of the world. Light means revelation or truth. Light also brings visibility. This is the hour of glory when God is made visible through his Word to the world. The trial of Pilate will address the truth about Jesus who reveals the Father. At first it appears as if Pilate is placing Jesus on trial, but actually the narrative reveals that Jesus is placing the "world" on trial. The reader knows from previous texts that he is a judge; he is declared a king, he has the truth, and he asks questions. In this trial, Jesus behaves and acts as if he is a judge. This is a criminal trial. In fact, Jesus is going to offer indisputable evidence that sin has been committed during the

---

[363] J. Blank maintains that there is a role reversal. The accused Jesus becomes judge and accuser. See his "Die Verhandlung vor Pilatus Joh 18, 28-19, 16 im Lichte johanneischer Theologie," *BZ* 3 (1959): 64-65.

[364] Brown, *John*, 713.

trial itself. A thief on trial, for example, is not going to steal the jurors' wallets. That would give the jurors conclusive evidence to convict. There is undisputed evidence in Jesus' court because the crime is committed during the trial. The sin that is judged in this trial is rejection of the truth.[365] Jesus tells Pilate that those who "handed me over (παραδίδωμι) to you are guilty of a greater sin. The word he uses to identify sin is παραδίδωμι (hand over). Rejection is expressed by "handing over." Judas is not the only rejecter to hand Jesus over (παραδίδωμι) to the soldiers in the garden.[366] The crowd hands Jesus over to Pilate: "If this man were not a criminal, we would not have handed him over (παραδίδωμι) to you" (18:30). Later, Pilate will hand Jesus over (παραδίδωμι) to the executioners: "Then he handed

---

[365] Both Bultmann and Ernst Käsemann argued the passion narrative focuses on revelation and the atonement for sin is "a foreign element," not a central theme for the passion narrative. Rudolf Bultmann, *Theology of the New Testament*, trans. Kendrick Grobel (2 vols. New York: Charles Scribner's Sons, 1951 and 1955), 2:54. See also Ernst Käsemann, The Testament of Jesus: A Study of the Gospel of John in Light of Chapter 17 (London: SCM, 1968), 24; Martinus C. de Boer, *Johannine Perspectives on the Death of Jesus, Contributions to Biblical Exegesis and Theology 17* (Kampen: Kok Pharos Publishing House, 1996), 20-30. Those who argue otherwise must admit that any atonement theme is subtle, "under-the-radar," and can be missed by the reader. Gieschen, "Atonement for Sin," 245.

[366] Eight times Judas is named as the agent who hands Jesus over (παραδίδωμι). Three times the Jews are named (18:30, 35, 19:11), and Pilate once (John 19:16).

him over to them to be crucified" (19:16). Jesus' trial finds unquestionable proof of sin.[367]

This is the final day of preparation for the Passover when the lambs are slaughtered at noon, the same time that Pilate appears before the crowd for the last time and declares Jesus as king (19:14). Just before the last Passover, Jesus multiplied the loaves and fish and fed the crowd. He also offered himself as food for everlasting life. One recalls early in the Gospel when John twice proclaims Jesus as the "Lamb of God" who takes away the sin of the world. Here while the world is on trial for sin, at the time the lambs are slaughtered, Jesus takes away sin. He is the judge, though he did not come to condemn the world but to save it. The judge and king will save the world by providing eternal life. All of these earlier texts prepare the reader to understand the meaning of the trial and death of Jesus as a revelation and salvific act. All the pieces come together at the trial.

For the second time, Pilate goes outside to meet the Jews and gives them an offer. Their response will expose them as frauds (18:38). Pilate will pardon one of the condemned. One can assume that three were scheduled to be crucified because Jesus died with two thieves. Pilate offers any one of the four. They chose Barabbas who is a bandit (18:40). None of the other three are labeled with this title, making him stand out among the others. The Greek word for "bandit" is λᾳστής. It is used to describe those revolutionary or guerrilla warriors with a predisposition to wage conflict against Rome. Josephus used the term in the first century for those who were rebels

---

[367] "Sin for John, therefore, is primarily unbelief. Sins are the result of unbelief and lead to judgment and death (8:21, 24)." Culpepper, "Theology," 419.

against Rome.³⁶⁸ He called them the worst enemies of his people since they put the Jews at risk by inciting Roman retaliation. How does the reader know this is the meaning that the author intends? Is there evidence in the narrative that can support this interpretation? I suggest that the term exposes the Jews as hypocrites and further demonstrates their illegitimate claims against Jesus. Their choice of Barabbas is ironic: they reject "truth" that will offer them eternal life by selecting the one who will put the nation in danger with Rome. One recalls the high priest: "It is better for you to have one man die for the people than to have the whole nation destroyed" (11:49). Jesus is not a danger to the people because Pilate recognizes him as a legitimate king: "Do you want me to release for you the King of the Jews?" (18:39). Caiaphas's wisdom would have been good council in this decision. Do they put a rebel back on the street that can harm a nation with his propensity toward violence or choose someone who is legitimate in the eyes of Rome? ("I find no case against him," 19:6). The irony is striking. The Jews put themselves in danger of death

---

³⁶⁸ Josephus, Ant, 9:183; 14.159, 415, 421, 424; 16.276, 277, 279, 280, 281, 282, 283, 285, 291, 347). On the definition of the term, see Karl Heinrich Rengstorf, "λῃστής," *TDNT*, 4.258. See also Bultmann who sees irony in the Jews request for Barabbas against Jesus, in his *Theology*, 657. Schnackenburg claims the text does not support Johannine irony where the Jews prefer a political freedom fighter against Rome. Yet the text does highlight the Jews declaring Caesar as king which is a political decision. Also, Schnackenburg does not address Caiaphas and his concern to save the nation against one who seeks to kill Romans which would put the Jews in danger much more than it would for Jesus. The author of John describes the λῃστής as a murderer in 10:10. Neither Jesus nor the other two who are crucified are described as λῃστής. See Schnackenburg, *John*, 3:252-53.

rather than choose the true son of the Father (*bar abba*) who can provide eternal life.

Due to the Passover, the Jews cannot defile themselves by entering into Pilate's headquarters. Pilate must come outside to meet them. When he meets Jesus privately, he returns inside. The "outside" "inside" transitions allow the author to produce another chiastic formation similar to the literary structure that was reflected in Jesus' meeting with Annas.[369]

> A (outside) Pilate and the Jews: first dialogue
>   B. (Inside) Pilate and Jesus: the kingship of Jesus
>   C. (Outside) Pilate and the Jews: Barabbas
>   D. (?) **Coronation** (location of this activity is omitted)
>   C. (Outside) Pilate and the Jews: Ecce Homo
>   B. (Inside) Pilate and Jesus: Pilate's power
> A. (Outside) Pilate and the Jews: "Behold your King"

It appears that the coronation of Jesus is centrally located in the trial narrative which is indicated by the chiasmus structure. I will argue that the purpose of Jesus' kingship is to establish his origin with the Father. This is how Pilate finds him innocent of the charges

---

[369] Those who favor this structure are Brown, John 858-59; J. Blank, "Die Verhandlung vor Pilatus joh 18, 28–19,16 im Lichte johannneischer Theologie," *BZ* 3 (1959): 61; David Rensberger, "The Politics of John: The Trial of Jesus in the Fourth Gospel," *JBL* 103 (1984): 401; Ignace de la Potterie, *The Hour of Jesus: The Passion and the Resurrection of Jesus according to John* (New York: Alba House, 1989), 58.

brought against him. Although the soldiers use this moment to mock him, it best describes the kind of king Jesus represents. His power and authority come from God. His kingship governs by divine justice because he has the truth and is the provider of eternal life. He is the "Word." The violence toward Him, point to Jesus authenticity as a king because this is the habitual practice among rejecters of truth.

When Pilate brings Jesus inside his headquarters for the first time, he asks Jesus if he is a king? It is an odd question because the Jews never said that Jesus claimed to be a king. They accused him of a crime without the mention of kingship: "If this man were not a criminal, we would not have handed him over to you" (18:30). Jesus answers a question with a question: "Do you ask this on your own, or did others tell you about me" (18:34). It is a legitimate inquiry: how did Pilate know that Jesus is a king? Pilate does not change the subject with his next question. In fact, he wants to know what kind of king he is by knowing his activity: "What did you do?" (18:35). Jesus reveals where he is from by citing his signs and words, using an analogy Pilate can understand. The Father's bosom where Jesus receives the truth is a place distinct from the world. Nothing came into being without the divine Word according to the prologue. He was sent into the world to bring about a new birth, but this birth comes from above, not below: "No one can see the kingdom of God without being born from above" (3:3). It is the Word from above that reveals God. Those who believe become children of God: "All who received him, who believed in his name, he gave power to become children of God" (1:12). Those who are born from above by the Word form a family; they are children of God. When Jesus says "kingdom," he means "family." The king is responsible for the family of believers.

Pilate can relate better to this imagery: "So you are a king?" (18:37). Jesus' response to this second reference to his kingship is packed with meaning. The reader has been collecting information throughout the Gospel to understand each element of Jesus' rejoinder. First, he states: "You say I am a king" (18:37). The "I am" statement confirms the claim. He is a king but Jesus needs to qualify the term. First, he is king because he provides the truth: "I came into the world, to testify to the truth" (18:37). The reader also knows that the king/messiah is one who has all knowledge from the Samaritan Woman: "The woman said to him, "I know that Messiah is coming" (who is called Christ). 'When he comes, he will proclaim all things to us.' Jesus said to her, "I am he" (4:25-26). The term "I am" and "Messiah" are linked together. The reader recalls from reading the Gospel that truth sets people free, produces believers, and provides eternal life. Before Pilate, Jesus also states that some belong to the truth. This statement is also understood from previous texts. Everyone who obeys his commands abides in Christ. Just as the Father and the Son are one, so those who believe and obey abide in the Word. They can only bear fruit if they abide in Christ, just as a branch can bear fruit when it is attached to the vine (15:4). Finally, he reveals to Pilate that believers "listen to my voice." The reader has seen this expression in the good shepherd narrative. The gatekeeper opens the gate for the shepherd who calls his sheep by name. The raising of Lazarus was a fitting example. Jesus goes to the tomb, the stone is removed, Jesus calls Lazarus by name, and he hears Jesus' voice and comes out of the tomb. Jesus' response to Pilate can be summed up in this way: Yes, I am a King. I was sent to reveal the words of God (truth) which produce children of God, which is a family that will inherit eternal life. In this sense, one can understand the kingdom as a family of believers and Christ as the king. But it is a kingdom from above because He is from above.

Ironically, Jesus answers Pilate's question, "What is truth?" (18:38), before he asks the question. His word, which is truth, creates a family or kingdom. That is why Jesus can be called a king. Pilate's question "What is truth" is not a rejection, a denial, or indifference as some commentators conclude.[370] Pilate's uncertainty fits a pattern. Nicodemus questions how one is born back in chapter 3. The Samaritan woman asks where one can find living water. The man born blind does not know where Jesus is from. John that Baptist did not know who "He" was until the Spirit came. Mary Magdalene does not know where they took the body of Jesus. All those who eventually believed in Jesus began the long journey with a lack of understanding. The reader knows that the believer is one who progresses in knowledge. Pilate, likewise, will grow in his conviction of Jesus' innocence and his identity as a king. Pilate will acknowledge Jesus as a king just as Nicodemus will declare him a king with his royal burial. Before Pilate progresses, he exposes his limitations. At the beginning of the trial, Pilate asks if he is a king. At the end of the

---

[370] Schnackenburg claims that Pilate's effort is "not a serious search for truth." It is a sign of his "rejection" of Jesus. However, such a conclusion does not explain why Pilate wants to release Jesus under extreme pressure to have him condemned. See his *John*, 2.251. De la Potterie describes Pilate's "tone" as "indifferent"; see his *The Hour of Jesus: The Passion and the Resurrection of Jesus According to John* (New York: Alba, 1989), 67.

trial, he introduces him as a king. He even finalizes the claim with a legal document: "What I have written I have written" (19:22).

After Pilate calls Jesus a king, he orders him to be flogged.[371] Unlike the synoptic Gospels where scourging is included as part of the death sentence, here Jesus is sent to be chastised without condemnation of death. The narrative has reached the literary center of the trial. There will be two more outside appearances with the Jews and one inside encounter with Jesus. The kingship of Jesus is the interpretive key to the trial. Remember that "Messiah" in this Gospel means "one who knows all, who has the truth." In this scene Jesus is presented as a king then rejected, and the typical behavior for rejecters is violence. The prologue announced that the Word came to his own but his own people would not accept him (1:11). As king among his own, Jesus is rejected. The soldiers weave a crown of thorns and place it on his head. They also put a robe on him with the imperial color purple. Those who reject Jesus justify their blindness by veiling his identity with a costume and then mocking him. Ironically, they chose a covering that reveals who he is and his role in the world. He is the king who produces a kingdom by his Word.

One recalls the incident that occurs after the feeding of the crowd in chapter 6. Jesus is forced to retreat to the mountain alone because the Jews wanted to force him to be their king. Jesus' kingdom is not of this world. The world is the location for non-believers. The Jews will end up rejecting Jesus as their king: "We have no king

---

[371] Scholars find it hard to understand why Pilate has Jesus scourged in the middle of the proceedings. See Brown, John, 886-89; Schlier, "Jesus," 67-68; David Rensberger, "The Politics of John: The Trial of Jesus in the Fourth Gospel," *JBL* 103 (1984): 402.

but the emperor" (19:15). The term "king" occurs more times in John than any other book in the New Testament. appearing 12 times during the passion narrative alone. Jesus allows the people to greet him as king when he enters Jerusalem because his throne is the cross. Jesus reigns from the cross; the cross lifts him up so that he can reveal God's glory to all. Both are introduced here. Again, those who reject are blind by their own free will. In this particular case, blindness comes by cloaking a real king who offers the Word of everlasting life. One notes that the whole Passion scene is free of spitting, blows to the head, and insults that are present in the other Gospels. There are two moments of humiliation during this passion narrative. The first was the slap of the guard. I pointed out above that the blow by the attendant is at the center of a chiasm as well. The second is the crowning of thorns, found at the literary center of Jesus' trial narrative. The two chiastic centers represent rejection, one from his own people, the Jews, and one from the kingdom of the world. Likewise, both confirm the statement in the prologue: "His own people did not accept him" (1:11).

Pilate returns outside and presents Jesus as they have never seen him before, wearing the crown of thorns and purple cloak: "Behold the man" (19:5). What is the significance of the word "man?" The Samaritan woman reported to the crowd of her encounter with an extraordinary "man": "Come and see a man who told me all that I ever did" (4:29). This statement is a description of the messiah who will know everything according to the Samaritan woman. In addition to this, the prologue announces that "the Word became flesh" (1:14). For the reader, the Word is a man which means revelation.

God wants to put on the flesh so that he is seen. When Pilate introduces Jesus as the "man," the reader understands Pilate as saying, "behold revelation and truth in the flesh." This is what rejection looks like when one comes "among his own."[372] The chief priests and police demand death by crucifixion. Pilate cannot accept their demands because they have not provided any evidence against him: "I find no case against him" (19:6). The Jews clarify to Pilate that they want him executed, not because Jesus is a king, but because he claims to be the Son of God. Indeed, Jesus does, in fact, claim to be the Son of God, because it is true. The rejecters fail to recognize the evidence that validates Jesus' claim. They are self-blinded to authentic testimony. From the accusers' perspective, Pilate chastised Jesus for being a king, but this was the wrong reason. The crowd never handed him over as a king. Pilate believes Jesus: he is innocent, he is a king, and the charges are unfounded.

The crowd presents their case with more exacting detail: he claims to be the Son of God. This new accusation is beyond Pilate's competency. Pilate is no longer a disinterested third party in the midst of religious squabbling. The crowd is making it personal for Pilate. He fears. He is threatened by the obstacle for all believers, which is forcing his hand to do something he does not want to do: "hand him over." He calls for one more meeting with Jesus inside his headquarters (19:8). This time the "where" question arises one more time: "Where are you from?" (19:9). The reader is quite familiar with the significance of this question. It is the right question to

---

[372] See de la Potterie's "Jésus," 245-46; Rensberger, "Politics of John," 404.

ask because this is now a religious issue. The reader knows that Jesus is from God. Jesus' origin validates his claim as the Son of God. Those who testify to Jesus need to know where Jesus is from. Pilate needs to acquire this knowledge if he is to testify to the truth before the Jews. Jesus does not answer the question immediately. He allows Pilate to struggle in the silence: "Do you refuse to speak to me? Do you not know that I have power to release you, and power to crucify you?" (19:10). This question generates the opening Jesus needed in order to discuss his origin on Pilate's terms. Jesus tells Pilate that power has its origin from above.[373] The Jews are in violation because they have rejected the Son of God by handing him over (παραδίδωμι). Pilate sides with Jesus. He is confident with the evidence: "Pilate tried to release him" (19:12).

The Jews have no counterclaims or evidence to suggest that Jesus is a fraud and so they resort to threats against Pilate: "You are no friend to the emperor. Everyone who claims to be a king sets himself against the emperor" (19:12). For the last time Pilate returns outside to confront the Jews. Jesus is present. The text says that "He brought Jesus outside and sat on the judge's bench" (12:13). The Greek is unclear as to whether Jesus or Pilate is the one sitting on the bench. It is philologically possible for either of the two. I contend that the confusion is intended by the author to suggest to the reader that there are two judges who have been conducting two alternate trails and are soon ready to render a verdict, one to judge Jesus the other to judge sinners.[374] However, scholars argue for one or the other. Some

---

[373] Ibid.

[374] De la Potterie argues that Jesus is being seated on the Judgment seat because he is king and judge. See his "Jésus," 221-33.

contend that Pilate is the one who sits on the chair. Schnackenburg claims that the author intends to offer information that is historical rather than theological: "It cannot be denied that the obvious meaning according to the historical situation, that Pilate sat himself on the judgment seat."[375] De la Potterie, who favors Jesus as the occupant of the seat, argues for the transitive meaning of the verb to sit, noting a lack of the article for βῆμα (seat, 19:13).[376] Brown cites Matthew's account where "the whole trial seems to have taken place with Pilate seated on the judgment bench and Jesus standing before him."[377] An anarthrous βῆμα (chair) would have a broader meaning: "on the platform," rather than the more precise "judgment seat." Brown is correct, observing that Pilate's intention is not to further mock Jesus by placing him in the judgment chair.[378] Sitting on the seat stabilizes the narrative and offers the impression that Pilate's verdict is legitimate, later, backed by legal documentation ("What I have written I have written"). Pilate also makes a judgment from his investigation. He concludes that Jesus is a king and announces his verdict: "Behold your King" (19:15). The imperative "behold" is the same word that John the Baptist used to announce Jesus to his disciples: Behold the Lamb of God (1:36). Pilate, like John, witnesses to Christ. Both the trial of Jesus and the trial of Pilate yield the truth. Pilate declares that Jesus is a king. Pilate appears to be a believer who has progressed by upgrading Jesus title as King.

---

[375] Schnackenburg, *John*, 2.263-64.
[376] De la Potterie, *Hour of Jesus*, 83-84.
[377] Brown, *John*, 881.
[378] Brown, *Passion Narratives*, 844.

Jesus, on the other hand, proves that sin has been committed and he, "the lamb of God" will take away the sin of the world. This means he will replace rejection with belief by offering revelation.[379] He is also the good shepherd and will save by giving up his life for the sheep. At this moment, Jesus is about to accept the cross as an act of judgment because only Jesus can lay down his own life. The reader knows that Jesus is a judge: "The Father judges no one but has given all judgment to the Son" (5:22); "he has given him authority to execute judgment, because he is the Son of Man" (5:27); "as I hear, I judge; and my judgment is just" (5:30). No one has authority over him. Jesus is the one who has the truth. Jesus has indisputable evidence that sin—handing over—has been committed because the crime takes place while the trial is in progress.

"They have no king but Caesar" can be understood as a rejection of God himself, but it is hard to know if the author has certain biblical texts in mind that declare God as the king of Israel (Judg 8:23; 1 Sam 8:7; 2 Sam 7:11-16). The claim that Caesar is king, nevertheless, indicates a clear rejection of Christ. Irony once again is strong. The crowd claims to be friends of Rome after they picked Barabbas, a condemned enemy of Rome.

The hour is noon on the day of the preparation of the Passover. The last time in the Gospel it was noon, Jesus sat at the well because he was tired from a journey. This literary connection suggests that Jesus sat again at noon who would have been tired from the torment, and back and forth travel from inside/outside of the praetorium.

---

[379] Craig R. Koester, *The Word of Life: A Theology of John's Gospel* (Grand Rapids: Eerdmans, 2008), 115.

This time he sits, not as the bridegroom meeting a woman with marital issues, but as the judge sitting before sinners. It is from the seat of judgment that Jesus' words can be best understood and implemented: "I do not come to condemn the world but to save it" (3:17). He says this just after he announced that God so loved the world that he gave his only Son (3:16). The Gospel writer had planted information earlier in the text so that the reader can interpret this passage. The terms that describe the trial provide literary connections for the reader. These literary ties actively engage the reader to draw meaning from previous texts.

The Crucifixion

However, after the verdict, the threat becomes too real: "we have no king but the emperor" (19:15). Pilate, who proclaims the truth, succumbs to the fear, and he too rejects Jesus by handing him (παραδίδωμι) over just as Judas and the Jews: "Then he handed him (παραδίδωμι) over to them to be crucified" (19:16). The suddenness of the shift is a warning. Peter too shifted his allegiance at the moment he fell to fear, and now Pilate joins the company of the parents of the man born blind and Peter who yielded to fear. The Jews knew if they could get Pilate to fear, they could control him. That has been their strategy throughout the Gospel. The one who claimed to have power to release and the power to crucify did not have the power to rule according to his convictions. Pilate represents those who accept the truth but later fall victim to the threats of those who reject the truth.

The Inscription

Jesus bears the cross alone. There is no mention of the crimes of the two others who are crucified with Jesus. The Gospel only cites a document describing Jesus' crime: "Jesus of Nazareth, the King of the Jews" (19:19). John is the only Gospel to use a definite article with "king," and the phrase is the same one used by the soldiers at the crowning of thorns: "the king of the Jews" (ὁ βασιλεὺς τῶν Ἰουδαίων, 19:3,19). The place of Jesus' origin on the inscription is obviously incorrect to the reader. Jesus is from the Father, not from Nazareth. Philip made the same mistake. The Jews, however, complain that the inscription is wrong and needs to be amended. They are correct. The inscription is inaccurate, but they identify the mistake incorrectly. They want Pilate to change the part that is not in error: "Do not write, 'The King of the Jews,' but, 'This man said, I am king of the Jews'" (19:21).[380]

Once again one can see the advantage of intratextuality. The attentive reader will know, based on previous testimony about Jesus' origin, that half of Pilate's inscription is inaccurate. True, Jesus is a king, but he is simply not from Nazareth. The prologue confirms Jesus' origin as the pre-existent being with God, according to 1:1-4. The "Word" is not created but always existed before creation (1:2) with a special relationship "with God" (1:1), and "in the bosom of the Father" (1:18). In the Gospel, Jesus never states that he is from Nazareth. Others have made a claim (i.e., Philip, the police in the

---

[380] Rensberger argues that Pilate uses the king of the Jews reference to antagonize the Jews. This interpretation, however, does not consider a theological purpose as I do. See his "Politics of John," 402.

garden), only to be followed by a correction. In the garden, the police are seeking "Jesus of Nazareth." Jesus responds by saying "I am," which is a statement of origin. There is an unusual cluster of three "I am" statements in the garden to counter the two "Jesus of Nazareth" declarations by the police. The reader recalls that Jesus had used the "I am" statement earlier in the Gospel to clarify his origins: just before Jesus claims he is from above to the Pharisee, he announces that he is the light of the world with an "I am" statement (8:12). Later in the conversation, Jesus again clarifies his origin with an "I am" statement: "Before Abraham was, I am" (8:58). In 15:1 Jesus uses the "I am" phrase to highlight his relationship with the Father: "I am the true vine, and my Father is the vine grower." The author has used the "I am" statement consistently to indicate Jesus' origin and place with the Father. We have already seen how often the origin of Jesus is underscored throughout the Gospel. Scholars such as Raymond Brown conclude that Jesus is simply confirming his Nazorean roots in the garden by saying "I am" to the arresting soldiers.[381] However, in light of the prologue and other conversations, Jesus seems to be correcting the arresting officers' misconception by countering with his "I am" statement, indicating his true origin. Jesus' origin continues to be an issue during the trial. Shortly after the arrest, Pilate asks Jesus two questions in his interviews. He

---

[381] Heil argues that "Jesus' reply, "I am he," or more literally, "I am" (ἐγώ εἰμι, 18:5,6,8), not only identifies him as the Nazorean but resonates with all of his previous "I am" predications (4:26; 6:20, 35, 41, 51; 8:12, 18; 10:7, 9, 11, 14; 11:25; 15:1, 5)." See his "High Priest," 731. Also see Brown, *Passion Narratives*, 260. For a discussion of the Johannine "I am" statements, see Brown, *John,* 533-38, 735 n.15.

inquires if he is a king, and where he is from. Jesus answers both with reference to his origin; first, he states that his kingdom is not of this world and second, that power is from above. Jesus' kingship and power are clearly from above. Nazareth has nothing to do with the origin of Jesus' authority.

After Jesus clarifies his origin, the chief priests of the Jews are correct to complain about the inaccuracy of the inscription, but ironically they want to change the part that is correct: "Do not write, 'The King of the Jews,' but, this man said, 'I am King of the Jews'" (19:21). They ignore the true inaccuracy: "Jesus the Nazorean." The attentive reader can pick up that subtle detail which highlights an important theological point. People who reject Jesus do not know his origin. This is true throughout the whole Gospel. If a commentator isolates a text from the prologue or other texts in the Gospel that have interpretive value, he or she will risk losing pertinent information, such as the irony when the leaders insist on changing the inscription. If the prologue is the interpretive key/blueprint for the Gospel, then it will be necessary for interpreting later passages. One can also use the narrative progression as an interpretive guide because it follows a consistent message, reechoing the plan that was articulated in the prologue.

Again, those who reject Jesus do not know his origin.[382] Pilate is no longer a believer and so he does not have the truth. The inscription is inaccurate. At first, Pilate arrived at the truth, but fear turned him into another non-believer. Those who believe and testify to the

---

[382] "For Pilate has asked Jesus what the world can never know, namely, 'Where are you from?' (19:9)." Rensberger, "Politics of John," 409.

truth know that the decree would be more accurate if it read: "Jesus, who was sent from the Father, is king of all." The irony is subtle, but the attentive reader, who has recall of past passages, will understand the point. Many of those visiting the city for the feast will be misinformed because rejecters control the press.

The soldiers crucify Jesus, raising him up for all to see. The multiple languages on the inscription invite many nations to draw close to read the notice. Jesus is lifted up and begins to draw all to himself as he predicted in 12:32 (cf. 10:16; 11:49-52). The expression "lifted up" occurs three times (3:14-15; 8:28; 12:32) as the three passion predictions for this Gospel. Jesus is now visible to all nations and who is about to offer eternal life to all who believe.

The Outside Garment and the Inside Garment

Jesus has two sets of garments: the outside piece is divided, the one closest to the skin remains seemless. The garments represents two parties. Note that the divided garment comes right after the division we see among the non-believers, Pilate and the Jews, as they cannot agree on the inscription. The seemless garment represents the united family of believers that Jesus will bring together when he addresses His mother and the beloved disciple. So the two sets of clothing, one that is divided the other that remains whole, can reflect two ways in which revelation is received. Some reject others believe.

There are numerous examples of division among the people as I described in the introduction. During the feast of Tabernacles, the people are divided: "so there was a division of the people over him" (7:43). Also in the story of the man born blind: "There was a division among them" (9:16), and "There was again a division among the Jews because of these words" (10:19). When Jesus reveals, he causes division because some believe and some will not.

Jesus also promoted unity which is symbolized by the undergarment: "Abide in me as I abide in you" 15:4); "So they may be one as we are one" (17:22). The soldiers agree not to tear the seamless garment. The word "tear" is also used to describe the net that was not torn despite the 153 large fish in 21:11. The description of the seamless condition of the garment is peculiar. It is woven "from the top." The term "from the top" (ἄνωθεν) jumps out at the reader because it was the word that befuddled Nicodemus (3:3, 7, 31). The adverb can mean both "again" or "from above." Nicodemus understood the word to mean "again" during Jesus' teaching of one's birth. He assumed Jesus was talking about a second birth, "again." Jesus, however, used the term to discuss how one is transformed into a child of God: birth that is "from above." According to the prologue, those who receive the Word through belief are given power to become children of God (1:12). This is the purpose of the creative Word coming into the world.

The conversation that took place surrounding this particular word now resurfaces just before Jesus unites his mother with the beloved disciple, the two witnesses. They now share the same home, a family of witnesses. Witnesses have the truth; they know where Jesus is from, and they abide in God. It is a family made from heaven "above." The term "from above" is a fitting introduction to Jesus' first words from the cross. He is responsible for producing a family of witnesses. He is the Word that came into the world. Those who believe become children of God. The mother of Jesus is the witness at the beginning of his ministry. The beloved disciple appears for the first time at the end of Jesus' ministry where he will play the role of a witness: "He who saw this has testified so that you also may believe" (19:35); "This is the disciple who is testifying to you these things and has written them, and we know that his testimony is true" (21:24). Both remain nameless throughout the Gospel. Both symbolize those who believe and give witness. Together, they represent the first moment that the "hour" was mentioned at the wedding of Cana and the moment blood and water, the fluids that represent eternal life, are made available. The entire ministry of Jesus from Cana to Golgotha is embodied by their unification. "Woman, here is your son… Here is your mother" (19:26-27) is the final instruction of Jesus to finish the work of the Father: "After this, when Jesus knew that all was now finished" (19:30). Jesus uses the same imperative verb that John the Baptist used to instruct his two disciples: "Behold" (Ἴδε, 1:36). Pilate uses Ἴδε (behold) three times to try to win over the Jews (19:4, 5, 14). However, they cannot "look" because they are blind. The mother of Jesus, who first introduced her son with the words "Do whatever he tells you" is asked to obey his command "Love one another as I have loved you" (15:12). The seamless garment is a symbol of the community of witnesses and, despite opposition against them, their union, like the garment, will not be torn apart and divided.[383] The garment that was torn represents the divided world that does not accept divine revelation.

---

[383] "The fact that Jesus' seamless tunic is woven "from the top" or "from above" (εκ των ἀνωθεν) indicates that its emphasized unity has a divine origin." Heil, "High Priest," 724.

"I Thirst"

Once again, Jesus fulfills Scripture when he thirsts: "for my thirst they gave me vinegar to drink" (LXX Ps 68:22).[384] The last time Jesus appeared thirsty, he was seated at Jacob's well around noontime.[385] He asked a Samaritan woman for water: "give me a drink" (4:7). She came up with three excuses for why she should not: the well is deep, he had no bucket, and Jewish men should not seek favors from Samaritan women. One finds out that Jesus' intention was not for her to give him a drink. His objective was to give her a drink: "If you knew the gift of God, and who it is that is saying to you, 'Give me a drink,' you would have asked him, and he would have given you living water" (4:10). Because of similar details that one finds in the passion narrative, the whole Samaritan scene comes to mind for the engaged reader. Recall the many connections between these two texts: both mention the action of sitting ("and Jesus, tired out by his journey, was sitting by the well" 4:6, and "When Pilate heard these words, he brought Jesus outside and sat on the judge's bench" 19:13).

---

[384] There are four Old Testament citations during the crucifixion of Jesus. The casting of the dice (John 19:24) fulfills Psalm 22:18. Jesus' thirst (John 19:28) fulfills LXX Ps 68:22. The soldier chooses not to break Jesus' legs, fulfilling Psalm 34:20, and the side of Jesus is pierced, fulfilling Zech 12:10. See also Matthew D. Jensen, "The Fourth Gospel and the Apostolic Mission: John's Common Evangelical Theology." *Unio cum Christo* 2 (2016): 204.

[385] Scholars suggest that Jesus' thirst is another example of Johannine irony: that the very source of living water would be thirsty (Senior, *The Passion of Jesus*, 118; Mannucci, V., Giovanni, *Il Vangelo narrante* (Bologna: EDB 1993), 113.

Both describe Jesus' physical thirst (4:7; 19:28) and one can assume that Jesus is the giver and source of the living water (4:10; 17:37-38). Both passages discuss moments of physical weakness: Jesus' fatigue "from a long journey" (4:6), and his flogging, crowning with thorns, and being struck on his face (19:1-3). Both share the same verb to express Jesus' intention to finish his work ("My food is to do the will of him who sent me and to complete [τελειόω] his work" (4:34), and "After this, when Jesus knew that all was now finished" [τελειόω] 19:28). Both narratives have characters who call Jesus a "man" (4:29; 19:5) and the messiah/king (4:29; 19:14), and both have a water container (Jacob's Well and the Messianic pierced side). Finally, both texts discuss living water. The Samaritan asks Jesus where to find living water: "Where do you get that living water?" (4;11).

Jesus sits at noon and appears thirsty. Perhaps Jesus was physically thirsty on the cross, but to the reader who calls to mind the scene in John 4, Jesus' intention is to give others a drink. The reader is interpreting the words "I thirst" from the cross by drawing on the words Jesus spoke to the Samaritan woman: "If you knew the gift of God, and who it is that is saying to you, 'Give me a drink,' you would have asked him, and he would have given you living water." The power of suggestion continues to filter to the next passage when Jesus' side is pierced and blood and water flow. If the reader continues to connect the passion narrative to the Samaritan passage, the answer to the Samaritan's question is finally answered: "where do you get that living water?" (4:11). The beloved disciple is able to witness to the blood and water so that "you can believe," because he knows what all witnesses need to know: "where." He knows "where" you can get this living water. There is no greater love than to give one's life for one's friends. Jesus, the model witness, testifies to the truth, making available revelation that offers the believer eternal life. The blood and water symbolize eternal life: "The water that I will give them will never be thirsty. The water that I will give will become in them a spring of water gushing up to eternal life" (4:14); "Those who eat my flesh and drink my blood have eternal life" (6:54).

Jesus dies, but the imagery resounds with the theme of eternal life. He is the grain that falls to the ground and dies that bears much fruit. Jesus is king; his kingdom belongs to members born from above, a family of believers. God becomes most visible when the Son of God offers his life for the benefit of others: "No greater love than this, to lay down one's life for one's friends" (15:13). The crucifixion narrative is beautifully constructed. The inscription, gambling for a t-shirt, a mother and disciple, and the thirst are not isolated events. They string together a harmonious and coherent picture of God to inspire believers to imitate the two model witnesses that now form a family. Jesus offers eternal life by testifying to the truth so that others will have eternal life. The death of Jesus is more about the celebration of life: "If you love me you would rejoice that I am going to the Father" (14:28). The cross is a sacrifice for others, but even more, it represents a revelation, which provides eternal life for others.

"It Is Finished"

The term τετέλεσται ("finish") in v. 30 is the same word used in 19:28: "After this, Jesus, knowing that all are now finished" (πάντα τετέλεσται). Note that the singular verb in verse 28 has a plural subject (πάντα).[386] Often the neuter plural refers to Jesus works. Earlier in 5:19-20 πάντα ("all things") referred to the "works" (ἔργα) that Jesus did in imitation of his Father: "Amen, amen I tell you, the Son is not able to do on his own even one thing unless he sees the Father doing it. For the things which that one ['the Father'] is doing— these things also the Son is doing likewise. For the Father loves the Son and shows him all things (πάντα) that he himself is doing, and greater works (ἔργα) than these he will show him, that you may marvel." Note also in 7:21 when Jesus says: "I have done one work, and you all marvel." Also is 4:45: "Therefore, when he [Jesus] went into Galilee, the Galileans welcomed him, because they had seen all things (πάντα), as many as they were (ὅσος), that he had done in Jerusalem during the festival."[387]

---

[386] It is common for a plural neuter subject to take a singular verb in Greek usage. Thus, "all things are now finished."

[387] The two terms "works" and "signs" are often found in the plural: 13 times in the case of ἔργα (5:36 (2x); 7:3; 9:3, 4; 10:25, 32b, 37, 38; 14:10, 11, 12; 15:24), 10 or 11 times in the case of σημεῖ (2:11, 23; 3:2; 6:2, 14 v.l., 26; 7:31; 9:16; 11:47; 12:37; 20:3). See Robert H. Gundry, "New Wine in Old Wineskins: Bursting Traditional Interpretations in John's Gospel (Part 1)," *BBR* 17 (2007): 293-94. He argues rather successfully that the plural neuter subject in 19:30 refers to the works and signs of Jesus meaning that Jesus completes his revelation of the Father on the cross with his death. He concludes: "In summary, τετέλεσται in 19:30 means 'they are finished' in an echo of ἤδη πάντα τετέλεσται, 'all are now finished,' in 19:28. 'They' refers to 'all,' and 'all' (πάντα, neuter plural) likely refers to Jesus' 'signs,' 'works,' and 'words' (σημεία, ἔργα, and ῥήματα, neuter plurals). His finishing them enables him to give the Spirit over to the disciples, those who believe in him." Ibid., 296.

Jesus was sent into the world to create children of God by way of revelation. He finished what he came to do. It is on the cross that he gives access to eternal life to everyone. Revelation is no longer offered to just selected groups or individuals. Everyone has access because Jesus was lifted up. After he announces the completion of his creative work, it is now time for the Word to return to the Father. He gives up his Spirit. Irony is once again used. Non-believers tried to prevent revelation by killing Jesus, however, they provided for him the finish line of success. Jesus finished his work. The Word came into the world to create children of God. Now the Word returns back to the Father.

The expression to give up the Spirit is intensely significant. Those who reject him can only resort to violence in their desperation to silence the Word of God. Yet they have no evidence to support their charges. Jesus pays the ultimate price. Still, he is king so he rules. As ruler and judge, he puts sinners on trial. During the trial, they sin by rejecting Jesus. Judas, the chief priests, and Pilate all hand Jesus over (παραδίδωμι). He has indisputable evidence of their sin because the crime happens during his trial. However, Jesus did not come to condemn the world but to save it. He saved it by the way he died: "Then he bowed his head and handed over (παραδίδωμι) his spirit" (19:30). Remarkably, the word that was used to describe sin is now employed to describe the fulfillment of a promise: "Now he said this about the Spirit, which believers in him were to receive" (7:39). Jesus said he would give believers eternal life, a promise that was set for the future "for as of yet there was no Spirit" because Jesus was not yet glorified. Jesus, who is now glorified on the cross by revealing God's love for the world, hands over his Spirit. Jesus' response to sin is not condemnation, but a gift to believers. Believers need the Spirit to authenticate their testimony. Witnesses will not be left orphans and without legal support. Jesus truly delivered on all his promises while he was on the cross. He provided a home (family) for believers, living water, his blood to drink, his body as the unblemished Lamb of God (his bones were not broken, cf. Psa 34:20-21; Exodus 12:10, 46; Num 9:12) who takes away sin, and his spirit. Lastly, the reader was told that Jesus returns to the Father. Death is not an end but a passage. The believer knows where Jesus abides after his death. The cross is the "hour of Jesus": "When a woman is in labor, she has pain, because her hour has come. But when her child is born, she no longer remembers the anguish because of the joy of having brought a human being into the world" (16:21).

The Burial of Jesus

The hour of glory has a transforming effect on believers. They no longer have a reason to fear. After Jesus' death, believers who fear or who have a history of fear are beginning to come out of hiding and go public. The first is Joseph of Arimathea, who is introduced as a believer who fears.: "Joseph of Arimathea, who was a disciple of Jesus, though a secret one because of his fear of the Jews, asked Pilate to let him take away the body of Jesus" (19:38). Apparently, he no longer fears as he approaches the Roman governor. He is a work in progress. Also Nicodemus, who met Jesus at night, likewise arrives at daytime to assist with the burial. Another work in progress. The bodies have to be buried before sunset. This is the day of glory; the body of Jesus could not be more visible than on the day of his Passion. After the resurrection, Mary, who runs from the tomb in fear, will witness to the disciples that the Lord has risen. The disciples, who gather in fear in the upper room, are transformed with overwhelming joy. Peter, who denied Jesus three times because of fear, will tell him his love three times, the remedy and antidote for fear. During the trial, Pilate represented those who believe but succumb to threats made by opponents to the truth. Jesus, who provides eternal life, has robbed his opponents of their sole weapon. Their threats against those who witness to the truth are no longer an issue because death is now a passage to eternal life for those who believe. After the resurrection, Jesus resolves the believers' problem. No longer do they have a reason to fear opponents. The reader is already aware that Jesus defines himself as the resurrection and the life, and that through him, death is no longer permanent. He is the Good Shepherd who leads his flock out of the gate, a metaphor that was made real in the raising of Lazarus. The reader now sees how this is played out in the death and resurrection of Jesus.

If Jesus' "sleep" is not permanent, then one expects that his burial will not be out of the ordinary, and, indeed, it is not. Nicodemus brings a mixture of myrrh and aloes, weighing about a hundred pounds. It is an extraordinary amount for the task. Myrrh, a resin that is put on the burial clothes, is used for embalming the body. The application of such a large amount will have a considerable effect on the burial clothes. As I discussed in my treatment of Nicodemus, when myrrh is exposed to the air, the gum hardens. The volume of resin will bond the strips of cloth, encasing the body in a sealed shell: "They took the body of Jesus and wrapped it with the spices in linen cloths" (19:40). This presents a problem. The material used for the burial and the brief description in the Gospel suggests an Egyptian burial. However, the text explicitly says that this is a Jewish burial: "according to the burial custom of the Jews" (19:40). Typically, the Jews treat the body with washings and anointing, none of which is described in the text. It is not entirely clear if Jews regularly treated the cloth with myrrh and aloes, which can be either in the form of powder (incense) or liquid. Unfortunately, neither substance can be ascertained from the text. With so many variables, it is hard to determine what the author intended by including such peculiar procedural details in the text. Also extraordinary is the fact that he is placed in a tomb "in which no one had ever been laid" (19:41). This means that there will be no previous stench from death and decay, and the myrrh and aloes will fill the tomb with a pleasant aroma. One recalls the anointing of Mary in preparation for Jesus' burial, which also filled the room with a fragrance (12:3): "So that she might keep it for the day of my burial" (12:8). Finally, the burial is in a garden: "in the garden was a new tomb" (19:41). One recalls the many references in the Gospel to plants bearing much fruit, and the metaphor of the seed that dies in order to bear much fruit comes to mind. Finally, the author reminds the reader that he is buried during the preparation of the Passover: "it was the Jewish day of Preparation" (19:42). It is impossible to know with certainty if the author intends to use the significance of the Passover, when the angel of death passes over the Jewish households in Egypt, to anticipate the celebration of the life of Christ after death. The reminder about the Passover may suggest to the reader that Jesus' death will not be permanent.³⁸⁸ I will now argue that the extraordinary details in the burial description are used to lead the reader to understand death as something temporary, whose meaning has been transformed to a passage to reunification with God.

The Empty Tomb

One of the characteristics of a believer is that they are a work in progress. Throughout the resurrection scenes we will encounter flawed disciples. The resurrection corrects the flaws and transforms them into believers who will reveal the truth to others. Nine of the disciples have fear behind a locked door, Mary Magdalene does not know where Jesus is, and Thomas does not believe despite receiving indisputable evidence by having multiple witnesses. The encounter with the risen Lord will change all of these limitations.

It was still dark when Mary Magdalene went to the tomb and found it empty.³⁸⁹ She runs to inform Peter and the beloved disciple. The last time the reader encountered the two, Peter denied Jesus three times out of fear, and the beloved disciple witnessed "so that you also may believe" (19:35). They go together to the tomb, one representing believers who fear, the other representing those who love by witnessing. Jesus said he loves those who obey his commands: "If you keep my commandments, you will abide in my love

---

³⁸⁸ Jesus dies at the hour when the Passover lamb was slaughtered on the day of the Preparation of the Passover (19:14). Neyrey, *John*, 313.

³⁸⁹ John is the only Gospel in which the burial was not witnessed by any of the women. However, Mary Magdalene is unaccompanied when she visits the tomb, suggesting she had prior knowledge of the location.

just as I have kept my Father's commandments" (15:10). This may imply that the beloved disciple is one who bears much fruit from his testimony. He testifies which means he loves. The comparative genitive suggests a tension between the two: "the other disciple outran Peter" (20:4). The emphasis should not be placed on the one who arrives at the tomb before the other, but what the two see when they arrive. The beloved disciple has a better vision than Peter because his seeing leads to belief. The disciple who "loves" by testifying sees differently from the disciple who has acted out of fear in the past. When the beloved disciple gets to the tomb first, he bends down and "sees" the burial wrappings. That is, he sees a mound of clothing that has been oversaturated with an extraordinary amount of resin. It is not until one goes inside the tomb that the details appear. Peter arrives second and enters the tomb first. Inside he can see that there are two sets of clothes that are distinguished. One is rolled up and placed on the side as if it did not receive the same treatment as the strips that covered the body. Why would the face cloth be differentiated from the body covering? One cloth represents the permanence of death with all its myrrh, the other cloth suggests otherwise. The rolled-up head cloth is soft and moveable, free of the heavy coatings of the stiffening resin. One set of clothing represents the permanence of death, while the other suggests temporary sleep. Both death and sleep are represented.

This is not the only time in the Gospel where the two are juxtaposed. Lazarus was dead and asleep: "Our friend Lazarus has fallen asleep, but I am going there to awaken him… Then Jesus told them plainly, Lazarus is dead'" (11:11, 14). The garden also suggests death turns to life as I argued above with the seed analogy. The unused tomb shows no evidence of death, such as stench, decay, or corpses. When the two disciples enter the tomb with no evidence of death, they see different realities. The verb, θεωρέω (inspect, speculate, theorize), that expresses Simon Peter's seeing in 20:7 is different from the word that will describe the beloved disciple when he enters the tomb: he saw (εἶδον, 20:8). While Peter is observing the linens (θεωρέω), the beloved disciple enters, sees, and believes. Peter is not a believer who witnessed to the truth as the beloved disciple did, so his visual abilities are limited. However, limitations are subject to change in the presence of the risen Lord who will give believers power to overcome fear. Peter's sight can improve just as Jesus gave sight to the man born blind. Therefore, Christ's appearance can advance Peter's progress, as the reader will see in the next chapter when Peter transforms from a state of fear to love: "You know I love you" (21:15, 16, 17).

Appearance to Mary Magdalene

Mary cries. The text repeats the word cry twice for emphasis. The two angels in white question her about her tears: "Woman, why are you weeping?" (20:13). In the story of Lazarus in the tomb, Jesus appeared disturbed at the weeping, taking it to be a lack of faith in the resurrection and the life which the Son of Man provides. She also does not know "where": I do not know where they have laid him" (20:13). She does not possess the elements of a witness; she does not believe because of her weeping, and she does not know "where." Yet, the resurrection of Jesus will transform her. When she first encounters Jesus, she thinks he is the gardener. One recalls when Jesus called his father the vine grower who cleans the branches so that they can bear much fruit (15:1). One is made clean by the Lord's Word (15:4). "Go to my brothers and say to them, 'I am ascending to my Father and your Father'…Mary Magdalene went and announced to the disciples, 'I have seen the Lord'" (20:17-18). After Jesus speaks her name, Mary, He addresses both her lack of faith and her ignorance of "where."[390] First, he restores her faith. The good shepherd calls the sheep by their name and the sheep recognize his voice: "Jesus said to her, 'Mary'" (20:16). Next, he informs her where he is from: "Do not hold on to me, because I have not yet ascended to the Father" (20:17). Now armed with the essentials, she is sent out to witness to his disciples. Schneiders suggests that the forbidden touch is understood as a misunderstanding on Mary's part about Jesus' transformed body. He no longer belongs to this world and so she should not "encounter him as if he were the earthly Jesus resuscitated."[391] I rather argue that it is Mary who is transformed from a weeping, non-believer to a witness. I argue instead that the forbidden touch is the author's way to introduce Jesus' origin in the narrative. Mary needs to know where He is from if she is going to be a witness, the necessary prerequisite for testifying. The reader knows this from other Gospel narratives as I have argued above. It is consistent from other texts that Jesus uses the imagery of ascending

---

[390] Only seven women appear in the Gospel of John: the mother of Jesus; a Samaritan woman; a woman caught in the act of adultery; the sisters of Lazarus, Martha and Mary; Mary of Magdala; and Mary, the wife of Clopas. This is the only instance that Jesus addresses a woman by her name.

[391] Schneiders, "Encounter," 219.

(ἀναβαίνω) to refer to his origin (cf. Nathaniel, 1:51; Nicodemus, 3;13; and the Jews, 6:62). I contend that the text is rather addressing Mary's lack of understanding "where" Jesus is from. Jesus forbids her to touch as a teaching opportunity to address her ignorance. Once she knows where Jesus is from, she can be sent to witness to the disciples. Again, intratextuality allows the reader to interpret a passage by picking up clues from a sequential reading of the Gospel. In this case, the reader knows that witnesses need to know "where."

Jesus Appears to His Disciples

The disciples are locked inside a house due to fear. Immediately upon arrival, Jesus replaces the fear with joy. In 14:27 Jesus said that he leaves them with peace, with the instructions not to be afraid: "And do not let your hearts be troubled, and do not let them be afraid." So peace counters fear. He showed them his hands and his side which still hold the marks of crucifixion. He breathed on them and said to them receive the Holy Spirit. He promised them that when he left them, he would not leave them orphans. They would have support. They are now equipped to testify: fear is removed and they have legal support to authenticate their testimony. They will encounter some rejection so they will need to manage sin, which is rejection of the truth. Sin is a rejection of the Word either by self-inflicted blindness of the evidence or by fear. The reader has seen examples of both during the trial. Here the disciples have the power to manage any opposition to their testimony. Jesus and his resurrection has transformed the disciples to become believers who testify, and they do so when they encounter Thomas.

Thomas is not in the room when Jesus arrived. Either he is not afraid or he did not gather with them in the house. The text does not say why he was not with them. Even though there are multiple testimonies, Thomas refuses to believe the witnesses to the resurrection; he needs tangible proof. Even with indisputable evidence of multiple witnesses he still does not believe. He wants a visible sign for proof. Jesus will clarify for him that the testimony itself is sufficient proof: "Have you believed because you have seen me. Blessed are those who have not seen and yet have come to believe" (20:29). Thomas is now a believer, and that he upgrades his reaction by saying "My Lord and my God."

John 20:30-31 summarizes the purpose of the Gospel: "³⁰ Now Jesus did many other signs in the presence of his disciples, which are not written in this book. ³¹ But these are written so that you may come to believe that Jesus is the Messiah, the Son of God, and that through believing you may have life in his name." No doubt that belief in Jesus generates life for the believer. It is a constant theme throughout the Gospel. There is a general consensus among scholars that the last sentence in John 20 was the original ending and that chapter 21 was appended later.[392] There is never a time in the transmission history that chapter 21 was missing from John. Still, it is impossible to say whether the chapter was written by the original author or a redactor.[393] It is also unclear why the redundancy created

---

[392] Paul Trudinger, "Subtle Ironies and Word-Plays in John's Gospel and The Problems of Chapter 21," *St Mark's Review* 162 (1995): 22.

[393] Tom Thatcher states that "John 21:24-25 should be viewed as an unknown editor's attempt to wrap up the revised narrative by returning to

at the end of John 21 was not avoided. Twice it states that many other things/signs that Jesus did were not recorded. John 21, however, clarifies that the beloved disciple testifies and that the testimony is backed up by other voices: "We know that his testimony is true" (21:24). The reader does not know this from the ending in 20:30. Likewise, 20:30 offers information that 21 leaves out, that the testimony leads to belief: "So that you may come to believe that Jesus is the Messiah, the Son of God and that through believing you many have life in his name." My intention is to read the Gospel in light of the final redactor/editor. I see the repetition in 20:30 and 21:30-31 as bookends to underscore the role and importance of the final chapter.

Peter and Jesus: Fear to Love

Chapter 21 has a number of parallels with the rest of the Gospel. Seven disciples gather at the Sea of Tiberias. It is the location of the feeding of the five thousand in chapter 6. The last time the disciples were on the sea they were in a boat when they encountered Jesus who they did not recognize. In both stories, the boat is not far from shore. Also, along the sea in chapter 6, Jesus feeds the five thousand with bread and fish. Again in chapter 21, Jesus feeds with fish and bread. In both scenes, an abundance of food appears through Jesus'

---

the theme of John's closing remarks." See his "John's Memory Theater: The Fourth Gospel and Ancient Mnemo-Rhetoric," *CBQ* 69 (2007): 504.

word, more than enough to satisfy all.³⁹⁴ The charcoal fire (ἀνθρακιά) brings the audience back to the courtyard where Peter denied Jesus three times.³⁹⁵ Light breaks through the darkness, recalling once more the prologue, "light shines in the darkness" (1:5). During the dark of the night they catch nothing. Without the light and the Lord they cannot do anything (cf. 9:4; 12;35). Without Jesus, the seven cannot even produce enough fish to put on a cracker for an appetizer (hors d'oeuvre, προσφάγιον). With Jesus' help, they catch 153 very large fish, an extraordinary amount (21:6).³⁹⁶ The Gospel often boasts of extraordinary amounts (100 pounds of myrrh, 300 days wages of perfumed oil, etc.).³⁹⁷

Themes of the resurrection scene also appear in the narrative. There is a contrast between Peter and the beloved disciple. The beloved disciple recognizes Jesus quicker than Peter. Due to the fact

---

³⁹⁴ For example, the verb ἑλκείν (drag) occurs five times in John. and in four of these with a theological significance relating to the theme of ingathering (6:44, 12:32, 21:6, 21:11).

³⁹⁵ The word ἀνθρακιά is only used twice in the New Testament (18:18 and 21:9).

³⁹⁶ There are similarities with the call of Peter in Luke in Luke 5:1-11. Both narratives report of fishing all night, Jesus giving directives to cast out the nets, an extraordinary haul, a net that almost rips, Peter's reaction to the haul, Jesus addressed as Lord, and that other fishermen help with the haul. There are also differences in John's account: Jesus is not recognized, Jesus is on shore, and Peter rushes to the Lord whereas in Luke, Peter asks Jesus to depart.

³⁹⁷ The Gospel often refers to numbers: "the tenth hour" (1:39); "46 years" (2:20) "five porticos" (5:2) "38 years" (5:5) "100 pounds" (19:39); "153 large fish" (21:11).

that chapter 21 has many features and themes of the Gospel, I contend that the author/redactor intended a seamless and continuous flow building on the theological thesis of the Gospel. For this, I will continue to examine the chapter as I have done with the others using composition theory.

Once again, Jesus' death and resurrection has transforming effects on believers who have failed to witness due to fear. The three denials around the charcoal fire in the high priest's courtyard are replaced with three emphatic statements of love.[398] After Peter confesses his love, Jesus confirms his conviction by telling him the kind of death he would die, recalling Jesus' words: "There is no greater love than this than to lay down one's life for one's friends" (15:13). He is asked to feed lambs, tend sheep, and feed sheep. The food Jesus provided in chapter 6 is food for everlasting life which the reader understands as God's Word/revelation. As a witness, Peter will pro-

---

[398] There are two distinct terms for the word love in the exchange between Jesus and Peter: φιλέω and ἀγαπάω. These two terms are interchangeably used throughout the Gospel. Frequently, John uses words that are polyvalent in meaning. The Gospel of John demonstrates a predisposition to use terms that have multiple lexical definitions and double entendre. There is no need to strictly assign significance to each one. Brown warns not to draw distinctions between synonymous terms such as γινώσκω (know) and οἶδα (know) as does de la Potterie in his "ΟΙδα et γινώσκω: Les deux modes de connaissance dans le Quatrième évangile," *Bib* 40 (1959): 709-25. Brown argues that "John may tend to use one verb in one way and the other verb in another way, but it is really a question of emphasis and not of sharp distinction. The evangelist is not so precise as his commentators would make him." Brown, *John*, 731 n. 5.

vide eternal life to others by his witness to the truth. His death, predicted by Jesus, will be the direct consequence of his feeding, just as Jesus died to offer life to others. There are a lot of recognizable features in this passage that characterize witnesses, such as obedience to Jesus' word, knowledge of Jesus and his location, and a water container (Sea of Tiberius). Peter obeys Jesus when he asks to bring more fish from the catch (21:11) and none of them dare ask, including Peter, if it is Jesus (21:12).

Since Jesus' death, believers have been transformed into witnesses. They no longer have a reason to fear because death now is a gate, a passage that leads to eternal life. Jesus' words lead to everlasting life. The sheep follow the voice of the good shepherd: "When he has brought out all his own, he goes ahead of them, and the sheep follow (ἀκολουθέω) him because they know his voice" (10:4). Peter is told to feed, but he still remains a sheep: "After this he said to him, 'Follow (ἀκολουθέω) me'" (21:19).

As Jesus takes the lead and moves out, Peter turns and sees the beloved disciple following Him. The text identifies the beloved disciple as the one who asked about the betrayer and had reclined next to Jesus at table. Peter asks about him, but Jesus again instructs him to follow—that is, do the very thing the beloved disciple is doing just behind him: "following." Now that Peter is a believer who witnesses, he must understand that some will pay a price for witnessing and some will not. Some will be rejected like the witness of the man born blind, and some will be well received like the Samaritan woman. Peter's testimony will bring about his death, and the beloved disciple may not die. The two, however, find common ground by following Jesus.

Bultmann claimed that the theme of John's Gospel can be summed up in one simple phrase: "Jesus the revealer."[399]

Closing Thought

The purpose of this study was to advance composition theory or intratextuality as a legitimate method for understanding the intention of the human author. Often scholars use intertextuality as the primary resource. That is, seeking outside texts to understand what the author wants to imply. Intratextuality is a more precise tool for understanding authorial intent than other historical critical methods.

The purpose of the Gospel addresses fears that have arisen in the community of believers. Fear prevents one from witnessing to the truth so that others may believe and have access to filial life with God and eternal salvation. Using the Christ story, one could replace fear with love because Christ destroyed death and allowed one to abide in the presence of God. There is no greater love for another than to provide access to God. I contend that the author/redactor of the canonical Gospel (*textus receptus*) presents a detailed divine plan to create a family through the power of revelation, beginning with the divine Word coming into the world and ending with the inheritance of eternal life for believers. The Word, or revelation, is the key element in this dynamic. A witness is sent to reveal divine truth, the Word of God, a divine gift because it does not have human origin.

---

[399] Rudolf Bultmann, *Theologie des Neuen Testaments* (Tübingen, 1961), 402-422.

So, there is a tension between believing the Word and not. In order to believe, the word has to be authentic. The only way to validate the authenticity of the revelation is by knowing the origin of the Word. Those who believe must know that the origin of revelation is from God. So, anyone exposed to revelation must immediately contend with the first obstacle of verifying the validity of the revelation. To overcome this obstacle, the revealer presents two witnesses. Jesus introduces his Father as a second witness, and the believer abides in the Holy Spirit as his or her own witness. The one who accepts the revelation as true will encounter a second obstacle: fear. They fear non-believers who have the potential to become violent towards them. To overcome this obstacle, Jesus offers eternal life, thereby routing out any death-threats from non-believers. Once the believer surpasses this fear, he or she becomes a testifier for others to believe. They have access to the Holy Spirit to provide proof for their testimony. As for those who refuse to believe, they typically fail to disprove authenticity of the testimony, resorting instead to violence and threatening the believer. Their threats are weakened by Christ who gives the Spirit, truth, and eternal life. The behaviors of the believers and the rejecters are polar opposites of each other: the activity of non-believers is violence which leads to death, while the activity of believers is testifying to the truth which leads to life.

I argued that the dynamic between the activities of believers and non-believers makes up the theological framework of the entire Gospel. This structure is first introduced in the prologue, which provides the interpretive background for what follows. The section-by-section examination of the Gospel allowed me to offer evidence to substantiate these claims with textual support. I pointed out the reoccurring themes (revelation, witness, origin, and belief) in the narrative progression. Some of these terms and themes were represented by various symbols and expression of thought: water represented revelation, eating Christ's flesh and drinking his blood represented acceptance of Christ as the creative Word which produces an intimate relationship with God (children), and the gate represented a passage from death to life. Expressions and terms have been given special meaning. Even the Jewish feasts are given new Christological meaning. Due to the fact that familiar terms have been altered in significance, it is difficult to understand the Gospel by importing meaning from other sources. This is why there are so many varied and unresolved disputes among scholars who attempt to understand the Gospel in terms of historical critical methods alone.

In the first century, many people did not have immediate access to the Gospel. It was imperative to reach out. I know if I lived in the first century and no one gave me the opportunity to have access to eternal through the gospel, I would have been very upset. It was urgent for Christians to offer the gift of the Gospel to others. People, however, were denied this valuable information due to fearful Christians. This Gospel addresses this fear.

Finally, the Gospel offers the modern-day reader an opportunity to appreciate the value of revelation that has been passed on to us. Many sacrificed so that we could have access to God through Christ. The gift of faith puts us into a family of God and promises us eternal life. Revelation allows us to have divine knowledge so that we, too, have the privilege and benefit of being in the bosom of God.

Appendix
Woman Caught in Adultery

Many scholars, including myself, contend that the passage on the Woman caught in adultery was an interpolation. There are many commentaries that discuss this, so I will leave it to these to elaborate on this issue. The constant theme of revelation is missing in this passage, so I will make some observations about the text without referencing the rest of the Gospel of John.

A woman is caught in adultery. The first question that comes to mind is where is the guy, since they only have the woman? One gets the impression that this was a setup. There was a sinister plot behind this. They needed a sinner to get to Jesus and expose Him to a no-win situation. The problem with the plotters is that their scheme is a greater sin than adultery. The sin of adultery pales in the light of a plot to destroy the Son of God. There is no record of what Jesus wrote in the sand, but it caused the accusers to leave, beginning with the elders, who were most likely the masterminds of the plot. The writing suggests that the men are all gravely sinful, and Jesus knows about the plot.

Jesus, of course, lets them all go. What is the difference between the men who were plotting the death of the son of God and the woman caught in adultery? The men leave disappointed because their trap was foiled. They will continue to find a way to plot against Christ and put him to death. They experience no change, and their horrible past stays with them. The woman, however, goes away with a reason to begin a new life. Her past can be erased easily as a marking in the sand.

Bibliography of Texts Used

Aland, Kurt. "Eine Untersuchung zu Joh. 1.3/4 Uber die Bedeuting eines Punkte.'" *ZNW* 59 (1968): 174-209.

Alter, Roberts. *The Art of Biblical Narrative*. New York: Basic, 1981.

Aloisi, John. "The Paraclete's Ministry of Conviction: Another Look at John 16:8-11." *JET* 47 (2004): 55-69.

Anderson, Paul N. *The Christology of the Fourth Gospel: Its Unity and Disunity in the Light of John 6*. Valley Forge, PA: Trinity Press International, 1996.

Attridge, Harold W. "The Samaritan Woman: A Woman Transformed," Pages 268-81 in *Character Studies in the Fourth Gospel: Narrative Approaches to Seventy Figures in John*. Edited by Steven A. Hunt, D. Francois Tolmie, and Ruben Zimmermann; WUNT 314; Tubingen: Mohr Siebeck, 2013.

Auwers, Jean-Marie. "La nuit de Nicodème." *RB* 97 (1990): 482.

Bassler, Jouette M. "Mixed Signals: Nicodemus in the Fourth Gospel." *JBL* 108 (1989): 635-46.

Balfour, Glen. "The Jewishness of John's use of the Scriptures in John 6:31 and 7:37-38." *Tyndale Bulletin* 46 (1995): 357-80.

Barnabas, Lindars. *The Gospel of John: New Century Bible*. London: Marshall, Morgan & Scott, 1972.

Barrett, Charles K. "John and the Synoptic Gospels." *ExpTim* 85 (1973-74): 228-33.

_____, *The Gospel According to St. John*. London: SPCK, 1955.

Barrosse, D Thomas. "The Seven Days of the New Creation in St. John's Gospel." *CBQ* 21 (1959): 507-16.

Bauckham, Richard. "Historiographical Characteristics of the Gospel of John." *NTS* 53 (2007): 17-36.

_____. *The Testimony of the Beloved Disciple: Narrative, History, and Theology in the Gospel of John*. Grand Rapids: Baker Academic, 2007.

Beasley-Murray, Craig L. *John*. Waco: Word, 1987.

Beutler, Johannes. "Greeks Come to See Jesus (John 12:20f)." *Bib* 71 (1990): 333-47.

Bennema, Cornelis. *Encountering Jesus: Character Studies in the Gospel of John*. Milton Keynes: Paternoster, 2009.

Blackwell, J. Miriam. "The Hour of Jesus in the Gospel According to John." *Journal of Theta Alpha Kappa* 3 (1980): 15-19.

Blank, J. "Die Verhandlung vor Pilatus Joh 18, 28-19, 16 im Lichte johanneischer Theologie." *BZ* 3 (1959): 60-81.

Blomberg, George R. "The Globalization of Biblical Interpretation: A Test Case—John 3-4." *BBR* 5 (1995): 1-15.

Boismard, Marie-Emile. "Du Bapteme a Cana (Jean 1.19-2.11)." *Theology Digest* 13 (1965): 39-44

_____. "Les Tradtions,"

_____. *Moses or Jesus: An Essay in Johannine Christology*. Translated by B.T. Viviano; Leuven, Belgium: Leuven University Press, 1993.

Borgen, Peder. "God's Agent in the Fourth Gospel," Pages 137-148 in *Religions in Antiquity: Essays in Memory of Erwin Ramsdell Goodenough*. Leiden: Brill, 1968.

_____. "Logos Was the True Light: Contributions to the Interpretation of the Prologue of John." *NT* 14 (1972): 115-130.

Born, J. Bryan "Literary Features in The Gospel of John (An Analysis of John 3:1-21)," *Direction* 17 (1988): 3-17.

Bouma-Prediger, Steven. "Water in Biblical Reflection." *Word & World* 32 (2012): 42-50;

Brodie, Thomas, *The Quest for the Origin of John's Gospel: A Source-Oriented Approach*. New York: Oxford University Press, 1993.

Brown, Raymond Edward. *The Death of the Messiah: From Gethsemane to the Grave: A Commentary on the Passion Narratives in the Four Gospels*. New York: Doubleday, 1994.

_____. *The Community of the Beloved Disciple: The Life, Loves, and Hates of an Individual Church in New Testament Times*. New York: Paulist, 1979.

_____. *The Dead Sea Scrolls and the New Testament*. London: Geoffrey Chapman Pub, 1972.

_____. *The Gospel of John, A Commentary on the Gospel of John*. Garden City, NY: Doubleday, 1966, 1970.

_____. "The Paraclete in the Fourth Gospel." *NTS* 13 (1967): 113-38.

Brown, Sherri. "Water Imagery and the Power and Presence of God in the Gospel of John." *Theology Today* 72 (2015): 289-98.

Brown, Tricia Gates. *Spirit in the Writings of John*. London: T &T Clark, 2003.

Bulembat, Jean-Bosco Matand. "Head-Waiter and Bridegroom of the Wedding at Cana: Structure and Meaning of John 2.1-12." *JSNT* 30 (2007): 55-73.

Bultmann, Rudolf. "Der religionsgeschichtliche Hintergrund des Prologs zum Johannes-Evangelium." Pages 1-26 in *Eucharisterion: für H. Gunkel II*. Göttingen: Vandenhoeck &Ruprecht, 1923.

———. *The Gospel of John: A Commentary.* Translated by G. R. Beasley-Murray, R. W. N. Hoare, and J. K. Riches; Philadelphia: Fortress, 1971.

———. *Theologie des Neuen Testaments.* Tübingen, 1961.

———. *Theology of the New Testament.* Translated by Kendrick Grobel, 2 vols. New York: Charles Scribner's Sons, 1951 and 1955.

Bussche H. Van den. "Le signe du Temple." *BVC* (1957): 92-100.

Caneday, Ardel. "The Word Made Flesh as Mystery Incarnate: Revealing and Concealing Dramatized by Jesus as Portrayed in John's Gospel." *Jets* 60 (2017): 751-65.

Carmichael, Calum M. "Marriage and the Samaritan Woman." *NTS* 26 (1980): 332-346.

Carson, D. A. *The Gospel according to John.* Grand Rapids: Eerdmans, 1991.

Carroll, John T. and Joel B. Green. *The Death of Jesus in Early Christianity.* Peabody, MA: Hendrickson, 1995.

Carter, Warren. "The Prologue and John's Gospel: Function, Symbol and the Definitive Word." *JSNT* 39 (1990): 35-58.

Ceroke, Christian. "The Problem of Ambiguity in John 2:4." *CBQ* 21 (1959): 316-40.

Charlesworth, James H. "Exploring Opportunities for Rethinking Relations among Jews and Christians." Pages 35-53 in *Jews and Christians: Exploring the Past, Present, and Future.* New York: Crossroad, 1990.

Chennattu, Rekha. "On Becoming Disciples (John 1:35-51): Insights from the Fourth Gospel." *Salesianum* 63 (2001): 465-496.

Chilton, Bruce. "The Gospel according to John's Rabbi Jesus." *BBR* 25 (2015): 39-54.

Coloe, Mary L. "Welcome into the Household of God: The Foot Washing in John 13." *CBQ* 66 (2004): 400-15.

Cortes, Juan B. "Yet Another Look at John 7:37-38." *CBQ* 29 (1967): 75-86.

Cotterell, Peter. "The Nicodemus Conversation: A Fresh Appraisal." *ExpTim* 96 (1984-85): 237-42

Cullmann, Oscar. "Der johannische Gebrauch doppeldeutiger Ausdriicke als Schliissel zum Verstandnis des vierten Evangeliums." Theologische Zeitschrift 4 (1948): 360-72.

Culpepper, R. Alan. *Anatomy of the Fourth Gospel: A Study in Literary Design*. Philadelphia: Fortress, 1983.

_____. *The Gospel and Letters of John*. Nashville, Tn: Abingdon, 1998.

_____. "The Theology of the Gospel of John," *Review and Expositor* 85 (1988): 417-32.

Dale C. Allison, Jr. "The Living Water (John 4:10-14, 6:35c, 7:37-39)." *St Vladimir's Theological Quarterly* 30 (1986), 143-157;

Danna, Elizabeth. "A Note on John 4:29." *RB* 106 (1999): 219-223.

Davidson, JoAnn. "John 4: Another Look at the Samaritan Woman." *Andrews University Seminary Studies* 43 (2005): 159-168.

De Boer, Martinus C. *Johannine Perspectives on the Death of Jesus, Contributions to Biblical Exegesis and Theology 17*. Kampen: Kok Pharos Publishing House, 1996.

_____. "Narrative Criticism, Historical Criticism, and the Gospel of John." *JSNT* 47 (1992): 35-48.

Dennison, James. "The Prologue of John's Gospel." *Kerux: A Journal of Biblical-Theological Preaching* 8 (1993): 3-9.

De Jonge, Marinus. "Nicodemus and Jesus: Some Observations on Misunderstanding and Understanding in the Fourth Gospel." *BJRL* 53 (1971): 337-59.

De la Potterie, "*Charis* paulinienne et *charis* johannique," Pages in 252-285 in *Jesus und Paulus*: Festschrift für *Werner Georg Kümmel zum 70*. Geburstag. Edited by E. Earle Ellis and Erich Grässer; Göttingen: Vandenhoeck & Ruprecht, 1975.

_____. "De punctuatie en de exegese van Joh 1,3.4 in de traditie." *Bijdragen* 16 (1955): 117-35.

_____. "Jésus roi et juge d'après Jn 19, 13." *Bib* 41 (1960): 236-40.

_____. "L'emploi de eis dans Saint Jean et ses incidences theologiques," *Biblica* 43 (1962): 366-87

_____. *Maria nel Mistero dell'alleanza*. Genova: Mariet, 1988.

_____. *The Hour of Jesus: The Passion and the Resurrection of Jesus According to John*. New York: Alba, 1989.

Derrett, Duncan M. "Intoxication, Joy, and Wrath: 1 Cor 11:21 and Jn 2:10." *FN* 2 (1989): 41-56.

Destro, Adriana and Mauro Pesce. "Discipleship, and Movement: An Anthropological Study of John's Gospel." *Biblical Interpretation* 3 (1995): 266-284.

Dibelius, Martin and Hans Conzelmann, *The Pastoral Epistles*. Hermeneia; Philadelphia: Fortress, 1972.

Di Luccio, Pino. "La Risurrezione Di Lazzaro." *La Civilta Cattolica* 166 (2015): 17-29.

Do, Toan "Revisiting the Woman of Samaria and the Ambiguity of Faith in John 4:4-42." *CBQ* 81 (2019): 252-276.

Dodd, Charles Harold. *Historical Tradition in the Fourth Gospel*. London: Cambridge University Press, 1976.

Dodd, Chris H. *The Interpretation of the Fourth Gospel.* Cambridge: CUP, 1953.

Dolan, Mary Ellen. "Irony in The Gospel of John Part II: Specific Uses of Irony in the Fourth Gospel." *Journal of Theta Alpha Kappa* 11 (1987): 2-9.

Droge, Arthur J. "The Status of Peter in the Fourth Gospel: A Note on John 18:10-11." *JBL* 109 (1990): 307-11.

Duke, P. D. *Irony in the Fourth Gospel.* Atlanta: John Knox, 1985.

Dunn, James D. B. "The Washing of the Disciples' Feet in John 13:1-20." *ZNW Zeitschrift fur die Neutestamentliche Wissenschaft* 61 (1970): 247-52.

Edwards, R. B. "Charin anti charitos (John 1:16): Grace and Law in the Johannine Prologue." *JSNT* 32 (1988): 3-15.

Ellens, J. Harold. "A Christian Pesher: John 1:51." *Proceedings* (2005): 143-55.

Esler, Philip F. *Community and Gospel in Luke-Acts: The Social and Political Motivations of Lucan Theology.* SNTSMS 57; Cambridge: Cambridge University Press, 1987.

Farelly, Nicolas. "An Unexpected Ally: Nicodemus's Role within the Plot of the Fourth Gospel." *TrinJ* 34 (2013): 31-43.

Fiorenza, Elisabeth Schussler. *In Memory of Her: A Feminist Theological Reconstruction of Christian Origins.* New York: Crossroad, 1984.

Fokkelman, J. P. *Reading Biblical Narrative: An Introductory Guide*, trans. Ineke Smit. Louisville, KY: Westminster John Knox, 1999.

_____. *Narrative Art in Genesis: Specimens of Stylistic and Structural Analysis.* Sheffield: JSOT Press, 1991.

Forma, Robert T. *The Gospel of Signs: A Reconstruction of the Narrative Source Underlying the Fourth Gospel*. SNTSMS 11; Cambridge: Cambridge University Press, 1970.

Förster, Hans. "Die Begegnung am Brunnen (Joh 4.4-42) im Licht der 'Schrift': Überlegungen zu den Samaritanern im Johannesevangelium." *NTS* 61 (2015): 201-218.

Freed, Edwin D. "Egō Eimi in John 1:20 and 4:25." *CBQ* 41 (1979): 288-91.

Frye, Northrop. "Literary Criticism" in *The Aims and Methods of Scholarship in Modern Languages and Literatures*. Edited by James Thorpe; New York: Modern Language Association of America, 1963.

Gangel, Kenneth O. *John*. Holman New Testament Commentary Series; Nashville: B&H Publishing, 2000.

Gieschen, Charles A. "Baptism and the Lord's Supper in the Gospel of John." *CTQ* 78 (2014): 23-45.

_____. "The Death of Jesus in the Gospel of John: Atonement for Sin?" *CTQ* 72 (2008): 243-261.

Gingrich, W. "Ambiguity of Word Meaning in John's Gospel." *Classical Weekly* 37 (1943): 77;

Grassi, Joseph A. "The Role of Jesus' Mother in John's Gospel: A Reappraisal." *CBQ* 48 (1986): 67-80.

Gorman, Michael J. "John: The Nonsectarian, Missional Gospel." *Canadian-American Theological Review* 7 (2018): 138-62.

Guelich, Robert A. *Mark 1-8:26*. WBC 34A; Dallas: Word, 1989.

Gundry, Robert H. "New Wine in Old Wineskins: Bursting Traditional Interpretations in John's Gospel (Part 1)." *BBR* 17 (2007): 115-130.

Haenchen, E. *John I*. Hermeneia; Philadelphia: Fortress, 1984.

Häfner, Gerd; Pettinger, Diana; Witetschek, Stephan. "Die Salbung Jesu durch Maria (Joh 12,1-8)." *Biblische Notizen* 122 (2004): 81-104.

Hakola, Raimo. "Burden of Ambiguity: Nicodemus and the Social Identity of the Johannine Christians." *NTS* 55 (2009): 438-55.

Harnack, A. von "Über das Verhältnis des prologs des vierten Evangeliums zum ganzen Werk.'" *ATK* 2 (1892): 189-231.

Harrington, H. K., "Purification in the Fourth Gospel in light of Qumran." Pages 117-38 in *John, Qumran, and the Dead Sea Scrolls: Sixty Years of Discovery and Debate*. Edited by M. L. Cole et al.; SBLEJL 32; Atlanta: Society of Biblical Literature, 2011.

Hays, Richard, *The Moral Vision of the New Testament: A Contemporary Introduction to New Testament Ethics*. San Francisco: HarperSanFrancisco, 1996.

Heil, John Paul. "Jesus as the Unique High Priest in the Gospel of John." *CBQ* 57 (1995): 729-45.

_____. *Jesus Walking on the Sea: Meaning and Gospel Functions of Matt 14:22-33, Mark 6:45-52 and John 6:15b-21*. AnBib 87; Rome: Biblical Institute, 1981.

Hengel, Martin. "The Prologue of the Gospel as the Key to Christological Truth," Pages 265-94 in *The Gospel of John and Christian Theology*. Edited by R. Bauckham & C. Mosser; Grand Rapids: Eerdmans, 2008.

Hooker, Morna. *Jesus and the Servant*. London: SPCK, 1959.

Hoskyns, Edwyn Clement. *The Fourth Gospel*. Second edition; London: Faber, 1947.

Hultgren, Arland J. "The Johannine Foot-Washing." *New Testament Studies* 28 (1982): 539-46.

Hylen, Susan E. *Imperfect Believers: Ambiguous Characters in the Gospel of John.* Louisville: John Knox, 2009.

_____. "The Shepherd's Risk: Thinking Metaphorically with John's Gospel." Bibint 24 (2016): 382-99.

Infante, Joan Salazar. "Jesus Shed Tears in Frustration: The Contribution of dakryō and klaiō to the Interpretation of John 11:35." Pacifica 27 (2014): 239-252.

Janzen, J. Gerald. "How Can a Man Be Born When He Is Old?: Jacob/Israel in Genesis and the Gospel Of John." *Encounter* 65 (2004): 339-40.

Jeremias, Joachim. *Parables of Jesus.* London, S.C.M, 1972.

Johnson, Luke T. *The Writings of the New Testament: An Interpretation.* London: SCM, 1986.

Jojko, Bernadeta. "Eternity and Time in the Gospel of John." *Verbum Vitae* 35 (2019): 245-78

_____, *Worshiping the Father in Spirit and Truth: An Exegetico-Theological Study of 4:20-26 in the Light of Relationships Among the Father, the Son and the Holy Spirit.* Tesi Gregoriana 193; Roma: Gregorian & Biblical Press 2012.

Jones, Larry P. *The Symbol of Water in the Gospel of John.* JSNT Sup 145; Sheffield: Sheffield Academic, 1997.

Karakolis, Cristos. "Recurring Characters in John 1:19–2:11" in *The Opening of John's Narrative (John 1:19–2:22): Historical, Literary, and Theological Readings from the Colloquium Ioanneum 2015 in Ephesus.* Wissenschaftliche Untersuchungen zum

Neuen Testament 385; Edited by R. Alan Culpepper and Jörg Frey; Tübingen: Mohr Siebeck, 2017.

Käsemann, Ernst. "The Structure and Purpose of the Prologue to John's Gospel," Pages 138-67 in *New Testament Questions of Today*. Philadelphia: Fortress, 1969.

_____. *The Testament of Jesus: A Study of the Gospel of John in Light of Chapter 17*. London: SCM, 1968.

Keener, Craig. *The Gospel of John: A Commentary*. Vol. 1; Peabody, Mass: Hendrickson, 2003.

Kilpatrick, George Dunbar. "The Punctuation of John vii 37-38." *JTS* 11 (1960): 340-42.

Kim, Seyoon. *The Origins of Paul's Gospel*. WUNT 2/4 Tübingen: Mohr, 1981.

Kim, Stephen S. "The Significance of Jesus' Raising Lazarus from the Dead in John 11," *Bibliotheca sacra* 168 (2011): 53-62.

Kirk, David R. "Heaven Opened: Intertextuality and Meaning in John 1:51." *Tyndale Bulletin* 63 (2012): 237-56.

Klingbeil, Gerald, "Water." Pages 818-21in *The New Interpreters Dictionary of the Bible*, ed. Katharine Sakenfeld; Vol 5. Nashville: Abingdon, 2009.

Knoppler, Thomas. *Die theologia crucis des Johannesevangelium*. WMANT 69; Neukirchen-Vluyn: Neukirchener Verlag, 1994.

Koester, Craig R. "Hearing, Seeing, and Believing in the Gospel of John." *Biblica* 70 (1989): 327-48.

_____. "Messianic Exegesis and the Call of Nathanael (John 1:45-51)." *JSNT* 39 (1990): 23-34.

_____. *Symbolism in the Fourth Gospel: Meaning, Mystery Community*. Minneapolis: Fortress, 1995.

_____. *The Word of Life: A Theology of John's Gospel*. Grand Rapids: Eerdmans, 2008.

Kostenberger, Andreas. *A Theology of John's Gospel and Letters*. BTNT; Grand Rapids: Zondervan, 2009.

Kowalski, J. A., "On Water and Spirit: Narrative Structure and Theological Development in the Gospel of John." Ph.D. diss., Marquette University, 1987.

Kurek-Chomycz, Dominika A. "The Fragrance of Her Perfume: The Significance of Sense Imagery in John's Account of the Anointing in Bethany." *NovT* 52 (2010): 334-354.

Kysar, Robert. "Anti-Semitism and the Gospel of John." Pages 113-137 in *Anti-Semitism and Early Christianity*. Edited by Craig A. Evans and Donald A. Hagner; Minneapolis: Fortress, 1993.

_____. *The Fourth Evangelist and His Gospel: The Examination of Contemporary Scholarship*. Minneapolis: Augsburg Publishing House, 1975.

Lausberg, H. *Handbuch der literarischen Rhetorik: Eine Grundlegung der Literaturwissenschaft*. 2d ed.; Munich: Hueber, 1973.

Lee, Dorothy A. "Abiding in the Fourth Gospel: A Case-study in Feminist Biblical Theology." *Pacifica* 10 (1997): 123-36.

_____. "Creation, Ethics, and the Gospel of John," Pages XXX in *John and Ethics*. Edited by S. Brown &

_____. "Creation, Matter, and the Image of God in the Gospel of John." *St Vladimir's Theological Quarterly* 62 (2018): 101-17.

_____. "Signs and Works: The Miracles in The Gospels of Mark and John." *Colloquium* 47 (2015): 89-101.

_____. "The Significance of Moses in The Gospel of John." *ABR* 63 (2015): 52-66.

Leon-Dufour, Xavier. *Lecture de Vévangile selon Jean*. Paris: Editions du Seuil, 1988.

Lightfoot, Robert H. *St. John's Gospel: A Commentary*. Oxford: Clarendon, 1983.

Lincoln, Andrew T. *The Gospel According to Saint John*. BNTC; Peabody, MA: Hendrickson, 2005.

Lindars, Barnabas. "Rebuking The Spirit a New Analysis of the Lazarus Story of John 11." *NTS* 38 (1992): 89-104.

_____. *The Gospel of John: New Century Bible*. London: Marshall, Morgan &Scott, 1972.

Loader, William. "John 1:51 and Johannine Christology" in *Historical, Literary, and Theological Readings from the Colloquium Ioanneum 2015 in Ephesus*. Wssenschaftliche Untersuchungen zum Neuen Testament 385. Edited by R. Alan Culpepper and Jörg Frey; Tübingen: Mohr Siebeck, 2017.

Maccini, Robert Gordon. "A Reassessment of the Woman at the well in John 4 in Light of the Samaritan Context." *JSNT* 53 (1994): 35-46.

Marsh, J. *St John*. Philadelphia: Westminster, 1968.

Martyn, J. Louis. *History and Theology in the Fourth Gospel*. Nashville: Abingdon, 1979.

McHugh, John. *Mother of Jesus in the New Testament*. Garden City, NY: Doubleday, 1975.

Meeks, Wayne A. "The Ethics of the Fourth Evangelist." Pages 318-319 in *Exploring the Gospel of John. Essays in honour of Dwight Moody Smith*. Edited by R. Alan Culpepper and C. Clifton Black; Louisville, Ky.: Westminster John Knox, 1996.

_____. "The Man from Heaven in Johannine Sectarianism." *Journal of Biblical Literature* 91 (1972): 44-72.

_____. *The Prophet-King: Moses Traditions and the Johannine Christology*. Leiden: E.J. Brill, 1967.

Menken, Martinus J. J. *Old Testament Quotations in the Fourth Gospel: Studies in Textual Form*. Kampen, Netherlands: Kok Pharos, 1996.

Michaels, J. Ramsey. "By Water and Blood: Sin and Purification in John and First John." Pages 149-62 in *Dimensions of Baptism: Biblical and theological Studies*. Edited by S. E. Porter and A. R. Cross; JSNTSup 234; Sheffield: Sheffield Academic Press, 2002.

Miller, Ed. L. *Salvation-History in the Prologue of John: The Significance of John 1:3/4*. Supplements to Novum Testamentum LX; Leiden: Brill, 1989.

Moloney, Francis J. *Belief in the Word: Reading the Fourth Gospel, John 1–4*. Minneapolis: Fortress, 1993.

_____. "Can Everyone Be Wrong? A Reading of John 11.1-12.8." *NTS* 49 (2003): 505-527.

_____. *Gospel of John*. Collegeville, MN: Liturgical, 1998.

_____. "'In the Bosom of' or 'Turned towards' the Father." AusBR 31 (1983): 63-71.

_____. *Love in the Gospel of John: An Exegetical, Theological, and Literary Study*. Grand Rapids, Ml: Baker Academic, 2013.

_____. "The Faith of Martha and Mary: A Narrative Approach to John 11,17-40." *Biblica* 75 (1994): 471-493.

_____. *The Gospel of Mark: A Commentary*. Peabody, MA: Hendrickson, 2002.

_____. "The Structure and Message of John 13:1-38." *AusBR* 34 (1986): 1-16.

Moore, W. E. " Sir, We Wish to See Jesus. Was This an Occasion of Temptation?" *SJT* 20 (1967): 75-93.

Morris, Leon. *Reflections on the Gospel of John. II. The Bread of Life, John 6-10*. Grand Rapids: Baker, 1987.

_____. *The Gospel According to John*. Grand Rapids, MI: Eerdmans, 1995.

Moule, Charles Francis Digby. "A Note on 'under the Fig Tree' in John 1:48. 50f." *Journal of Theological Studies* 5 (1954), 210-11.

Moulinier, Louis. *Le pur et L'impur dans la pensée des Grecs d'Homère à Aristote*. Paris: Klincksieck, 1952.

Myers, Slicia D. "The Ambiguous Character of Johannine Characterization: An Overview of Recent Contributions and Proposal." *PRST* 39 (2012): 289-98.

Neeb, John Herman Conrad. "Jacob/Jesus typology in John 1:51." *Proceedings* (1992): 83-89.

Neirynck, Frans. "John and the Synoptics." Pages 73-106 in *L'Évangile de Jean: Sources, Rédaction, Théologie*. Edited by Marinus de Jonge; BETL44; Leuven: Leuven University Press, 1977.

Neyrey, Jerome H. *The Gospel of John*. Cambridge: Cambridge University Press, 2007.

_____. "The Jacob Allusions in John 1:51." *CBQ* 44 (1982): 586-605.

Ng, Wai-yee. *Water Symbolism in John: An Eschatological Interpretation*. New York: Peter Lang, 2001.

O'Grady, John F. "The Prologue and Chapter 17 of the Gospel of John." Pages 215-28 in *What We Have Heard from the Beginning: The Past, Present, and Future of Johannine Studies*. Edited by Tom Thatcher; Waco: Baylor University Press, 2007.

Okure, Teresa. *The Johannine Approach to Mission: A Contextual Study of John 4:1-42*. WUNT, 2; Tübingen: J.C.B. Mohr [Paul Siebeck], 1988.

O'Neill, Jon Cochrane. "Son of Man, Stone of Blood (John 1:51)." *NT* (2003): 143-155.

Oudtshoom, Andre van. "Where Have All the Demons Gone?: The Role and Place of the Devil in the Gospel of John." *Neotestamentica* 51 (2017) 65-82.

Painter, John. "Earth Made Whole: John's Reading of Genesis." Pages 65-84 in *Word, Theology, and Community in John*. Edited by R. A. Culpepper, F. F. Segovia & J. Painter; St Louis, MO: Chalice, 2002.

_____. "John 9 and the Interpretation of the Fourth Gospel." *JSNT* 9 (1986): 31-61.

_____. *John, Witness and Theologian*. London: SPCK, 1975.

_____. *The Quest for the Messiah: The History, Literature, and Theology of the Johannine Community*. Second edition; Nashville: Abingdon, 1993.

Palatty, P. "Discipleship in the Fourth Gospel: An Acted Out Message of Disciples as Characters." *Biblebhashyam* 25 (1909): 285-306.

Pliny the Younger, *Complete Letters*. Translated by P. G. Walsh; Oxford World's Classics; Oxford: Oxford University Press, 2006.

Poirier, John C. "Day and Night and the Punctuation of John 9.3." *NTS* 42 (1996): 288-294.

_____. "Some Detracting Considerations for Reader-Response Theory." *CBQ* 62 (2000): 250-63.

Pontifical Biblical Commission, "The Interpretation of the Bible in the Church," (1994).

Pyle, William T. "Understanding the Misunderstanding Sequences in the Gospel of John." *Faith and Mission* 11 1994): 26-47.

Quasten, Johannes. "Parable of the Good Shepherd (Jn. 10:1-21)." *CBQ* 10 (1948): 151-169.

Rand, J. A. du. "Narcological Perspectives on John 13:1- 38." *Hervormde Teologiese Studies* 46 (1990): 367-89.

Rensberger, David. "The Politics of John: The Trial of Jesus in the Fourth Gospel." *JBL* 103 (1984): 395-411.

Richard, Earl, "Expressions of Double Meaning and Their Function in the Gospel of John." *NTS* 31 (1985): 96-112.

Richter, Georg. "The evangelist argues that the death of the cross is integral to Jesus' role as Messiah, "Die Fusswaschung Joh 13, 1-20." *Münchener Theologische Zeitschrift* 16 (1965): 13-26.

Ricoeur, Paul. *Interpretation Theory: Discourse and the Surplus of Meaning.* Fort Worth: Texas Christian University Press, 1976.

Ringgren, Helmer. *The faith of Qumran: Theology of the Dead Sea Scrolls.* Philadelphia: Fortress, 1963.

Robinson, J.A.T "The Relation of the Prologue to the Gospel of St. John." *NTS* 9 (1962-63): 120-29.

Romanowsky, John W. "'When The Son of Man Is Lifted Up': The Redemptive Power of the Crucifixion in the Gospel of John." *Horizons* 32 (2005): 100-16.

Rowland, Christopher "John 1.51, Jewish Apocalyptic and Targumic Tradition." *NTS* 30 (1984): 498-507.

Sabbe, Maurits. "The Denial of Peter in the Gospel of John." *Louvain Studies* 20 (1995): 219-40.

Saxby, Harold. "The Time-Scheme in the Gospel of John." *ET* 104 (1992): 9-13.

Schapdick, Stefan. "Religious Authority Re-Evaluated: The Character of Moses in the Fourth Gospel." Pages 188-189 in *Moses in Biblical and Extra-Biblical Traditions*. Edited by Axel Graupner and Michael Wolter; Berlin: Walter de Gruyter, 2007.

Schnackenburg, Rudolf. *The Gospel According to St John: Commentary on Chapters 5-12*. Burns & Oats, 1980.

Schnelle, Udo. *Theology of the New Testament*. Translated by M. Eugene Boring; Grand Rapids: Baker Academic, 2009.

Schneiders, Sandra M. "John 20:11-18: The Encounter of the Easter Jesus with Mary Magdalene—A Transformative Feminist Reading" in *What Is John?: Readers and Readings of the Fourth Gospel*. Edited by Fernando F. Segovia; SBLSymS 3; Atlanta: Scholars, 1996.

_____. *Written That You May Believe: Encountering Jesus in the Fourth Gospel*. New York: Crossroad, 2003.

Schulz, S. *Komposition und herkunft der johanneischen reden*. Stuttgart: Kohlhammer, 1960.

Schwankl, Otto. *Licht und Finsternis: Ein metaphorisches Paradigma in den johanneischen, Schriften*. Herders Biblische Studien 5; Freiburg: Herder, 1995.

Sciberras, L. *Water in the Gospel of St. John According to the Greek Fathers and Writers of the Church*, (Thesis for the licentiate, Studium Biblicum Fanciscanum, Jerusalem, 1975.

Scott, Brandon. *The Word of God in Words*. Philadelphia: Fortress, 1985.

Segovia, Fernando. F. F. "John 13:1-20: The Footwashing in the Johannine Tradition." *ZNW* 13 (1982): 31-51.

_____. "'Peace I Leave with You; My Peace I Give to You': Discipleship in the Fourth Gospel." Pages 76-102 in *Discipleship in the New Testament*. Philadelphia: Fortress, 1985.

_____. *What Is John? Readers and Readings of the Fourth Gospel*. SBLSymS 3; Atlanta: Scholars, 1996.

Skinner, Christopher W. "'The Good Shepherd Lays Down His life of the Sheep' (John 10:11, 15, 17): Questioning the Limits of a Johannine Metaphor." *CBQ* 80 (2018): 97-113.

Siliezar, Carlos Raúl Sosa. *Creation Imagery in the Gospel of John*. LNTS; London: Bloomsbury T&T Clark, 2015.

Stanks, Thomas. *The Servant of God in John 1:29, 36*. Louvain dissertation, 1963.

Steinberg, Meir. *The Poetics of Biblical Narrative: Ideological Literature and the Drama of Reading*. Bloomington: Indiana University Press, 1987.

Stibbe, M. W. G. *John as Storyteller: Narrative Criticism and the Fourth Gospel*. SNTSMS 73; Cambridge: Cambridge University Press, 1992.

Smalley, Stephen. "Joh 1,51 und die Einleitung zum vierten Evangelium" in *Jesus und der Menschensohn*. Edited by R. Pesch, R. Shnackenburg, O. Kaiser; Freiburg: Herder, 1975.

Smith, D. Moody. *The Composition and Order of the Fourth Gospel: Bultmann's Literary Theory*. New haven, Yale University Press, 1965.

_____. "The Setting and Shape of a Johannine Narrative Source." Pages 80-93 in *Johannine Christianity: Essays on Its Setting, Sources, and Theology*. Columbia: University of South Carolina Press, 1984.

Somov, Alexey and Vitally Voinov. "Abraham's Bosom" (Luke 16:22-23) as a Key Metaphor in the Overall Composition of the Parable of the Rich man and Lazarus." *CBQ* 79 (2017): 615-633.

Sylva, Dennis D. "Nicodemus and His Spices (John 19:39)." *NTS* 34 (1988): 148-51.

Rensberger, David. *Johannine Faith and Liberating Community*. Philadelphia: Westminster, 1988.

Richter, G. "Die Fusswaschung Joh 13, 1-20." *M.Th.Z* 16 (1965): 13-26.

Ringgren, H. *The faith of Qumran*. Philadelphia: Fortress, 1963.

Teeple, Howard Merle. *The Mosiac Eschatological Prophet*. JBL Monograph, X; Philadelphia: Society of Biblical Literature, 1957.

Thatcher, Tom. "Jesus, Judas, and Peter: Character by Contrast in the Fourth Gospel." *Bibliotheca sacra* 153 (1996): 435-448.

_____. "John's Memory Theater: The Fourth Gospel and Ancient Mnemo-Rhetoric." *CBQ* 69 (2007): 487-505.

Thate, Michael J. "Conditionality in John's Gospel: A Critique and Examination of Time and Reality as Classically Conceived in Conditional Constructions Journal of the Evangelical Theological Society." *JETS* 50 (2007): 561-72.

Theobald, Michael *Die Fleischwerdung des Logos: Studien zum Verhältnis des Johannesprologs zum Corpus des Evangeliums und zu I Joh.* Münster: Aschendorff, 1988.

Thomas, John C. *Footwashing in John 13 and the Johannine Community.* JSNTSup 61; Sheffield: JSOT, 1991.

Thompson, Marianne Mey. "Baptism with Water and with Holy Spirit: Purification in the Gospel of John" Pages 59-78 in *Historical, Literary, and Theological Readings from the Colloquium Ioanneum 2015 in Ephesus* (Wissenschaftliche Untersuchungen zum Neuen Testament 385) ed. R. Alan Culpepper and Jörg Frey (Tübingen: Mohr Siebeck, 2017).

Tire, Philip. "A Community in Conflict: A literary and Historical of John 9." *Religious Studies and Theology* 15 (1996): 77-100.

Toussaint, Stanley D. "The Significance of the First Sign in John's Gospel." *Bibliotheca sacra* 134 (1977): 45-51.

Trible, Phyllis. *Rhetorical Criticism: Context, Method, and the Book of Jonah.* Minneapolis: Fortress, 1994.

_____. *Texts of Terror: Literary-Feminist Readings of Biblical Narratives.* Philadelphia: Fortress, 1984.

Trudinger, Paul. "Subtle Ironies and Word-Plays in John's Gospel and The Problems of Chapter 21." *St Mark's Review* 162 (1995): 20-24.

Tovey, Derek. "Stone of Witness and Stone of Revelation: An Exploration of Inter-Textual Resonance in John 1:35-51." *Colloquim* 38 (2006): 41-58.

Valentine, Simon R. "The Johannine Prologue—a Micorocosm of the Gospel." *EQ* 68 (1996): 291-304.

Viviano, Benedict T. "The Structure of the Prologue of John (1:1-18): A Note." *RB* (1998): 176-184.

Wan der Woude, A. S. *La secte de Qumran*. Recherches Bibliques, IV; Louvain: 1959.

Voorwinde, Stephen. "John's Prologue: Beyond Some Impasses of Twentieth-Century Scholarship." *WTJ* (2002): 15-44.

Wahlde, C. von. *The Latest Version of John's Gospel: Recovering the Gospel of Signs*.Wilmington, Del.: Michael Glazier, 1989.

Wai-yee Ng, *Water Symbolism in John: An Eschatological Interpretation*. New York: Peter Lang, 2001.

Wead, David. "The Johannine Double Meaning," *Restoration Quarterly* 13 (1970): 106-20.

Wengst,Klaus. *Das Johannes evangelium*. W. Kohlhammer Verlag, 2007.

Williams, R. H. "The Mother of Jesus at Cana: A Social-Science Interpretation of John 2:1-12." *CBQ* 59 (1997): 679-92.

Whitenton, Michael R. "The Dissembler of John 3: A Cognitive and Rhetorical Approach to the Characterization of Nicodemus." *JBL* 135 (2016): 141-159.

Whitters, Mark F. "Discipleship in John: Four Profiles." *WW* 18 (1998): 422-427.

Woll, D. Bruce. "The Departure of 'The Way': The First Farewell Discourse in The Gospel of John." *JBL* 99 (1980): 225-239.

Wyer-Menkhoff, Karl. "The Response of Jesus: Ethics in John by considering Scripture as Work of God." Pages 159-174 in *Rethinking the Ethics of John*. Wisssenschaftliche Untersuchungen zum Neuen Testament. Edited by Jan

Yee, Gale A. *Jewish Feasts and the Gospel of John.* Wilmington, Del: Michael Glazier, 1989.

www.ingramcontent.com/pod-product-compliance
Lightning Source LLC
Chambersburg PA
CBHW050850160426
43194CB00011B/2104